GUN RACKS
AND
SIX-PACKS

Gun Racks and Six-Packs

*The Life and Times
of the Genuine, Original,
All-American Redneck*

The Best of
Bo Whaley

Rutledge Hill Press
Nashville, Tennessee

Copyright © 1986, 1987, 1988, 1989, 1990, 1991, 1992, 1993, 1995, 1996 by Bo
Whaley.

These stories have been published previously.

Published in Nashville, Tennessee, by Rutledge Hill Press, Inc.
211 Seventh Avenue North, Nashville, Tennessee 37219

Typography by E. T. Lowe, Nashville, Tennessee.

Illustrations by Will Owen.

Library of Congress Cataloging-in-Publication Data

Whaley, Bo, 1926–
    Gun racks and six-packs : a redneck compendium / by Bo Whaley.
        p.   cm.
    ISBN 1-55853-445-8 (pbk.)
    1. Rednecks—Humor.   2. Southern States—Humor.   I. Title.
PN6231.R38W43   1996
814' .54—dc20   96-20574
                                                                    CIP

Printed in the United States of America

1 2 3 4 5 6 7—99 98 97 96

*To Jeremy
and Brett.
They make me proud
to be a grandfather.*

CONTENTS

GUN RACKS
AND
SIX-PACKS

Rednecks Really Are for Real

WHAT, EXACTLY, IS A REDNECK? THIS IS A QUES-
tion that has cried out for an answer ever since Adam
popped the first wad of Levi Garrett in his mouth and Eve
cautioned him not to spit on the astro-turf.

Here, then, are the conclusions of one redneck researcher
who has considered the question for more than forty
years.

A redneck is a mysterious sort of character who drives
a four-wheel drive pickup with oversize tires on the first
floor and a cab perched on the eighth, flanked by twin CB
antennas, with a fish stringer hanging from the inside
rear-view mirror. He's a shaggy-haired varmint who hasn't
seen a barber since Sal Maglie retired from baseball,
sports a beard, and wears a Cat Diesel cap, black with
yellow patch. In his left shirt pocket is a barely visible

pouch of Levi Garrett chewing tobacco, with an equally subdued pack of Winstons in his right. A 30-06 rifle (with scope) and a .12 gauge Remington Model 1100 shotgun, along with a reel and rod, hang in the back window above the decal of a Confederate flag that bears the reminder: Hell No! I Ain't Forgettin! And there are three bumper stickers: How 'Bout Them Dawgs?!, Get Your Heart in America or Get Your (picture of a donkey) Out!, and next to it is one with a forefinger pointed skyward that says I Found It!

Those are the back bumper. On the front under the grille is a personalized tag that reads, Joe Boy and Willie Kate.

He's driving with a long-neck Bud in one hand, a large portion of Willie Kate in the other, and they listen as Waylon and Willie and the boys knock out their theme song, "Luckenbach Texas," on the AM-FM stereo tape player.

And, they're headed to . . . wherever, to do . . . whatever.

With complete disregard for my own safety, I've gone to great lengths to gather data regarding the stereotyped redneck. Throwing caution and good judgment to the wind, I invaded beer joints, all-night coffee houses, VFW dances, juke joints, and wrestling matches from Dry Branch to Donalsonville. I still don't have the answer to my question, "What is a redneck?"

Some replies are printable; some not. Here are a few that are:

"A guy with a chip on his shoulder lookin' for somebody to knock it off."

"Troublemaker. A born troublemaker. That's what a redneck is."

"A rebel. Anti-everything. Lives off beer, cigarettes, and beef jerky."

"A know-it-all who don't know nothin'."

"He's stupid. People laugh at him but he ain't got the sense to know it."

"Thinks he's a real ladies' man. Hah! Couldn't get a date in a women's prison."

There's more to this research business than meets the eye.

I walked into a cafe next to a pool room down near the Florida line. The front door screen was torn and a lug wrench was on the pinball machine next to a tattered copy of *Parts Pups*. What really caught my eye was the sign above the grill: "Notice—We Don't Cook No Omlits."

Next, I had a memorable experience in a quaint little establishment between West Green and Broxton. Not only did I inquire about rednecks there, I wound up face to face with one—and he did all the questioning.

I played it straight, asking the waitress my well-worn question, "In your opinion, what is a redneck?"

"A redneck? There's one right over there in that booth by the juke box. Hey, Buster! Drag it over here and talk to this here newspaper man," she shouted.

Caught! I was caught in a REDSCAM of my own design. I'd have been glad to buy Buster an omlit and vamoose. Ever seen an elephant get up? Lord, I thought Buster never was gonna get through gettin' up. He finally made it and ambled over to the counter where I stood—trembling.

"Yeah, what is it, Hoss?" he grunted, settling his 6' 6"- 280-pound frame on the next stool.

I didn't get to answer. Miss Big Mouth did it for me. "Man's wantin' to learn somethin' 'bout rednecks. He's from the newspaper," she blurted out before I had a chance to lie or run.

"Newspaper man? Where 'bouts you from, Cuz, Atlanter?" he asked through his beard and kitchen match.

"No, sir, but I'll move there if you want me to. I'm from Dublin," I stammered.

I explained my mission and, thank God, he understood. Actually, I was all set to go flyin' over the counter to join the dirty dishes and cold French fries. My epitaph flashed before my eyes: "Bo Whaley. Died March 28, 1981, Between the Dirty Dishes and Cold French Fries, From Multiple Head Wounds in Leona's Lunch."

"Really, I don't know what a redneck is. I'm just trying to . . ."

"Well, put this down in your little book, Cuz. Damn right I'm a redneck. Don't take nothin' off nobody. I drink Blue Ribbon beer, been married twice and was drunk both times. Shacked up more times than I can remember and got little Busters strewed from here to Nashville, and I ain't through yet. I'm thirty-seven years old, a veteran, and don't hit a lick at a snake 'less I have to. Chew Levi Garrett and ain't got no use for them B—'s in Washington, and Atlanter ain't no better. Live in a trailer, by myself most of the time, down by the river. I got a '68 pickup and listen to Willie Nelson, Moe and Joe, and Loretter Lynn. Ain't had a tie on since grandpa's funeral in '63. I like my eggs fried hard and can't

remember a week when I ain't got drunk. Fact is, I'm runnin' late, Cuz. Anything else you wanna' know?"

"No, sir, Mr. Buster. That's fine, sir, just fine. Thank you,
sir," I said, humbly.

He spanked Leona on the rear and ambled out the front
door. A redneck? I have to think so. A thoroughbred.

Like I said in the beginning, "with complete disregard
for my own safety. . . ."

I was eating breakfast in a place near Darien. I had the
guy at the next table pegged as a redneck. His table man-
ners were awful. He slurped his coffee, propped his feet
on a chair, and ate his sausage with his hands. When he
finished he struck a stick match with his thumbnail and lit
a Camel. Filter? Perish the thought.

He and the waitress were obviously at odds. I heard her
mutter something about, "the night you whupped up on
Ralph," before taking a swing at him with a butcher knife.
Such upbringing! When she swung the butcher knife, I
dang near dropped a whole handful of grits!

Take it from me, you gotta' go south to find pedigreed
rednecks, the real thoroughbreds.

The best place to find them is in juke joints, and notice
I didn't say night clubs, supper clubs, cabarets, or social
halls. Rednecks come to roost in juke joints Friday and
Saturday nights. Now then, when I say juke joint, I mean
a down-yonder, roll-up-your-sleeves, bring-me-another-
beer, every-man (and woman)-for-himself, three bucks to
get in and $37.85 to get out, Willie Nelson-Conway
Twitty-Loretta Lynn establishment where they stamp
your hand when you spring for the three and suck up
your $37.85 like an Electrolux. That, good buddy, is where
you find the thoroughbreds.

I went south on my motorcycle. Credentials, man; you
gotta' have 'em. I wouldn't leave home without 'em on a
juke joint excursion.

I found a redneck roost near the Altamaha River. The sign said, "Daisy Mae's Place—Cold Beer and Fish Baits." I parked between a four-wheel-drive Blazer and a Jeep featuring pink carpet. Are you with me? The bumper sticker on the Jeep suggested a solution to a Sunday morning problem: Sure Cure for Hangovers—Don't Sober Up.

The clock on the Blue Ribbon sign indicated it was 8:40 P.M. as I dropped three ones on the table at the door and had my hand stamped.

"Been here before, buddy?" she asked.

"No ma'am, first time," I replied.

"O.K. The stamp means you can go outside and to the men's room as many times as you want to. Just stick it under the light when you come back in."

"My hand?"

"Right. You got it, good buddy. Next? That'll be three dollars. You been here . . . ?"

Properly branded, I felt my way into the main arena and sat at a table near the bandstand, but not for long because this girl waitress wearing either very short shorts or a wide belt suddenly appeared.

"Can't sit here, mister. This is Rooster's table," she said.

"Oh? Who's Rooster?"

"Never mind. Rooster just don't like nobody settin' at his table 'less he asks 'em."

Know what I did? I moved to another table. I didn't pass Good Judgment 101 at Georgia Southern by taking foolish chances. After all, a table is a table, right?

I sat and waited, eyeing Rooster's table. I wanted to see that cat. At 8:55 by the Blue Ribbon clock he strolled in, walked right by the handstamper like she wasn't there, slowing down just long enough to sling a little currency her way. Hand stamp? Forget it! When Rooster wants to go to the men's room he don't need no hand stamp to get back inside.

Rooster walked straight to "his" table, but didn't sit down. He never sat down all night, just propped his cowboy-boot-clad foot in the chair and leaned on the back of it. He could have had a spot on the bandstand. Rooster is definitely the "cock of the walk" at Daisy Mae's.

When Rooster Roberts walks in a juke joint, everybody who is able stands up and takes notice. Those unable to stand simply wave as he strolls by. You can't miss him. He wears Western shirts, Levis held up by a belt with a buckle only slightly smaller than a sheet of plywood, and Western boots with toes sharp-pointed enough to thread a needle with. Rooster's real trademark, though, is the ever-present stick match in his mouth.

"Ain't never seen Rooster without his match," Rita, the waitress, allowed. "Stays right there whenever he eats, drinks, smokes, dances, or, uh, whatever."

I knew I had to try it even if I got my head knocked off, so I walked over to Rooster's table and asked him, "Excuse me, sir, but do you have a match?"

"Nope, not since Superman died," he replied. Of course, I could have asked for the one stuck in his mouth, but would have had more success attempting to extract his wisdom teeth.

"Pretty slim pickins tonight, Hoss," he said.

"How's that?" I asked.

"Gals. Nothin' much worth lookin' at 'cept maybe that'n over there by the juke box. Hey, Rita!" he yelled.

"Yeah, whatcha' want, Rooster, a beer?"

"Naw, give that ol' gal over there by the juke one an' tell her I bought it," he ordered. Then, turning back to me he said, "Set y'self down if y'want to."

I pulled up a chair, propped my foot in it and watched Rita deliver the beer and the message to "that ol' gal" who, by my arithmetic, measured in the neighborhood of 37-22-36, and that ain't a bad neighborhood. Once, when she stood to adjust whatever women stand up to adjust, I had to change my calculations because if those jeans with the little pony on the back pocket ever busted, the measurements would change to 37-22 and a bunch. Swift never packed a tighter package.

Rooster sent a steady stream of Blue Ribbons to "that ol' gal" and finally made his move shortly after midnight when he called for Rita, peeled a ten-spot off a roll, and said, "Tell them jokers to play my song." Rita was well-schooled and shortly them jokers played "For the Good Times," and Rooster danced with "that ol' gal." The jeans held, thank God.

When the song ended, Rooster returned to his table and propped.

"You really like that song, huh?" I asked.

"Only one I dance to, Hoss. You can have that fast mess. I ain't dancin' with no gal I can't squeeze."

That, friends and neighbors, is Rooster Roberts, cock of the walk at "Daisy Mae's Place—Cold Beer and Fish Baits."

Country songs are mostly sad songs with such tear-jerking lines as "Three hungry children and a crop in the field; you picked a fine time to leave me, Lucille," "Ruby, don't take your love to town," "When your girlfriend writes a letter to your wife." Sad words, sure, but not nearly as sad as those sung to Rooster by "that ol' gal."

She was busy collecting her Salem 100s and Bic lighter and stuffing her shoulder bag when Rooster hit her with, "Come on, baby. Let's go to my place down on the river."

"Can't. Goin' to S'vanner with the guitar picker," she said. The saddest lyrics ever written? You better believe it. After Rooster invested twelve dollars in beer and the guitar picker hadn't even bought her a Slim Jim, she comes up with, "I'm goin' with the guitar picker."

Rooster watched him put his Fender electric in the case, grab what was left of the last Blue Ribbon Rita had delivered to "that ol' gal," and leave with her. Rooster couldn't believe it.

"Damn, Rita! He looks like a commercial for embalming fluid. What's he got that I ain't got?" Rooster asked.

"I can tell you but you won't like it, Rooster."

"Go ahead!"

"A Fender electric guitar that he knows how to pick, 'that ol' gal' you been buyin' beer for all night, and what's left of the last Blue Ribbon you bought her."

"Yeah, guess you're right. I'll wait for you in the truck, Rita."

"Ten-four, Rooster."

I left and headed home, thinking about Rooster. Somebody ought to write a song about him. I hummed the lyrics, sad lyrics, as I tooled up U.S. 1 on my Harley: "Sorry, but I'm goin' with the guitar picker."

The Official Redneck Aptitude Test

Self-appointed experts from the deep South and the far North keep trying to identify and classify the redneck. Some of them know what they're talking about, and some don't.

To aid them in their efforts I have designed what I believe is a foolproof aptitude test for the purpose of determining an individual's redneck traits or tendencies. You would do well to take the test. Better still, take it with a friend who is convinced he's a bigger redneck than you are. Make a friendly wager. Let the loser pay for the long-neck Buds.

	Me	You

1. You get five points if you chew tobacco. Add two more if you dip snuff. You get an additional fifteen points if your grandmother dips snuff. Double that if you've ever kissed a woman who had snuff in her mouth at the time.

2. You get five points if you go swimming in cut-off Levis. If you are female and you wear cut-off Levis and a T-shirt swimming, you get double points. Both male and female subtract ten points if you do your swimming in a swimming pool. But add five points if your dog goes in swimming with you.

3. If you own a polyester leisure suit, give yourself five points. Add five more if you still wear it. Add three more points if you got it from your daddy. Double that if it has any embroidery on it.

4. Give yourself three points if your belt has your name on the back. Add one point for each inch wide the buckle is. Add five points if you carry a knife in a case on the belt. You get five bonus points if you wear a white belt. If you wear white shoes to match the belt, add ten points. And if you wear white socks, add fifteen points.

	Me	You

5. Give yourself five points if you wear cowboy boots. Double it if you sleep in them. Triple it if the boots are made of snake or lizard skin. Subtract fifteen points if they're made in Taiwan or in Massachusetts. Add ten points if you own a horse.

6. You get ten points if you live in a mobile home. Add five more if it's a single-wide. Add two more for every dog that sleeps under it and one point for every tire that's rotted out. Add three for every sliding closet door that works but subtract three points if its skirted, unless the skirting is rusted tin roofing or cardboard. Add one point for every dish in the sink that needs washing, but subtract a point for every pair of clean socks in the trailer.

7. Give yourself ten points for every car in the yard that's up on cement blocks. Subtract two points for each cement block that you bought. Add one point for each year if it's older than a 1972 model. Subtract five points if it has a battery. Subtract ten points if it's a European sports car. Add ten if you painted it yourself with a brush. Add five if you had it painted by Earl Scheib.

Me	You

8. Score ten points for yourself if you can whistle through your teeth. Add five more if your wife can.

9. Give yourself two points for every rifle you own, and add one point for each one with a scope. And give yourself five points if you carry a pistol in the glove compartment of your vehicle. Double that if your wife carries one, too. Triple it if she knows how to use it. Subtract ten points if either of you have a permit.

10. You get five points if you drive a pickup truck. Add five more if it's a four-wheel drive. Add five more if it has over-sized tires with raised white letters. Add another five if there's a dog box in the back, but subtract ten if the dog is registered. Add one point for every beer can in the back, add one point for each can that is hand-crushed. Subtract three points if the cooler is clean.

11. Give yourself four points if you smoke non-menthol cigarettes; and add five more if you smoke non-filter Camels. Subtract five if you don't smoke cigarettes. Add five points if you use stick matches, and two more if you can strike them with your thumbnail or on the seat of your britches. Add another for every hour you keep one in your mouth.

	Me	You

12. Give yourself five points if you've got a boat parked in the yard. Add three if it's a bass boat but subtract three if there are no dead worms in the bottom. Subtract five points if the motor cranks on the first pull. Subtract fifteen if it's a sailboat.

13. Give yourself five points if you have a beard, but subtract three if you bathed yesterday. Subtract three if all the plumbing works and all your utilities are paid and current.

14. You get five points if you wear a white shirt with the sleeves rolled up. Add five more if the shirttail is out. Subtract one point if it only has one pocket but add a point for each missing button. You must subtract two points if the collar button has ever been buttoned.

	Me	You

15. You get five points if you dropped out of high school. Double that if you were kicked out for fighting. Triple it if you attended for twelve years but failed to graduate.

16. Give yourself twenty points if you listen to country music. Add ten more if you've ever been to Nashville, and ten more if you went to the Grand Ole Opry. Subtract ten if you attended but didn't yell. You lose five more if you don't know where Johnny Cash and Merle Haggard served time. But add five if you can find WSM on your radio.

17. You lose ten points if you know who Pat Benetar is. And you lose twenty if you've ever listened to a whole song by Pat Benetar without changing to another station. You're out of the game and lose by forfeit if you own a Pat Benetar album or tape. But you can be considered for a future game if you can name all four members of the Alabama band.

Total

Well, how did you make out? If you feel that you scored high enough to seriously consider making the move South, then you need to keep reading for some helpful hints before making a final decision.

Speakin' Redneck Made Easy

Don't think for a minute that you can just up and move to redneck country and know what's goin' on right from the very start. Not so. Therefore, it is strongly suggested that you burn the ol' midnight oil in an attempt to memorize as many redneck words and phrases as possible before making the move. Otherwise, you will be just as lost as a redneck in China. You probably wouldn't understand a thing that's said.

There are certain key words that you'll need to know, words that come as natural as rain to a redneck. Having these words at your disposal will greatly ease the transformation.

The words selected have the same meaning north of the Mason-Dixon Line as they do south of it; the only real difference lies in their pronunciation.

By the way, no attempt is being made here to list the words in alphabetical order because it really don't make no difference as I see it. After all, we don't talk in alphabetical order, right?

The redneck spelling of the word is followed by the correct spelling of the word in parentheses. I figure you'll know that, but I ain't takin' no chances. Then there will be an example of how the word can be used in a sentence.

It is also suggested that this section of the book be clipped and saved because you never know when it might come in handy in your new surroundings.

NEVER LEAVE HOME WITHOUT IT!

Word	How It's Used
Kreck *(Correct):*	The kreck spellin' of kreck is "Correct." Lak "My mommer is a skool teecher and tonight she has to kreck tes' papuhs."
Fem *(Film):*	"Me an' Buster went to th' maountins an' I tuk my camra, but I'll be dadgummed if'n I did'n f'rgit to buy some fem."
Doc *(Dark):*	"I'm 19 yeers ol' but I steel sleep with a lite on 'cause I'm skeert o' th' doc."
Idnit *(Isn't it):*	"It shore is purty out t'nite with th' full moon an' all, idnit?"
Hard *(Hired):*	"My Daddy went to th' unemployment offis this mornin' to see 'bout gittin' a job at the new factry whut's openin' nex' month, but for some reason he wan't hard."

Idy *(Idea):* "I heered whut ya' sed at th' PTA metin' las' nite 'bout sponsorin' a chittlin' suppah to raise money f'r th' ban' uniforms, Charlotte, an' I thank thas a reel gud idy."

Jevver *(Did you ever):* "Bobby Joe tol' me ya' wuz daown at th' Chivverlay place lookin' at one o' them new Impallers. Jevver trade?"

Keer *(Care):* "Granny ain't gittin' 'long so good, what with her a' havin' roomytisem an' all. But she's a' doin' bettah since she got on a program called Home Hailth Keer whur nurses come t' visit her to home onc't a week."

Mere *(Mirror):* "We bin doin' th' crazies' thangs lately in Play Skool, Mary Frances. That new teecher has got us mem'rizin silly verses. Yistitty we had t' larn one whut goes, 'Mere, mere, on th' wahl, who's th' faires' uv them awl.' Now then, I ast ya, ain't thet plum' silly?"

Wail *(Well):* "I jis come fum th' doctor. I ain't rilly bin wail fer a while but wuz too busy to go an' find out whut wuz wrong. Found out I got shootin' pains, whatever th' heck that is."

Argy *(Argue):* "I ain't a' goin' to Lucy Mae's no more. She thanks she knows ever'thang an' she don't know nuthin' a tall. 'Sides, ever time I go to her haouse, all we ivver do is argy."

Bub *(Bulb):* "Johnnie Faye! Run daoun to Mr. Johnson's stow an' git me a lite bub—hunnert watt."

Earl *(Aerial):* "Josh, we plum' got to buy us a new earl fer th' radio. It's done got to th' pint whur I can't even git WSM an' they ain't no way I ain't gonna' lissen to th' Gran' Ole Opry come Sat'dy nite."

Far *(Fire):* "Bobby Joe, go git some stovewood an' bild a far in th' farplace in th' livin' room. Granny's a' comin' this afternoon an' you know how she hates col' weather."

Cocoler *(Coca-Cola):* "I want two hamburgers all the way, a awder o' Franch fries an' a Cocoler."

Hep *(Help):* "Tell ya' whut I'll do, Lunce. If'n you'll hep me dig my 'taters, I'll hep you cut yore hay."

Awduh *(Order):* "I'm gonna' awduh me two dresses an' a hat fum Sears. An'

I'm gonna' awduh two pair of ovalls fer Jayssie."

Wudnit *(Wasn't it):* "Boy! Thet shore wuz some scary movie on th' TV las' nite, wudnit?"

All *(Oil):* "Lemme hav five dollars wuth o' reg'lar an' a quat o' all, Goober. Ever'thin' ailse is awright."

Bard *(Borrowed):* "Lucy, I ain't loanin' Buster Bland nothin' ailse. He bard my shovel an' didn't brang hit bak. An' he bard my battry charger an' lost hit."

Bleeve *(Believe):* "Wail, I kin tail ya' one thang 'baout ol' man Jenkins. Ya' jus' can't bleeve a word he says. I wouldn't bleeve 'im if he wuz a' dyin' an' knowed it."

Kumpny *(Company):* "Git in heah an' blow yo nose an' warsh yore face, young'un! Don't ya' know we got kumpny a' comin t'nite?"

Gull *(Girl):* "Who wuz zat gull I seen ya' with las' nite, Bobby Jack? Man! She wuz a hum-dinger!"

Orta *(Ought to):* "I know dang wail I orta go ahead an' git my new car tag, but I jus' can't never thank uv it when I'm in taoun."

Nome *(No ma'am):* "Robert! Is ya' did yor Ainglish homework yit?" "Nome." "Wail, git on hit this minit! Fus' thang ya' know you'll be growed up an' won't have no idy haow t' write 'er tawk a tall."

Rench *(Rinse):* "I used to hav' a bunch o' troubl' with bad breath, m'sef. But I bought me some o' that stuff I seen on the TV whut ya' rench aout ya' mouth with an' I ain't had no more troubl'."

Tarred *(Tired):* "Why 'ont y'all go on to th' pitcher show, Zeke. I bin arnin' awl day an' I'm tarred aout."

Yale *(Yell):* "Wail naow, Bessie Faye, ya' can't be no cheerleader if'n ya' ain't willin' t' yale. Shoot! You can yale with the bes' uv 'em, so git on aout there an' yale."

Umurkin *(American):* "Did'ja see that feller on th' lebbum o' clock news las' nite burnin' that Umurkin flag up in New Yawk? Sumbody orta' raound him up an' teech 'im a lesson with a tar arn or sum'thin. I don't bleeve he's no Umurkin, nohow."

Treckly *(Later):* "Y'all go on home an' feed the cows an' slop th' hawgs, Lena. I'll be comin' on treckly."

Whirr *(Where):* "Whirr you bin, boy? Suppah's bin redy f'r mor'n two ouers."

Ovalls *(Overalls):* "Somebody answer that tellyphone, an' tell whoever 'tis I'll be there soon's I hang these ovalls on th' line."

Smore *(Some more):* "Ma, kin I hav smore greeuts?"

Spear *(Superior):* "Daddy said Buddy got coat-marshulled 'cuz he cuassed his spear officer."

Rernt *(Ruined):* "Know that new coat I bought at th' sale las' week? Well, Harvey spilt battry acid on it an' rernt it."

Prolly *(Probably):* "I ain't reel shore whut we gonna' do this Crismus. We'll prolly go to Mama's."

Summers *(Somewhere):* "I 'ont know zackly whirr Chicargo's at, but I believe hit's summers up north close to Illernoise."

Arn *(Iron):* "I tell ya', Hoss, thet ol' boy's tough as pig arn."

Aig *(Egg):* "Yeah, I bin t' Savanner twice't. An both times I went thet papuh meal smelt lak a rotten aig."

Plike *(Play like):* "Tell ya' whut, Billy Frank; you plike you Tonto and I'll plike I'm th' Lone Ranger."

Ahmoan *(I'm going to)* "Ahmoan ast Ma if I kin spen' th' nite at yore house."

Fur *(Far):* "How fur it is fum Atlanter to Chattnooger?"

Munt *(Month):* "Febererry is th' shortes' munt uf th' yeer."

Moanin *(Morning):* "Good moanin', Mr. Weeulson."

Hail *(Hell):* "Wail, I'll jus' tail ya' haow I feel 'bout it. If'n she don't lak th' way I dress, she can jus' go straight to hail."

Airs *(Errors):* "Anybody whut plays baseball is baound to make airs 'cause they ain't nobody purrfect."

Bay-ed *(Bed):* "I feel this way 'baout it. He made his bay-ed, so let 'im sleep in hit."

Lecktristy *(Electricity):* "I thank it wuz a feller name of Benjamin Franklin whut faound aout 'bout lecktristy when his Daddy los' patience with him an' tol' him to go fly a kite jus' to git Ben aout o' the haouse."

Cheer *(Chair):* "Jus' hang yore coat on the bak o' thet cheer."

Moanbak*:* *(Come on back)* "Cut th' stirrin' wheel to th' rite an' moanbak."

Dayum *(Damn):* "Frankly, mah deah, I don't giv' a dayum!"

Greeuts *(Grits):* "Pleez pass th' greeuts."

Saar *(Sour):* "Ma, this meeulk tastes lak hit's saar."

Stow *(Store):* "Ah'm goin' to th' stow an' git sum 'baccer. Be rat bak."

Thow *(Throw):* "Thayet uppity ol' Hortense Edwards jus' makes me want to thow up."

Spec *(Expect):* "I rilly wud lak to stay fer supper, but I spec I bes' be gittin' on home."

Sinner *(Center):*   "Ol' Charley won th' turkey shoot this mornin'. He flat hit thayet bull's eye dade sinner."

War *(Wire):*   "I cud fix this thang in nothin' flat if'n I had me a piece o' war."

Zat *(Is that):*   "This here's my cap. Zat yores?"

Zackly *(Exactly):*   "Frum Atlanter to Bumminham is zackly 158 miles."

Tawk *(Talk):*   "Yeah, I watch TV. But I don't watch none o' them tawk shows."

Sawt *(Salt):*   "This here taoun is gonna' miss ol' man Hipple. He was the sawt o' th' earth."

Pitcher *(Picture):*   "All right, you young'uns git in th' haouse an' git cleaned up some. We got to go to taoun an' git our pitcher took fer Chrismus."

Phrasin *(Freezing):*   "Somebody put some more wood on th' far. It's phrasin' cold in heer."

Shurf *(Sheriff):*   "If'n thayet pickup comes by heer jus' one more time a' speedin' I'm gonna' call th' shurf an' hav' 'im locked up."

Ose *(Oldsmobile):*   "Did'ja heer that Frankie Bennett traded cars las' week? Traded his '72 Ponyack fer a '79 Ose 88."

Ovair *(Over there):*   "I 'prechate th' offer uv a ride but I kin walk. I ain't goin' fur, jus' rite ovair."

Madge *(Marriage):*   "Says rat cheer in th' local papuh thayet Ralph Swilley has done ast Mollie Bentley fer her han' in madge."

Abode *(A board):*   "I promised the young'uns I wuz gonna' make um a see-saw, but fus I got to see if'n I kin fin' abode."

Tenshun *(Attention):*   "All right, class. I want all uv y'all to set up an' pay tenshun."

Venchly *(Eventually):*   "Naow then, don't git all upset 'cause we done los' owah fus' 16 ball games. Jus' wuk hard an' don' give up 'cause we gonna' win a game venchly."

Spishuss *(Suspicious):*   "I wudn't git too close to thayet new boy daown th' road if'n I wuz y'all. I bin a' watchin 'im an' he looks spishuss to me."

Skace *(Scarce):*   "Wail, Lem, looks lak th' pecan crop is gonna' come up short this yeer. Yessir, pecans is gonna' be skace as hen's teeth."

Po *(Poor):*   "Shoot, Roger, you don't know whut bein' po is. They's a fambly

ovah in Cedar Creek whut's so
po that ever' time they thow a
bone out th' bak door th' dog
signals fer a fair ketch."

Shaller *(Shallow):*

"Yeah, I guess you young'uns
kin go in swimmin'—but be
shore ya' stay in th' shaller
end."

Cutcha *(Cut you):*

"One thang 'baout ol' Ben, if'n he
gits drunk an' mad at th' same
time he'll flat cutcha."

Hesh *(Hush):*

"Hesh yo' maouth, boy! Jes' hesh
up!"

Mamanem:
(Mama and them)

"Howdy, Luke. How's yore
mamanem?"

Quair *(Queer):*

"I've always sorta' laked ol' Mr.
Woods, but he shore has some
quair ways, don't he?"

Shivry *(Chivalry):*

"Well, thanks fer openin' th' door
fer me, Jake. See chillun, th' age
o' shivry ain't daid."

Cawk *(Cork):*

"Anybody know whut happened
to th' cawk stopper whut I had in
this syrup bottle?"

Cad *(Carried):*

"I cad some peas ovah to Mrs.
Nelson lak ya' tol' me to, Pa. She
sed thank you."

Skeert *(Scared):*   "I'll go fus'. I ain't skeert."

Salary *(Celery):*   "Tossed salad jus' ain't tossed salad if'n it don't hav sum salary in it."

Less *(Let's):*   "Less go to th' ball game an' then go git a Big Mac."

Loud *(Allowed):*   "Mama said we wuzn't loud to go to taoun atter dark."

Foe *(Four):*   "I ain't memrized it all yet, but I know how it starts off . . . "Foe sco' an' sebum years ago . . .""

Fussed *(First):*   "Yes, ma'am, I know th' answer! Th' fussed man whut walked on th' moon wuz Neil Armstrong."

Doe *(Door):*   "Somebody open th' doe! I got a armload o' stovewood."

Astor *(Ask her):*   "I rilly don' thank Ma's gonna' lemmee go, but I'll astor."

Menshun *(Mention):*   "When ya' git to th' front doe, jus' menshun mah name an' you'll git a good seat."

Nudder *(Another):*   "Mama, kin I hav nudder piece o'cake?"

Leckshun *(election):*   "Can't buy no likker today, Henry. It's leckshun day. Can't nobody but th' politicians git drunk."

Pleese *(Police):* "Mus' be havin' trouble daoun at th' juke joint. I seen two pleese cars go by."

Lane *(Laying):* "I ain't worked none since I got laid off in Janawerry, but I'm goin' to wuk nex' week fer a haouse bilder lane tile."

Yistitty *(Yesterday):* "I gotta' go bak to DEE-troit in th' mornin'. I come in on th' bus late yistitty evenin'."

Rail *(Real):* "I seen Mr. Sullivan daoun at th' pig sale this mornin' an' I thot he looked rail good."

Blong *(Belong):* "I don't wanna' go to Sally Mae's birthday party. I jus' don't feel lak I blong there."

Paytrotick*:* *(Patriotic)* "One o' th' thangs I like bes' 'baout the Foth of July prade is the paytrotick music them bans play."

Sammitch*:* *(Sandwich)* "No, thank ya' m'am, I done et. Mama fixed me a bloney an' 'mater sammitch."

Tar *(Tire):* "Weeda' bin here 'fore naow but we had a flat tar jus' aoutside o' Waycross."

Wangs *(Wings):* "Oh yeah? Well, if'n a frog had wangs he wudn't keep a' bumpin his tail on th' groun."

Ax *(Ask):* "Jus' set there, Ned, an' don't ax so many questions."

Bail *(Bell):* "We bettuh hurry up. I thank I jes' heered th' skool bail rang."

Ball *(Boil):* "Can she cook? Heck, thet ol' gal cudn't ball watah 'thout scorchin' it."

Cane Chew: "Cane chew jus' see ol' Bobby Jack
(Can't you) all decked aout in one o' them monkey suits fer his sister's weddin'?"

Legible *(Eligible):* "Ain't no way Booger Creek kin win thet football game t'nite 'cause the qwatahbak ain't legible. He flunked Ainglish an' Hist'ry."

Coat *(Court):* "I guess we won't be a' seein' much of ol' Jay Bridges fer the nex' few yeers. He got sentenced to eight yeers in Circus Coat this mornin'."

Empire *(Umpire):* "Them Atlanter Braves shore got th' shawt end o' the stick agin' them Chicargo Cubs yistitty, did'n they? That fus' base empire flat missed thet play on Murphy at fus base. He wuz safe by two steps."

Tuck *(Took):* "I ain't never tuck a drink o' likker in muh life."

So much for the vocabulary. There are a couple of other tricks of the redneck trade that, if mastered, will prove invaluable to you in communicating with your new neighbors. These are cardinal rules of redneck grammar and musts for proper redneck speech:

- Never pronounce the "g" in words endin' with "ing."

- No matter if you're talkin' 'baout man, woman, child, a haoun' dog, or a pickup truck, put "ol" in front.

- Always put the accent or emphasis on the first syllable of words with two or more. For instance: DEE-troit, UM-breller; IN-shorance; and JU-ly.

And just as bonus, here's a great redneck line for you to store in your memory bank for future use. It is sure to melt a redneck girlfriend's heart:

"You jus' 'member this, Sugah. Long's I got a biscuit, you got half."

Sorta' chokes a feller up, don't it?

Bo Whaley

KINFOLK

Daddy's Notes

My father was a note saver. I'm glad he was. I wish he had put his collection, numbering in the hundreds, in the form of a book of some kind for others to read.

First, "The Preacher," that was surely written by one . . . or by his wife:

The Preacher

If he's young, he lacks experience; if he's old, he's "too old for our church."

If he has five or six children, he has too many; if he has none, he isn't setting a good example.

If his wife sings in the choir, she's being forward; if not, she's not interested in her husband's ministry.

If he uses a manuscript, he's preaching canned sermons and is dry; if he's extemporaneous, he rambles too much.

If he spend a lot of time in his study, he neglects his people; if he visits a lot, he's a gadabout.

If he's attentive to the poor, he's grandstanding; if to the wealthy, he's trying to be an aristocrat.

If he hunts or fishes, he's too worldly; if he doesn't, he's out of touch with the everyday world.

If he suggests improvements, he's a dictator; if he doesn't, he's merely a figurehead.

If he uses too many illustrations, he neglects the Bible; if not enough, he's not clear.

If he condemns wrong, he's cranky; if he doesn't, he's a compromiser.

If he preaches more than thirty minutes, he's long winded; if not, he's lazy.

If he fails to please everyone, he's hurting the church; if he does, he's hurting the church.

If he preaches tithing, he's money-hungry; if he doesn't, he's blamed for not meeting the church budget.

If he receives a large salary, he's mercenary; if a small one, it proves he's not worth much.

If he preaches every Sunday, people tire of hearing him; if he invites guest preachers, he's shirking his responsibility.

And there are those who think preachers have it easy. It takes much more than just showing up for a couple of hours Sunday morning.

Second, "Bag of Tools." I know this piece was very special to my dad. He used it often from his pulpit:

A Bag of Tools

Isn't it strange,
That princes and kings,

And clowns that caper in sawdust rings,
And common people,
Like you and me,
Are builders of eternity?
To each is given a bag of tools,
A shapeless mass,
And a book of rules,
And each must make,
Ere life has flown,
A stumbling block,
Or a stepping stone.

And finally, nobody enjoyed telling preacher stories more than my father. He was a mountain man. Story-telling was his forte, and I loved to listen to them when he told them. This was one of his favorites:

A young preacher serving his first church up in the North Georgia mountains was called upon to marry a young couple. It was his first wedding. He performed flawlessly, prompting the groom to compliment him in this manner.

"Preacher, ya' done real good. I'd like to give a few dollars, but I ain't got no money. So, I'll tell you what I'm gonna' do fer ya'. I got an old houn' dawg I been tryin' to sell for ten dollars. I'm gonna let you have him f'r five."

MOTHERS ARE SPECIAL

IT IS NO GREAT SECRET THAT IN ORDER FOR A woman to become a mother she must bear a child. That is the way God intended it, thank goodness! Should the roles have been divinely reversed, there is absolutely no doubt in my mind that kids would come one to a family, and those preoccupied with planned parenthood and the world population explosion would be out of business.

Should men bear the responsibility of birth, there would be no need for advocates of birth control, either. They would close up shop and look for another cause around which to rally.

I have never known a man who could go through what a woman must go through to bring a child into the world. But they pass out cigars and boast like they had done something great.

I don't think a man would make it through the delivery room door. He'd first fight—doctors and nurses. And he'd scream and cry.

The big thing going these days is for the husband to accompany his wife into the delivery room and then stand there while the baby is being born. Those promoting such madness lay claim to the fact that this is a procedure of love and support.

Friend, let me go on record right here and now that I ain't about to do that. Furthermore, not only would I not go into the delivery room, I wouldn't even want to be in the same building. That's the coward I am. Just yell down to the parking lot and say "Boy!" or "Girl!" and that all is well. I could handle that.

Mothers are very special people. I know, I have one, God bless her, who has been in a nursing home for eleven years. After two broken hips, a broken nose, and a broken knee, she doesn't walk any more and can't go out with me to eat like she used to. I see her every day when I'm in town, and the best we can do now is a milkshake. I never leave home to go and see her without one, usually chocolate.

The amazing thing about this lady is that she has seen more ups and downs than a yo-yo but never fails to ask two questions when I visit her: "Are you feeling all right, Bo? Are you eating right?" Yes, an eighty-eight-year-old lady in a wheelchair wants to know if her only son is all right and eating right. Does she complain? Never!

Maybe it would be well if we paused just long enough to consider what mothers are, anyway:

- A mother is a nurse, teacher, counselor, mediator, confessor, arbitrator, cook, seamstress, maid, taxi-driver, bookkeeper, laundry woman, programmer, censor, banker, planner, referee, umpire, cheerleader, and general Mrs. Fixit. She is all these and more.

- What does a mother do? She wipes away a tear, shares a laugh, spanks a bottom, cries when you fail, and laughs when you succeed. She prays with you and for you. She cooks your food, makes your bed, cleans your room, picks up after you, and takes you places.

You know about those things. But there is yet another dimension that you just may not think about. Remember?

Like the time when you were six years old and she watched you walk into that school for the first time, probably cleaner than you've ever been since. And I ask you, is there a prize for the mother who presents the cleanest first grader each September? When you walked in that schoolhouse that first day, you had been scrubbed from top to bottom, and your mama probably took a final swipe behind your ears as you walked through the door.

A mother can take a dainty hankie and a dab of saliva and clean the Empire State Building.

And don't think for a minute that the outfit you wore that first day was just something she happened to pick up at a yard sale the day before. Oh, no! She had shopped for it for months, and it made no difference that after that first recess you looked like a chimney sweep. When you walked in that first day, you were Mr. Spic and Span.

In addition to being very special, mothers are a strange breed. So tough, yet so tender. We break their hearts a thousand times over in the span of a lifetime, and they keep bouncing back.

Has there ever been a woman who experienced the miracle of childbirth who didn't harbor the hope that "this one is going to do something great"? I doubt it. And who can identify the mother who has ever said, "I know this one will never amount to a hill of beans"? Not I.

Mothers have a special way about them. They have a way of solving seemingly impossible problems, accomplishing the unbelievable. They know just the right thing to say when you feel bad and it seems that the whole world is caving in around you. Who never heard a mother say, "Well, maybe it's not all that bad. We'll find a way." And they do, magicians that they are.

What about the hours she spends on bended knee asking God to help you be the person she hopes you'll be? Or the hours she spends rubbing an aching stomach and then spends more hours watching as you sleep? What about the untold miles she's spent rocking you because she loved you and knew that you felt safe and secure nestling up close to her bosom from which she fed you?

Finally, no matter how many chores she had to do or the fact that the days didn't have enough hours for her to finish, she always seemed to find the time for you.

Mothers are tough.

The Joys of Becoming a Mother

For thirteen years since January 1978, I have written three columns a week for a daily newspaper. At least twice a year I offer my space to a high school student planning to pursue a career in journalism. Nora Cordell Hatchett is one of those. She wrote three guest columns while a student at Dublin, Georgia, High School.

After her marriage to Tommy Hatchett and the birth of their first child, I invited Nora to write another column on motherhood. What follows are Nora's thoughts on the subject of motherhood.

The Joys of Motherhood

Was it just yesterday the world was silent? I wondered as my alarm blared at 5:00 A.M., and the snooze button no longer worked. The sound that wakes me now comes from my baby monitor, which my husband calls "crying in stereo."

I well remember the first time I heard that sound, minus a few octaves. Everything moved in slow motion, like a movie. Masked people and sterile gloves hovered over me like some show on surgery I'd seen on television. The clicking of instruments and the bright aluminum lights fit together in perfect harmony, and everything was icy cold although I was quite warm—and nauseous.

The first cry was so anticipated. I lay there for what seemed like hours waiting, holding my breath, praying silently to hear that all important yelp—"the cry of life." A chill swept over my body when I heard it. Nothing could have sounded more beautiful until I heard it again . . . and again . . . and again.

I've decided all alarm clocks should have recorded baby cries instead of buzzers and bells. But then, no one would ever sleep!

I still never really think of myself as a mother. I keep waiting for her parents to come and pick her up and pay me. I guess that comes from years of babysitting. But every now and then reality strikes and certain events spark my motherly instincts, like the first time I changed Collier's diapers.

I had been looking after children since I was thirteen and had changed quite a few bottoms, but this time it was different. Suddenly brands became important, and questions clogged my mind. Like, should I use Pampers, Huggies, or Luvs? Should I scrimp and go with the cheap brand that might cause diaper rash or splurge and go for the prestige label? Am I being a terrible and lazy mother for not using cloth diapers? How much alcohol do you actually dab on the umbilical cord? And how much is a dab anyway? What would Mama do? And where the heck is she when I need her? I had never felt so alone.

Her temperature lit my concern like neon. Just what *is* the proper temperature for a baby? Her first day home I changed her outfit seven times, used the rectal thermometer five, and spent the rest of the day reading Dr. Spock. But no matter how many times I read him or how much I memorize and quote him, when a crisis strikes, I run all over the house looking for my Dr. Spock book while carrying a screaming baby in my arms.

All my life I had dreamed of the moment I would discover that I was pregnant. I knew exactly how it would be, too. An elderly and gentle nurse, dressed in a crisp snow-white uniform, would walk over to me gracefully wearing an angel's smile, take my hand in hers, squeeze it gently and lovingly, and whisper softly, "You are with child, my dear." Then I would blush, and my face would glow blissfully as I walked from the doctor's office with my secret buried deep within my heart to tell my beloved husband the good news.

It didn't happen exactly like that. The day I found out I was pregnant I had fallen from a fourteen-foot deer stand and landed on my head in twenty-five-degree weather at 4:30 A.M. The nurse was young, fat, and wore yellow pants and a pink shirt. She walked like an elephant and didn't look me in the eye, and her voice had two volume levels: loud and off.

"It's positive," she said matter-of-factly.

I threw up.

I continued to throw up—morning, afternoon, and night. I was tempted to paint a mural in the bottom of my toilet because that's what I looked at morning, afternoon, and night.

After five months of "re-tasting my food," I decided the final four were make-up months and that a milkshake a day would cure any ailment. I was right, with the exception of obesity.

My sister Rennie was married in the eighth month of my pregnancy. Originally, I had been scheduled to be matron of honor, but when my Mom started looking for a bush large enough for me to stand behind, I decided to bow out gracefully.

Finally, the time came, and just like Lucy Ricardo I woke Tommy at 3:00 A.M., standing by the bed with labor pains and a packed suitcase. Inasmuch as I was three weeks overdue, everything in my suitcase had to be ironed before I could wear it. The suitcase had been packed since the day the young, fat nurse with the yellow pants and pink shirt announced to the world, "It's positive!"

And little Collier was born.

When Collier was but three weeks old, I was celebrating my birthday a week late at the Dublin Country Club when my best buddy, Bo Whaley, stopped by my table, gave me a big hug, and asked me to write yet another column for him. He suggested that I write on being a new mother, and the only title I could come up with at the time was "The Jokes of Motherhood." You see, it has taken a little while for me to understand just exactly what a mother is, and the true meaning of joy.

Collier was born in July. I tiptoed into her room one night the following December and sat by her crib. Just the two of us. She smelled so fresh and clean, as only a baby can, with her clothes line-dried. Her tiny feet were tucked snugly under her bottom, resembling a frog. One arm rested by her side, the other above her head. I smiled and whispered, "Just like your Daddy." I thought she grinned at that, but maybe she didn't.

My heart felt so full, like the grinch when he realizes that Christmas is not about presents or turkeys or ornaments or stockings, but rather the spirit within every person that brings the true Christmas. It was at that moment that I realized why I shouldn't write an article about "The Jokes of Motherhood" because being a mother is not really about early morning alarms, diapers, clothing, pregnancy, or labor pains. No, instead I would write about the joys of motherhood and rediscovering the wonder and excitement of experiencing life for the very first time.

God doesn't just send us children to sustain or perpetuate the human race, but rather that they might recapture our spirit, enlarge our hearts, and make us aware of what a truly awe-inspiring world surrounds us. He sends us children to prevent the sterile preoccupation with material goods that prompts alienation from His everlasting love and strength.

If I could be granted but one wish for the children, it would be that their eyes would always be open to the wonders that surround them and that their ears would always be tuned to the sounds of nature.

I thank God that my world is no longer silent.

Why Mothers Get Gray Early

I know of no group more versatile than mothers, and I'm constantly amazed at what one can accomplish in a single day. Mothers are really miracle workers with aprons.

If there is an underrated segment of the American society, it has to be mothers. It's not so much that we don't appreciate them as much as it is that we don't tell them often enough that we do.

There are many reasons why I could never be a mother, other than my physical makeup. Foremost is that I don't have enough patience to be one, not when I look back on the years my own mother spent trying to guide me in the right direction. Let's face it, I was not a good little boy and hated vegetables. She saw to it that I ate them.

If I had to name the one thing that would cause me to blow my top if I were a mother, it would be meal planning and food preparation. I think this is the prime reason why mothers get gray. Let us take a hypothetical case that may not be as hypothetical as it seems.

You—mother and wife—have done the laundry, picked Judy up from baton class, delivered Evelyn to cheerleader practice, taken Robert to Boy Scout camp, attended your study group, picked up the dry cleaning, bought groceries and fought the checkout line, returned three books to the library, and engaged in a long and not so pleasant conference with little Ralph's teacher.

You walk in the back door, dog tired, put the grocery bag that contains the necessary ingredients for Sloppy Joes that you plan to prepare for dinner on the kitchen table, and steal four minutes in the recliner with a glass of tea before slipping into that beat-up, but comfortable, housecoat to cook supper.

The time is now 6:45 P.M., and you are well into the Sloppy Joes when the telephone rings. Howard, your dutiful breadwinner, is calling.

"Hi, Anne! Just thought I'd call to tell you that six men from the home office, including the company president, are here, and I invited them to have dinner with us. I'll pick up the wine. You take care of dinner. O.K.? Nothing fancy. See ya' 'bout 7:30. Love ya', Honey. Bye."

He loves you? Then how could he do that to you? It's good for fifteen gray hairs, and the urge to kill, or divorce, is upon you. But, wife and mother that you are, you race back to the supermarket and start all over, with a 7:30 P.M. deadline. But being a miracle worker, you make it.

Now, let's reverse the situation.

You have spent an entire afternoon preparing a great meal for the husband and kids. You have taken special pains to cook just what they like: roast beef, rice and gravy, potatoes, butterbeans, candied yams, homemade biscuits, and your very own prize-winning apple pie with vanilla ice cream. At the last minute, you rush out and buy a quart of milk for Judy and Robert. Your husband, Howard, will have his usual coffee while the rest of the flock will drink iced tea, sweetened, of course.

You are gone no more than fifteen minutes and return, milk in hand, to hear the telephone ringing. It's Robert.

"Hi, Mom! I won't be home for supper. I'm at Jimmy's, and we're gonna' cook hot dogs and build model airplanes. Bye!"

Then, a repeat call. This one from Evelyn, sweet and considerate Evelyn.

"Won't be there for supper, Mom! I'm going to the gym with Linda to help decorate for the Junior-Senior Prom. You can fix me something when I get home. Bye!"

You are into your second glass of iced tea, sweetened, of course, when hubby Howard calls.

"Hi, Anne! I'm going to Gene's after work to help him work on his boat. You and the kids go ahead and eat. I'll just grab a hamburger on the way. Love ya'! Bye."

So, what do you do? You do what any good and neglected housewife and mother would do. You find yourself a comfortable, secluded spot and sit and cry . . . and cry . . . and cry.

And when you've finished crying, you can count gray hairs. You should have a bumper crop.

Mothers Are Very Special People

Mothers really are very special people, a rare breed. They're strong as an ox and tender as a dew drop. No one has ever determined just how many burdens their frail shoulders can bear; how many heartaches and disappointments their hearts can sustain; or just how many times they will go that second mile.

Down through the years, recognized authorities of the written word have penned varied thoughts on mothers, who and what they are. This is the light in which I see them.

A mother is in reality a composite, a combination of many things. Above all she is a human being, but there are times when she surfaces as an almost superwoman. And a mother is as tough as she is tender. She has to be. Here are but a few things that a mother must be:

- A mother is a magician. She finds lunch money when there is seemingly none to be found. She makes tears disappear with a kiss and mends broken hearts with a hug. And she loves you when you least deserve to be loved, knowing that's when you need it most.

- A mother is a physician. She knows just where and how hard to rub when it hurts and kisses more stumped toes, bumped heads, scraped elbows, and cut fingers than anyone else in the world. She wipes dirty faces and runny noses, diagnoses from experience, treats with loving care, and heals through diligence and prayer.

- A mother is a detective. She needs no polygraph to decipher your answers. She knows when you've done right or wrong and weighs the evidence fully before rendering a verdict.

- A mother is a confidante. She listens to the details of a broken love affair, a disappointment, errors in judgment, the consequences of a bad decision, and offers advice that you never dreamed of.

- A mother is a judge. She listens to the evidence presented by both sides before rendering such monumental decisions as who gets to ride in the front seat, who gets the end piece of the chocolate cake, who gets the white meat, which television program to watch, whether or not you can go swimming, who hit whom first, and whether you can spend the night at a friend's house.

- A mother is a chef. She can do more with a pound of hamburger meat, a smidgen of cheese, a can of tomato paste, and a few slices of bread than Betty Crocker. And at the supermarket she can stretch a dollar from the canned vegetables to the meat department, and still manage to have enough left over to buy a few goodies.

- A mother is an athlete. She plays catch when she doesn't feel like it, pushes you in the wagon when her back is killing her, and fills in at shortstop when you can only come up with seven other baseball players. She'll take her turn at bat although her feet ache to the bone and there's dinner to be prepared or clothes to be washed.

- A mother is a chauffeur. She drives thousands of miles each year to make sure you're on time for majorette practice, a Little League game, cheerleader practice, piano lessons, a Boy or Girl Scout meeting, and school. She comes back again to pick you up.

- A mother is a person who can find things. She can find the baseball glove you left under the kitchen sink, the earring that has been behind the sofa for months, the composition book that was left behind the commode, the shoe that somehow ended up on top of the garage, the record album that nobody put in the stack of newspapers she's saving for the church, the knife that wound up in the laundry, the basketball that came to rest at day's end in the garbage can, and the tennis racquet that joined the lawnmower, rake, axe, gasoline can, and hedge trimmers at the end of summer. A mother can even find the tennis balls that rolled underneath the storage house all by themselves or the belt you said you'd never need again in a cardboard box in the storage room that also holds the deflated football that you'll ask her to find next week.

- A mother is a teacher. She teaches things like "Now I lay me down to sleep . . ." "Thank you God for the food that we are about to eat . . ." "The Lord is my shepherd, I shall not want . . ." "Thou shalt not steal . . ." "Do Unto Others . . ." "Jesus loves me this I know, for the Bible tells me so . . ." "One-Two-Three-Four-Five-Six. . . . " "I pledge allegiance to the flag of the United States of America. . . . " and "Oh, say can you see, by the dawn's early light. . . . "

And what does she expect in return? Nothing really, but it would be nice if sometime soon you took her in your arms and said, "Thanks, Mother. Thanks for everything. I love you."

DADDY'S LITTLE
GIRL GROWS UP

I FACE A WALL COVERED WITH PHOTOGRAPHS,
mostly of my daughter, Lisa. I see one taken when she set
a school record by scoring 1000 points in her basketball
career; one sitting on her throne when she was named
Homecoming Queen in 1976; one of her receiving her
diploma the night she graduated; and her official senior
photograph. I'm prejudiced, but I think she is the finest
and most beautiful daughter in the world. She inspires me
every day of my life.

Lisa has given me so many happy moments that to try
to list them would be futile. I reflect on some of them
every day.

Like trips to Daytona . . . ghost stories late at night, with
her hiding under the bed . . . weekends in Atlanta and
dining at the Midnight Sun . . . her first car . . . train rides

on the *Nancy Hanks* . . . sitting up all night talking and telling jokes.

And, just last week she was here for the play, *Look Homeward, Angel,* and saw her daddy-hero floundering around on stage—a hopeless drunk. (I am proud that this is the only time she has seen her daddy in such a condition.)

The pictures on the wall tell a story, the story of transition from little girl to young lady: the trampolines and toys turned to Toyotas and television; the Mouseketeers became The Young and the Restless; mama's old hats were replaced with cream rinse and hair rollers; and daddy's seat at the ball game, the movie, on the boat, and at the restaurant is now occupied by somebody else—Lisa's date.

Yes, no doubt about it, my little girl just up and became a young lady, a beautiful young lady. I'll never forget the night that the realization hit me right between the eyes. It was truly a date to remember. And I do. It happened this way.

I drove down to David Emanuel Academy in Stillmore to see her play basketball. She was a sophomore, age fourteen. I always followed the same routine when I went to see her play. I sat and watched the girls' game with a friend or two, and Lisa would come and sit with me for the boys' game. As far as I was concerned, this night would be no different. Boy! Was I wrong!

David Emanuel was playing Bartow Academy and the girls won their game easily. I walked to the concession stand between games. (I actually didn't want any coffee, but I couldn't pass up the opportunity to gloat as Lisa had played an exceptionally good game.) After finishing my coffee, I strutted back to my seat to wait for her as I always had. And true to form, she came bouncing up the bleachers as radiant as a sunrise. I shifted in my seat to make room for her. That's when she hit me.

"I've got a date, Daddy. I'm gonna' sit with Robert!"

Well, sir, I didn't know what to say! I don't think I could have spoken anyway with my heart in my throat! My little girl? A date? The little girl who just last year, it seems, sat on my lap and pulled at my glasses; went to sleep with a Barbie doll in her arms and a Pekingese, Chen-Chen, lying beside her; ran as hard as she could and jumped in my arms when I got out of the car when I got home from work; giggled all night when Audrey Ann or Debbie spent the night with her and I scared the pajamas off both of 'em with ghost stories and ugly faces; drove my car when she was twelve (and drove it well); walked hundreds of miles in high heel shoes playing "grown-up"? And now, she has the nerve to grow up on me and have a date? Unbelievable!

I really don't recall very much about the ball game, but I can sure describe Robert to you in full detail.

I watched Lisa as she left me to take her seat beside him. I wanted him to be ugly, with pimples, long hair, ears like Dumbo, and a nose like Pinnocchio, but he was a nice, clean-cut young man. I should have given Lisa the credit she deserved. I should have known he would be a nice boy. But I watched him like a hawk, anyway.

I tried hard to hear what they were saying as they giggled back and fourth but the cotton pickin' fans wouldn't be quiet so I could hear. Nevertheless I maintained my surveillance until the half when I eased back to the concession stand. I had to have a cup of black coffee and a few cigarettes! As I was devouring both, I saw them coming, Lisa and Robert. She was smiling from ear to ear, and I felt like cutting his throat from ear to ear! He had moved the old man out and had him singing the old song, "Somebody Else Is Taking My Place."

With a cigarette in one hand a cup of coffee in the other, I met Robert. I tried to remain calm and collected as I shook his hand and came out with a bald-faced lie.

"It's nice to meet you, Robert."

He shook my hand firmly and looked me right in the eye as he spoke.

"It's nice to meet you, Mr. Whaley. Lisa has told me a lot about you."

Con man, I thought. *What a con man. He ain't gonna snow me!*

"Would you and Lisa like to go to the Dairy Queen after the game and get something to eat?"

"Oh, no thank you, sir. We're going to a dance."

I felt weak, again. I could see the picture forming in my imagination. He would put her in the front seat of that hot rod with the mag wheels, lifters, tape player, portable bar, four-in-the-floor and take off like Cale Yarborough as his oversized wide-ovals slung gravel over the gymnasium. I would be able to hear him "get" all four gears as he roared out of town with the tape player turned up as high as it would go!

I was wrong, again.

I walked with them to his car, a conservative Chevrolet Impala. I felt like apologizing as I watched him open the car door for her and walk around to the driver's side and shake my hand again. He made a big point with me when he said, "I'll be careful, Mr. Whaley, and I'll have her home by 11:30."

I poked my head in the window after he was seated under the steering wheel and gave him a firm pat on the shoulder.

"Just call me Bo, Robert. All Lisa's friends do."

I watched him drive away, with my life in the front seat, and as his taillights disappeared from view, so did things like trampolines, ghost stories, train rides, mama's old hats, The Mouseketeers, Barbie dolls, trick or treating— gone. I had greeted my little girl when I arrived for the game and watched her ride away, a young lady.

Truly, a date to remember.

I look again at the wall above my typewriter and see some empty spaces, spaces for more pictures: one of her graduation from Georgia Southern; one of her as a "little sister" for the Kappa Sig fraternity; one as its sweetheart; one of her on her wedding day, and yes, there is a lot of space left on the wall. Who knows?

Because We
Love Them

I CAN'T REALLY PINPOINT JUST WHEN I DECIDED to write this, although the theme has tiptoed across my mind many times. It could have been when I had a recent conversation with a friend. We both shared a common concern: What to do about mama? Why? Because we love them.

Upon returning home later that evening, I was ready to reduce my thoughts to writing in the hope that my words, admittedly inadequate, might serve to help someone else, concerned about another mama, make a decision—because we love them.

I made mine within the past month. It was inevitable that I would have to make it. So far, I am comfortable with it because in my heart I know it was the right—and only—decision to make. That is important.

I had to remove a loved one from the confines of her home, the only one she ever owned, to place her in a care facility so that she might receive the attention she deserves.

It is done; she is there. We are comfortable with it. The long nights and days of indecision over. So why am I writing this? Simple. Because I know that there are literally thousands upon thousands of others who are faced daily with the same decision. The only question is just how long we shun the responsibility of making it. I am convinced that it may well be *the* major domestic concern in America. Why? Because we love them.

My decision was not a hasty one, and neither will yours be when you make it. There are certain definite and telltale signs that, individually, are insignificant; but, like snowflakes, when combined, they accentuate the passage of time and the necessity to pause and consider the options. Oh, we would like to turn the page and read another story to keep things in a form of status quo—like they used to be. We dream of a miracle and pray for guidance, and will accept either, because we love them. We eventually emerge from the confines of this "twilight zone"; we exit the world of fantasies and dreams and enter the world of realism, which is always there. Popular singer Jim Reeves echoes the feeling when he sings, "Make the World Go Away." It won't. We have to cope with it, and will, because we love them.

The signs? You'll see them. They sort of ease into your life—softly. Like when you first notice that it requires more and more effort for her to negotiate those two steps leading from the carport to the den; having to curtail the daily late-afternoon walks with her little canine companion, Mitzi, that both eagerly anticipated; not being quite strong enough to maintain her house and yard in the same manner she has been accustomed to for years, and with so much pride; finding it more and more difficult to sign checks, write a letter, or prepare her church envelope for Sunday morning, while you observe but remain silent. Partially because you don't know what to say, but primarily because you aren't prepared to receive her response—you are really treading water—you avoid the confrontation with the inevitable.

Days and weeks flit by. On visits you become acutely aware that a decision, a most important decision, is in the offing. Your observations become more microscopic and less discreet. Too soon they become fixtures in the reservoirs of your mind, only to surface later at seemingly the most unpredictable times and places.

In the middle of a hymn on Sunday morning you suddenly recall that she stumbled and nearly fell twice when you visited her the day before—once going into the kitchen and once coming out. As you ride to work you remember the words she mumbled when she tried to thread that needle to sew a button on your shirt the week before: "They just don't make the holes in these needles as big as they used to, son!" You smile and remain silent, still treading water. You just thread the needle for her and make yet another deposit in your memory bank.

As you watch a football game on TV you see those two bruised spots on her leg, that you should have asked her about.

Days become weeks, weeks become months. Your visits and your concerns become more frequent. And then, one day, you sit down with her in the den and take a closer and longer look—because you love her.

The needle holes continue to shrink; the impatient poodle hasn't been for a walk in weeks and doesn't understand; there are more bruised spots; the unanswered letters are beginning to pile up on the coffee table, alongside a stack of unread newspapers; the TV is as blank and mute as a shoe box; the refrigerator that once overflowed with the likes of chicken, pork chops, steak, sausage, eggs, meat loaf, vegetables of all kinds, and delicious home-made pies, now houses only a slice or two of boiled ham, a carton of milk, a partial package of wieners, and a frozen chicken pie. Tell-tale signs? Definitely.

The time is fast approaching when a decision must be made. You casually mention the bare refrigerator and she answers with a weak smile: "Well, I just don't seem to get as hungry as I used to."

However, she couldn't shrug off the bruised spots, the unanswered mail, the unread newspapers, the dormant TV, the ever-shrinking needle holes, the neglected poodle, or the delinquent church envelopes. Welcome back to the world of reality. The buck has stopped, and you have it! The game of pass the thimble is over and it has been dropped in your hands. You will handle it. You will do what you must, because you love her.

What do you do? You tread a little more water. She agrees that she needs help and you make a decision. You search and you search and search some more until you finally locate a lady to come, to help, to offer companion-ship. You are relieved, temporarily. You are comfortable in the knowledge that she is not alone during the daytime and you make an honest effort at commuting the fifty miles to be there at night. What you have really done is buy a little more time while you wait for a miracle.

The arrangement works, but only for a little while. Her companion confides in you that she needs professional care. You knew it but were waiting for another opinion. You weren't ready for it. You never would be, because you love her. It is decision time again.

As you sit with her in the den you try again to tread water, to put off. You put water on for a cup of coffee that neither of you really wants. You have the feeling that she is reading your mind.

You settle down with the coffee on your lap—Stone Mountain in your throat and the Sahara Desert on your tongue. It is a one-on-one situation, for you and Mama are the only two left. You have already made your decision. You would rather go to prison than relate it to her. But she's your mama, she can, and does, read you like a book. True to form, she makes things easier for you: "Son, I know I need some help. I'll leave it up to you. I'll do whatever you think is best."

The decision is made. From that point on it was just a matter of implementing it. Some call it "making arrangements." We did, and she is now in Dublin. I can, and do, see her every day.

So why have I written? To provide just a little insight into an area of concern that so many of us live with and, most importantly, to emphasize the need for "them" to fully realize that only one factor breeds our concern. We are concerned because we love them.

In My Father's Footsteps

SUNDAY WAS A VERY SPECIAL DAY FOR ME. I went to the United Methodist Church in Scott, Georgia, to be the guest speaker at the homecoming service. The fact that I drove from Chattanooga the night before to be there is incidental. I would have driven from Sacramento, California, just as eagerly.

For me, that's where it all started some fifty years ago, the day I was born in the Methodist parsonage at Scott, where my father was beginning what would be forty-three years as a minister in the South Georgia Conference.

I walked to the pulpit with some apprehension and stood in the very spot where my father had stood so proudly as a young minister.

For forty-three years I walked in his footsteps, as a child in Scott and later, as I grew older, in his beloved Middle and South Georgia woods and fields hunting quail. If he stepped on a log, I stepped on it, right where he did because I knew he would not steer me wrong. He always seemed to know just where the shallow places were, and the deep ones. If I had adopted a theme song in those beautiful years, it would have been, "Where He Leads Me I Will Follow."

As we both grew older, his steps shortened a bit and slowed down; but they were still *his* steps and I followed them until his death in 1969. He was my father. He was my buddy. He was my best friend. Do I miss him? Only twice every twenty-four hours—night and day.

The homecoming service was beautiful. As I stood in the pulpit and surveyed the scene, I couldn't help but reflect on days gone by. I was back in the atmosphere in which I had grown up, a small country church attended by good, hard-working and devout people. I wanted just to stand there and look at them. The character that radiated from their faces was so reassuring that I must have uttered a silent prayer that they stay that way. What I was really looking at was America, the way I think it should be. A few gathered together on Sunday morning to do the very thing this country was founded for them to do, worship.

No doubt there were many thousands of churches throughout America this morning that were more beautiful, with much larger congregations, but I feel certain that none was fostering the purpose for which it was built more than Scott Methodist, worshiping God. And I was there, standing proudly in the place where my father had stood half a century before.

The service ended with the singing of his favorite hymn, "Blest Be the Tie That Binds." I was still humming it as we all retired to the front lawn under the trees to partake of an American tradition, dinner on the ground. No restaurant in the world has yet come up with a menu to compare with a meal prepared by the ladies of the church. The flies were there but didn't stand a chance as the wooden-handle cardboard fans were there, too, compliments of Townsend Funeral Home.

I had to pause for a minute as I enjoyed a piece of delicious lemon cheesecake, my father's all-time favorite. I wished he could be there. I even told a joke or two, as he would have, but somehow they just don't come out as funny as when he told them.

What I am really trying to do is say a simple "thank you" to the good people of Scott for inviting me back to stand where my father stood, to walk where my father walked. I appreciate their allowing me to stand "in my father's footsteps." I just hope that someday I might have earned the right to do so.

Finally, we offer our thanks this day for the many blessings that you have bestowed upon each of us: the certainty that the sun will set and rise again; that the rain will come and the rivers will flow; that we are all equal in your eyes because you are a fair and just God; that the only way that any of us will not gain the eternal heritage of your heaven is to turn away from your outstretched and beckoning hand.

For your love and blessings, we are eternally thankful. May peace and love reign triumphant over strife and hate throughout the world and the coming year bring with it an even greater display of faith in Christianity than the world has ever known.

So ends our prayer this day. It is offered humbly but reverently, in the name of your only son, Jesus Christ. Amen.

A DAY WITH MOM

IT HAPPENS EVERY TIME I PICK MY MOTHER UP AT the nursing home to take her out. I hear the same song as we walk the hall, slowly, to leave.

"Have a good time, Mrs. Whaley!" they sing out as we pass each room. And some, without fail, add the verse, "It sure is thoughtful of you to take your mother out, Bo."

For more than a year now I've accepted their plaudits and taken my bows, returning regularly for encores— undeserved encores, I might add.

It happened again yesterday, Thanksgiving Day. I bowed and smiled, cautiously trying to keep my halo from falling off, as I escorted Mother to the familiar strains of the laudatory tune, "Have a good time, Mrs. Whaley!"

Ten minutes later we were seated in the dining room with mountains of turkey and dressing on the table before us. I looked around and found myself surrounded by the Hansley Horne table, the Wilbur Jones table, the Sarah Orr Williams table, and the Tal Orr table. I mused at the setting and stole a line from my friend, Ron Riley, "Where could I find better company?"

The waitress greeted us with, "It's so nice to see you and your mother out today. You sure are good to her."

I accepted her praise for what a good boy I was, bowing in familiar fashion while checking my halo. I retrieved my napkin from the carpet and sat back down to reflect on the pretty lady seated across the table and the praise and plaudits that had come my way.

I stirred my coffee and gazed at the familiar face reflected in the cup, pausing to sneak another peek at my Thanksgiving dinner companion. She was busy and paid no attention to my stares (actually she was wrestling with a turkey leg).

Then it happened. My halo fell to the carpet, replacing my napkin. I stopped stirring and began reflecting on my lady wrestler.

Wait a minute! Me? Good to my mother? An hour here or an hour there? A short visit periodically or an occasional trip to the mall? Hah! Let's focus the camera and get the true picture.

Isn't she the same lady who saw to it that there was always lots of icing left in the pan for me to scrape when she made my favorite chocolate cake? Then she scrubbed it off my face after I'd cleaned the pan.

Isn't she the same lady who went through the valley of death to bring me into this world over fifty years ago in Scott, Georgia? The same lady who cared for me, nursed and loved me, sacrificed so I might know the good life?

Isn't she the same lady who tolerated such critters over the years as white rats, goats, pet mules, turtles, pet chickens, snakes, rabbits, gophers, and dogs, attending their funerals with me when they died?

Isn't she the same lady who repeatedly put her longed-for dresses back on the rack and pulled jackets and shirts from another one, never bothering to let me know we were poor materially?

The picture was beginning to come into focus.

Me? Good to my mother? Hah! The halo lay dead on the dining room carpet.

She's the same lady who made mustard plasters and hot Vicks compresses, poured Groves chill tonic down my throat by the gallon every spring, bandaged and kissed stumped toes and mashed fingers, removed splinters, lanced boils, soaked sore eyes, and spread salve from my head to my feet. She bought salve by the ton. She had a medical theory: When all else fails, put salve on it. Calomel and castor oil, quinine and Dickey's eye water, I know about those things. I was spared the asafetida, though.

She put up with more teasing from me than a bouffant hairdo; played left field when my team was one player short; always did her magic trick every October, coming up with a few coins from out of nowhere when the county fair came to town. (She even beamed like an Academy Award winner when I brought home a ten-cent ash tray that I had spent a dollar to win by throwing rings over pegs.) Who signed all those report cards I was afraid to show to Daddy?

She played marbles with me and won most of the time, when all the other marble shooters had gone home; washed and mended my dirty, ragged britches with the hole in the right knee and pretended not to see when I sneaked my little bulldog Skippy under the covers when she came to say goodnight.

More? Sure, there's more.

Who always ate the dark meat and end pieces of bread? Who saw to it that when mail call came in such remote places in the South Pacific as Leyte, Mindanao, New Guinea, Guam, and Okinawa in World War II that my name wasn't omitted? Who sent such goodies as boiled peanuts, chocolate cake, and homemade fudge?

When I returned to the United States, who went to baseball games to watch me pitch when what she really felt like doing was turning out the light, going to bed, and nursing a sick headache? Who consoled me when I lost, and shared my thrill of winning?

I was looking at her across the table.

Me? Good to my mother? Bear with me.

Who took me in seven years ago when my wheels ran off and I was alone for the first time in twenty-five years? Mamas just know when you need them.

So, I ask you, who's been good to whom? I only know that the longer I focus upon her, the clearer the picture becomes.

What else can I say?

I picked up my halo off the floor, put it in my pocket, drove her back to the nursing home, and headed for my typewriter.

Thanksgiving? It was a great day. . . .

Take a minute, pause, and say, "Thanks, Mama." She'll understand. If you like, I'll lend you my halo. I don't really have any use for it anymore, now that the picture is in proper focus.

THANKSGIVING DAY BRINGS BITTERSWEET MEMORIES

WHEN THIS ROLLS OFF THE PRESS I SHOULD BE IN or near the small town of Sparta in Hancock County. I've been there on November 25 for the past seventeen years. It's a special day to me. It's the day I buried the greatest friend I ever had. On November 25, 1969, my mother and I sat and watched as my daddy was buried in the Sparta Cemetery.

I'll do the same thing today that I've done every November 25 since 1969. I'll go and sit and reminisce. Once again I'll follow him through the woods hunting quail, stand by his side and listen to his fox hounds bark their way through the branches of Macon County, wait as he patiently untangles my fishing line or dislodges the hook from a tree limb hanging over the Flint River.

I'll sit at his grave and once again listen to the great stories he told while sitting in front of Dan Kleckley's store in

Oglethorpe in the late 1930s. I'll hear him tell again how he won the Georgia State Liar's Contest with a story about his favorite rabbit dog and how surprised he was to see the headline in the *Macon Telegraph:* Methodist Preacher Wins Liar's Contest.

I'll have to smile when I recall the time he stopped preaching in the middle of a sermon in Alma and said, "Bo, go spit that chewing gum out."

I'll recall, too, the only time I ever ran from him when he was going to whip me. I ran under the house, only to get all tangled up in his trotline. He spent the better part of an hour removing fish hooks from my hands and seat. This done, he whipped me.

Then, there was the Saturday afternoon when he caught my boyhood friend, Jack Smith, and me smoking in the balcony of the Alma Methodist Church. I'd rather have tangled with his trotline. He whipped me, and Jack's daddy whipped him. I'll be thinking about that, too.

How can my visit be a sad one when I think about things like the Christmas many years ago when we were all at Grandma's house. It was Christmas Eve and all fifteen visitors had gone to bed. The presents were stacked neatly under the tree, appropriately marked. There were name tags like To Mama from Ruth, To Papa from Wales, To Margaret from Grace.

He got up and eased downstairs, pen in hand, and changed all the name tags so that they read, From Walker.

Christmas morning his little scheme worked well—for a little while. With his sister, Ruth, playing Santa Claus and giving out the presents, every one she picked up read From Walker. Grandma, Grandpa, Margaret, and Grace were all thanking him for their presents. He simply smiled and accepted their thanks.

In his early morning haste, however, he had written too fast for fear of being caught and his bubble burst when

Ruth finally picked up a package which read To Walker—from Walker, proving that even the greatest of practical jokes slip up now and then.

I'll laugh, too, as I sit at his grave and roll over in my mind the note I found in one of his Bibles. It was written by him on the day I was born, with copies sent to his mother, father, and six brothers and sisters. It is a typical example of the humor and wit of my friend and father.

Scott, Ga.
December 11, 1927

Well Hello:

We are the proud possessors of a fine eight-and-one-half pound BOY this morning at eight thirty. Leila is doing fine and the BOY has a splendid set of lungs. What makes me feel so good is that Leila is o.k. and the BOY is perfect in form.

God has wonderfully blessed us and we hope to make a bishop of this BOY. I am so happy I could almost shout this a.m.

Don (my bird dog) does not like the BOY much, but I feel sure he will get the good feeling from his master in a few hours when I take him hunting.

Dr. Fort says that Leila is doing the best he ever saw a young mother do. Also, he says the BOY is perfect.

Well, I will tell you the truth. He is ugly; looks like uncle Henry Collins, the ugliest man in Hancock County. Ha, Ha. But don't you dare tell me that when you see him because it wouldn't do for a preacher to get engaged in a fight.

Will try and write a letter next week if I'm back down to earth by then. Pray for us that we may do

(GUN RACKS AND SIX-PACKS)

what God would have us do and be the mother and father that He wants us to be.

Love to all. Yours devotedly.

Walker

A sad visit? No way. I'm just thankful that I had the benefit of his friendship and guidance for forty-two years of my life.

Next November I'll make the trip to Sparta again and relive the good times. When I do that it is hard to remember the bad ones.

SITTIN' UP WITH

UNCLE JAKE

I LEARNED DURING THOSE YEARS IN NEW YORK that Will Rogers was right when he said, "No matter how far away from home a man may roam, what degree of success he attains, or how dismal a failure he might become—he always has an inner desire to return home one day."

During the more than four years that I worked in New York and lived in New Jersey, I was fortunate to become friends with many fine people. We were close enough that they would laugh at me and my southern ways, and I would return the good-natured ribbing by ridiculing some of their northern peculiarities.

Oh, we didn't fight the Civil War all over again, but we did reminisce about it quite frequently. They would jab me about my grits and I would throw their Cream of

Wheat, a sick man's grits, right back at them. Sure, I was outnumbered, but so was the Confederate Army most of the time.

My best Yankee friend was Tony Piersante, from Brooklyn. We laughed a lot when we were with each other, and I liked that. Tony's friends joked with me about my southern heritage, but Tony would not allow them to insult me. At six-foot-six and 290 pounds, he was a good man to have around.

Tony called me at home late one Saturday afternoon. His brother-in-law, Joe Trabucco, had died that morning, and he invited me to go with him to the Trabucco home in the Bronx to pay our respects to Joe's family.

Joe, who had also been a friend of mine, had a nice wife, Maria, and seven children. Their ages ranged from three to fifteen, four boys and three girls. Maria was pretty, and an excellent cook. She prepared dishes I couldn't pronounce but had little difficulty digesting. (In her Italian household, if Maria had any doubt about the palatability of a particular dish, she just added more garlic.)

When we arrived at the Trabucco home about 10:00 P.M., I received the surprise of my life. The noise was deafening. It sounded like New Year's Eve, the Fourth of July, and Columbus Day all rolled into one. There must have been fifty people there, drinking, eating, laughing, and telling stories about Joe.

There was a bar, a bartender, a keg of beer, and tables loaded down with food, with more arriving at regular intervals. Over in a corner of the living room, quiet and sober, and stiff as a board, was Joe.

"What's going on?" I whispered to Tony.

"These are Joe's friends and relatives, honoring the memory of Joe," he explained. "It's called a wake. You mean you've never been to one?"

"Awake?" I questioned.

"Right, a wake. Most of these people will be here all night."

I glanced over at Joe, laid out in a coffin under a dim light. No doubt in my mind that ol' Joe was dead as Hillary Clinton's health care plan. Awake? No way. Asleep? You betcha'.

"Seems to me that it would more appropriately be called asleep than awake," I offered.

"Nope. It's always been called a wake. Don't you folks in Georgia sit up with the deceased the night before the funeral?"

"Sure. We call it sittin' up."

"And how is that different from a wake?"

"Well, first of all, there isn't any liquor. Also, it's a pretty solemn occasion. No jokes about the deceased. It's a pretty respectful time with lots of crying, mostly by distant relatives and businessmen to whom the deceased owed money," I explained.

"Sounds pretty dull to me," said Tony.

"It is most of the time, but not always. I remember one time in particular when excitement reigned."

"Tell me about it."

So I did.

Raymond Lofton turned thirteen a few days before the death of his uncle, Jake Lofton, who was slightly older than the Palace of Versailles at the time of his demise.

Raymond was a good boy, very obedient, who never shirked a family responsibility. So it was only natural that when his father, Luther Lofton, approached him and said he was old enough to take his turn, along with other family members, in the time-honored tradition of sittin' up with his uncle the night before the funeral, he raised no objection. But he wasn't too keen on the idea.

Raymond had always balked at being around anybody or anything dead. It was his nature. His assigned duty of sittin' up with Uncle Jake would be his initial participation in such a ritual, and although he didn't really cotton to the idea, he would do it because his daddy said he should.

At 9:00 P.M., Raymond entered the living room of the house, located near a swamp about eight miles from town. Uncle Jake was laid out in front of a window, reposing in a coffin underneath an open window. Raymond's cousin, James Barlowe, his uncle, Gus Lofton, and his daddy were seated in folding funeral home chairs, clutching hand-held cardboard funeral home fans. There was a picture of the McKibben Brothers Funeral Home on one side and an artist's conception of heaven, a lake, and Jesus on the other.

Raymond moved slowly to a folding funeral home chair, picked up the hand-held cardboard funeral home fan, and sat down, not knowing quite what to expect, or what was expected of him.

Outside, the weather was wet and unruly. Heavy rain beat on the windows and strong winds manhandled a lone, loose shutter on the living room window next to Uncle Jake's coffin, slamming the shutter roughly and repeatedly against the side of the house. Streaks of lightning sprinted across the dark sky, igniting explosive thunder that shook the house.

Uncle Jake had been injured severely in an automobile accident many years before his death, and a spinal injury had left him badly stooped. The McKibben brothers did a really fine job of running a leather strap from his heels to the back of his neck in order to straighten him up sufficiently to lay him in the coffin so the lid could be closed for the funeral. Raymond was not aware of this.

At 10:00 P.M., Raymond's daddy stood up and said, "Well boys, if y'all are gonna' sit up I b'lieve I'll go on up to bed," and left the room. That left Raymond, his Uncle Gus, and his Cousin James to sit up with Uncle Jake. They sat in relative silence, with the rain, lightning, and thunder continuing with an ever increasing tempo, until about 11:00, when Uncle Gus got up out of his folding funeral home chair, stretched, and said, "Well, if you two boys are gonna' sit up for a while I think I'll go on upstairs and get some sleep." With that, Gus was gone.

Raymond looked at James and James looked at Raymond. Both alternately looked at Uncle Jake.

Shortly thereafter, James followed Luther and Gus upstairs after saying, "Well, Raymond, if you're gonna' sit up for a while, I think I'll go on upstairs and go to bed." His departure left Raymond alone in the room with Uncle Jake.

Raymond sat motionless, holding his hand-held cardboard funeral home fan, listening to the constant ticking of the clock on the mantel. The family cat snuggled on his feet.

Suddenly, at the stroke of midnight, the rain, lightning, and thunder went crazy at the same time. It sounded like a train wreck. The rain was coming down harder than ever, repeated lightning dominated the sky, and a tremendously loud clap of thunder hit like a bomb, shaking the house from one end to the other. An oil lamp fell from the mantel, and the damaged shutter near Uncle Jake's coffin was blown off its hinges.

The cat scrambled to get underneath the sofa. A door slammed shut in the hallway. Yet Raymond, seated in his folding funeral home chair and clutching his hand-held cardboard funeral home fan, was unmoved. Then, the worst thunder of the night sounded across the sky. It shook Uncle Jake's coffin so fiercely that the leather strap running from his heels to the back of his neck snapped and Uncle Jake bolted upright in his coffin. At this point Raymond arose from the folding funeral home chair, cast down his hand-held cardboard funeral home fan, and

announced in a strong and determined voice, "Well, Uncle Jake, if you're gonna' sit up I think I'll go on upstairs and go to bed." With that, Uncle Jake was left alone, sittin' up with himself.

BREAKING THE
BAD NEWS

IT WAS A DAY MADE FOR WHISTLING; BRIGHT SUN-shine and 78 degrees at 3:22 P.M.

I stood in front of Oatts Drug Store and waited for the traffic light at W. Jackson and S. Lawrence to change. Across the street, in front of Lovett and Tharpe Hardware, a mother and her five-year-old daughter stepped off the curb and walked toward the bank, hand in hand. They almost didn't make it.

A late model sedan came cruising through the intersection, running a red light. The driver never saw either the red light or the mother-daughter duo and to this day I'm positive he has no idea how close he came to hitting the little girl, who jumped to one side to avoid a tragedy.

I know the driver well and it would have done him in had he hit the child.

The mother, visibly shaken, maneuvered the child to the curb and leaned against the bank, emotionally drained.

Replay of a Day in 1968

The year was 1968, the day, a day in February; Lyons was the town. And the driver? My Dad.

The telephone call came from a state trooper, a long-time friend of my Dad's. He'd hunted and fished with him, heard him say, "And now, I pronounce you man and wife," watched as he baptized his two daughters and officiated at the funeral of his mother. He loved my Dad. That's why he called.

"Bo, I want to talk to you about Brother Whaley," he said, almost apologetically. "It's his driving. He's reached the point where it's dangerous for him to continue. He just missed running over a boy in front of the school this morning. Ran right through a stop sign. It's happened before and I'm just afraid . . ."

"Thanks, Dave. I appreciate your call. I'll drive down this afternoon and talk with him," I promised.

"I wish you would. I've talked with the chief of police and the sheriff and none of us have the heart to tell him he shouldn't drive, but we love him too much to see him continue," he said.

I Didn't Have the Heart to Do It

I guess I really knew when I headed south on U.S. 1 that I wouldn't do it. Oh, I practiced my speech all the way from Swainsboro to Lyons, the full 30 miles. I had it down letter-perfect.

But answer me this: How do you tell the man who sat you in his lap when you were barely out of diapers, and let you steer on back roads, that his driving days are over? How do you explain that to the only driving instructor you ever had?

How do you just up and say, "You can't drive anymore?" to the man who balanced you on his knees in a 1934 Ford, taught you how to shift gears without "scraping" and let you blow the horn back in the dark ages when you blew the horn to pass?

What about all the times when you were but 14 and you anticipated him, saying, "Son, do you want to drive the rest of the way home?" Want to? He knew I'd have given my slingshot, pet goat, a pocketful of marbles and pocket-knife to get under the steering wheel.

Now, here I was on my way to break his heart. I was still rehearsing my speech as I passed the Lyons city limit sign and turned on N. Victory Drive. 303 was my destination. That's where I was scheduled to deliver my speech. I was still in a quandary.

Like, what would I say to the man who bought my first car in 1947 and made payments on it that I knew darned well he couldn't afford? Easy, huh? Yeah, just bust right in and say "Well, ol' fella', I hate to have to be the one to tell you this, but you just can't drive anymore."

To my Dad, who practically lived in his car, that would be like telling Herschel his running days were over, Grizzard that his typing days were finished or Jimmy Connors to hand over his tennis racquet.

Admittedly, I should have told him, but I didn't. I just plain didn't have the heart to break his.

March of 1969 Was a Bummer

Getting in his car and driving to the post office every morning was as normal as breathing and praying for my

Dad; next came stops at the drug store and the cafe. It was his morning ritual.

His bumpers and fenders bore visible signs of morning battles to park "between the lines," or "stop before bumping." And stop signs and red lights were fast becoming obsolete to him. Not that he ignored them, he simply never gave them a second thought when making his morning rounds.

Along came March, 1969. I was visiting and we were going fishing. He insisted on driving, as always. We threw our gear in the back seat and he backed out of the driveway, without looking.

He drove north on Victory Drive, east on Oglethorpe and zipped through a stop sign as he crossed U.S. 1, at the school. How the boy on the bicycle managed to avoid being hit I'll never know.

We never made it to Kovakos' pond. He pulled over like he'd done so many times when I was a boy and asked, "Do you want to drive back to the house?"

I parked his car under the carport. It was still there when he entered a hospital in Savannah two weeks later. It was still there when he died in Dublin seven months later, the day before Thanksgiving, 1969.

I was a year late in doing it but the hardest thing I ever had to tell him was, "Well, ol' fella', I hate to have to tell you this but you can't drive anymore."

He didn't dispute it. Somehow, I feel he knew it was far better to park his car than risk killing a child. He could never have taken that.

Somebody in Dublin Has a Job to Do

Somewhere out there a red light runner is waiting to be told. He probably won't park his car otherwise.

A son, a grandson or somebody is just going to have to up and say, "Well, ol' fella', I hate to have to be the one . . ."

It won't be easy, but it may ease the burden if you stop and consider the alternative.

THERE'S NO PLACE
LIKE THIS HOME!

I HADN'T GIVEN THE LEAST BIT OF THOUGHT TO Christmas, 1982, until last Saturday when a telephone call shook me with the realization that December 25th is just around the corner.

The call was from Abigail Rotchford, chairperson of the "Tour of Homes Committee." I was flabbergasted to hear from her and I'm sure she suspected the same after identifying herself.

"Oh, yes . . . yes ma'am. It's good to hear from you, Miss Abigail," I stammered.

"Thank you, Mr. Whaley. I'm looking forward to talking to you. The reason I called is this. Your house has been recommended for inclusion in the 'Tour of Homes,' and I was wondering if Rosemary Bartholomew could come out with me and tour your premises so that we might make a recommendation to the full committee Sunday afternoon?"

"My house? On the tour of homes? Gee! That's great! Certainly, you are welcome anytime. When would you like to come, Miss Abigail?" I stammered.

"I like to get right to things, Mr. Whaley. Rosemary is with me now and we'd like to come right on out," she said. "We can be there in 15 minutes, if that's satisfactory."

"Fine—just fine. Do you know where I live?"

"Oh, yes. It's the little red house on 441 North with the old blue, uh . . . I mean the uh, antique Mercury in the front yard, isn't it?"

"Right, and there's a not-quite-so-old green Mercury parked next to it. I'll see y'all in a few minutes," I told her.

Man! I was as nervous as a gallon of Jello. I mean, it just ain't every day that Abigail Rotchford comes visiting. Heck, she's been known to leave dinner parties because the deviled eggs didn't match. You talk about your uptown society with a capital "S" and you're talking about Abigail Rotchford. And . . . she was coming to my house . . .

A Tour of the Premises

I heard the knock on the door and opened it to find Abigail Rotchford and Rosemary Bartholomew standing there.

"Good evening, ladies! Come right on in," I said.

"Thank you, Mr. Whaley," replied Abigail. "We were just admiring your antique cars. Have you been collecting them long?"

"Oh . . . uh, well, just since the divorce. Do you like my collection?"

"They're very interesting," Abigail said.

"Yes, and quaint," added Rosemary.

"I see that you are a naturalist, permitting your grass, shrubs and trees to grow naturally," observed Rosemary.

"Well . . . yes, that's quite true. By not cutting the grass or trimming the shrubbery I feel quite close to nature. Nature knows best, I always say."

"Hmmmm, could be," Rosemary mumbled as we all three stopped in the living room.

"I honestly believe these are the most unique throw rugs I have ever seen. Where in the world did you ever get them?" asked Abigail.

"Are they original?" Rosemary inquired.

"Uh, the one over by the bookcase came from Statesboro about 1973. It belonged to my son who was an ATO there. He left it here when he came for the weekend about ten years ago," I explained.

"It looks almost like an old dirty sweatshirt, doesn't it, Rosemary?"

"Yes, complete with the Greek ATO on it," she said.

"And the other one?" asked Abigail.

"My daughter left it here last summer. Unusual, isn't it?" I stammered.

"Yes. It resembles a pair of ragged blue jeans," Abigail observed and moved on to the kitchen, stopping abruptly at the doorway. "Now then, I wish you would look at that, Rosemary," she said, pointing to my three-legged kitchen table. "Don't you just love the way he's incorporated the use of used brick into the kitchen decor? It has the look of ruggedness, Mr. Whaley."

"Oh, it's nothing, really. I just put the bricks under the short table leg to keep the table from tipping over from the weight of my elbows," I said, modestly.

We moved on into the kitchen where Rosemary made an observation. "Just look at that window box under the window, Abigail. Isn't that just the most original thing you've ever seen? He's even used glasses, cups, bowls, pots, pans and plates for effect. Just what is that green stuff growing in there, Mr. Whaley?"

"The county sanitation department was here last week and I heard one man say to the other that it appeared to be fungus and algae, whatever that is. They must have liked it, because each took samples and put them in little jars. And one said he just couldn't believe it. I guess fungus and algae must be rare in these parts and they wanted to take some home to their wives. And I didn't even charge them for it," I bragged.

"Yeeessss, I suppose that's a possibility," said Rosemary. "Let's go look in the bathroom."

"Do we have to?" Abigail asked.

"By all means. We must be thorough in our report to the committee," Rosemary answered.

"I suppose you're right. You go first, Rosemary."

The ladies gave my bathroom a quick once-over and commented only on the towels.

"Oh, I've heard of these, Abigail. They're replicas of Holiday Inn towels, right, Mr. Whaley?" Rosemary said.

"Uh . . . uh, yes ma'am, replicas. Exact replicas," I lied.

At the front door the ladies paused and thanked me for the tour of my house and said they would call me as soon as the "Tour of Homes Committee" made its decision on Sunday.

True to their word, I received a call from Abigail Rotchford late Sunday afternoon and she gave me the report of the committee's decision.

"Congratulations, Mr. Whaley! The committee feels your house is just what we're looking for," she said.

"Great! That's great!" I said. "What type of Christmas decorations should I use?"

"Christmas decorations? We were thinking more of pumpkins, witches and jack-o'-lanterns. The committee wants to use your place on the haunted house tour this Halloween, Mr. Whaley. Not Christmas . . ."

NORTH
VERSUS SOUTH

JUST WHAT IS A REAL SOUTHERNER ANYWAY?

I'VE ALWAYS BEEN REAL PROUD OF MY SOUTHERN heritage. "I'm American by birth and a Southerner by the grace of God" is how the bumper sticker puts it.

My Southern loyalty even extends to my bedroom as I sleep nightly under a 4' x 6' Confederate flag that hangs from the ceiling. Somehow, I feel more secure with that flag above my head.

I love the South for many reasons: the friendliness of its people, the wide open spaces, the diversity of its terrain, the beauty of its women and the delicious taste of its food.

Even on the streets our folks are friendly. Like when you meet a Southerner driving a motor vehicle he raises a forefinger to greet and recognize you. Of course, the folks in New Jersey do the same thing. Only they use a different finger.

As much as anything else, I love Southerners for their ability to poke fun at themselves. And that brings me to the following:

Are You from Dixie? Really?

- A real Southerner can sing all the verses of "Amazing Grace" with every book closed and every eye closed.

- A real Southerner thinks every airplane flight in the world passes through Atlanta.

- A real Southern woman knows her place: on the 50-yard line on Saturday afternoons.

- A real Southerner considers himself bilingual if he can understand Yankees when they talk, but will fight you 'til sundown if you call him a bilingual.

- A real Southern church-goer won't speak to other real Southern church-goers in the liquor store.

- A real Southerner puts Tabasco sauce on his hot sauce.

- A real Southern Republican probably moved here.

- A real Southerner is more scared of filter-tipped cigarettes than cancer.

- A real Southerner eats dinner at noontime and supper at night.

- A real Southerner thinks radar was meant for the Air Force and observes the 55-mile an hour speed limit only in his driveway.

- A real Southerner can kiss his girlfriend goodnight without shifting his toothpick or match stick.

- A real Southerner knows that tomatoes aren't any good unless they're grown in the same dirt he walks on.

- A real Southerner would rather have a cold biscuit than a hot tamale.

- A real Southern church-goer knows whose eyes are not closed during the prayer.

- A real Southerner knows that streak-o-lean is the best part of the hog.

- A real Southern housewife thinks we should have a national holiday for freezing corn and planting bulbs.

- A real Southern husband can't tell you the date of his wedding anniversary, but knows when it's the first day of deer season.

- A real Southerner says, if God hadn't intended us to eat grits then why did He give us red-eye gravy.

- A real Southerner knows that the real purpose of the Mason-Dixon Line is to separate "Y'all" from "Youse Guys."

PRECONCEIVED NOTIONS SOUTHERNERS HAVE ABOUT YANKEES

HERE ARE SOME PRECONCEIVED NOTIONS SOUTH-erners hold about those living north of the Youse-Y'all dividing line. Since most of these ideas are untrue, it is important to get them out into the open. Such ideas are:

- That everybody north of Baltimore is suspect.

- That all women living in the Bronx have hairy legs and eat garlic for breakfast every morning. (One true son of the South even went so far as to say that "the most effective form of birth control is a Bronx accent." Just not totally true, Beauregard. The garlic has to be a contributing factor.)

- That every man over the age of 18 in New York is a member of the Mafia.

- That lifelong residents of Brooklyn think Atlanta is located just over the Brooklyn Bridge somewhere in the vicinity of the Holland Tunnel.

- That California is a member of the United Nations.

- That there are continuous race riots in Detroit around the clock. Both sides riot in eight-hour shifts and are members of Race Rioters and Headbusters Local 609.

- That it snows year round in Michigan, and the sun only comes out on July 4th.

- That the only religion in Philadelphia is Catholicism.

- That everybody in New York goes to the ball park on Sunday afternoon. They sit in the bleachers, remove their shirts, drink beer, get sloppy and abusive, and curse the umpires. Not true. Some of them do not sit in the bleachers.

- That people in New York City actually live in telephone booths and public rest rooms. Also not true. Some have no roof over their heads at all, and there is a waiting list for telephone booths and public rest rooms.

- That cold-water flats (apartments) rent for as much as $1,000 a month. This is obviously in error. I have a good friend who lives in one, and he pays $1,500 a month.

- That everything in the North is overpriced. Probably. But there is one constant in both North and South: a fella' can still get five pennies for a nickel. The last time I visited in New York (July, 1985) I had a cup of coffee in my hotel, gave the cashier a $5 bill, and received $3.25 in change. I kept standing there with my hand out. He asked me what my problem was. "No problem," I said. "I'm just waiting for the deed to the restaurant." He had no sense of humor whatsoever and mumbled something that sounded like "Hick."

- That every nightclub and restaurant is filled to capacity with television, movie, and Broadway stars. Not true. I stayed in the city for five nights, and the closest I came to seeing a star was the visiting team batboy from Yankee Stadium at the Bronx Zoo and a Go-Go-Dancer who performs at Nudie Rudy's Skin Ranch in Times Square as she stepped out of a taxi and ran inside a side door to Nudie Rudy's. From the scant amount of clothing she was wearing, I think she was ready to perform when she arrived. I know she was wearing either a short skirt or a wide belt, but I'm not sure which. I just know that based on what I saw, or didn't see, a moth would starve to death in her clothes closest.

- That a large segment of the population of Brooklyn drink beer from the time the bars open at 7 A.M. until closing. This is another misconception of Yankees. Heck, some bars in Brooklyn don't open until 7:30 A.M.

- That every socialite in New York City has a poodle. Not so. Some have cats, and one I know has a jaguar.

- That Newark is a suburb of New York City. I don't know exactly what Newark is. I worked in the city for six years and, frankly, I'm convinced there ain't no reason for it to exist.

- That all Yankees eventually retire to the South. That is only partly true. Only those who can find The South retire here.

PRECONCEIVED NOTIONS YANKEES HAVE ABOUT SOUTHERNERS

HERE ARE SOME EQUALLY WRONG IDEAS NORTHerners have about those living south of the Youse-Y'all dividing line. These ideas hold up to scrutiny about as well as some of those Southerners have about Yankees. As you can see, I've added a few corrections of my own.

- That Southerners talk funnier than they do.

- That all women in the South are in the kitchen, barefoot and pregnant. Not anymore. Some spend a lot of time in the den.

- That moonshine is the regional drink and is served at all wedding receptions. This can't be true. If it were, the groom would never be able to back out of the driveway and get on with the honeymoon.

- That the majority of southern men spend most of their time hunting and fishing. I don't know a lot about that, other than that it takes almost as much time to scale fish and clean birds as it does to catch 'em and kill 'em.

- That all southern girls fourteen years of age and over are married. Ridiculous! I know a bunch in that age category who just shack up.

- That every man, woman, and child in the South owns a coon dog, a cat, or a frog.

- That grits grow on three-inch trees and are picked by midgets from Ringling Brothers during the off-season.

- That there really ain't no such thing as buttermilk. Sure is! It comes from a butter cow, and if your stomach looks anything like the glass it is downed from after it dries—heaven help you!

- That "Dixie" is sung at all weddings and funerals and is the official song of "Designing Women."

- That everybody down South talks with a drawl and sounds as if he or she is chewing homemade biscuits or boiled peanuts.

- That Southerners eat clabber as a substitute for yogurt.

- That mules are extinct.

- That Jack Daniel invented whiskey.

- That Atlanta Opera performers sing country songs.

- That hardly anybody down South watches "The David Letterman Show" that originates from New York. Well, more people would watch it if it wasn't on opposite "The Soybean Report" and "How to Whittle While the Mash Ferments." Priorities, you know.

- That Archie Bunker ain't a hero in the South. Wrong! He's right up there with Andy Griffith.

- That Sunday afternoons are spent mostly sitting under a giant magnolia tree, drinking mint juleps. Most Southerners outside of Louisville, Kentucky, ain't never seen a mint julep, and most of the giant magnolias have long since been cut for pulpwood along with all the other trees.

- That a man has two prized possessions—his bird dog and his wife—and prays long and hard that he'll never have to make a choice between them. While he can always stick something frozen in the microwave, it's just hard to find a wife who'll hold a point or retrieve quail.

Dixieland Entrance Examination

WHILE I HAVE NEVER SEEN IT, I UNDERSTAND there is an immigration station just north of Dillon, South Carolina, near the North Carolina line. I have it on good authority that it was built shortly after World War II and has been operational since 1949. Its purpose is to process Yankees bent on moving South.

The personnel who man the station are carefully selected, a prerequisite being that they be direct descendants of a Confederate soldier who served honorably and with distinction in the War of Yankee Aggression. Until his retirement in 1985, Beauregard P. Lee commanded the station and was replaced by Thomas J. ("Brickwall") Jackson who is now in charge.

The South Carolina immigration station is financed by a ten percent surcharge on all moonshine whiskey made in South Carolina, Georgia, and North Carolina, and since its opening in 1949 there has never been a shortage of funds.

Several years ago a friend of mine from Detroit, Michigan, retired after thirty years on the assembly line at Ford's River Rouge Plant, considered his options, and wisely chose to spend his retirement years in North Florida. Like hundreds of thousands of others had done before him, he bought a condominium and headed south. But he encountered one major obstacle: he almost didn't pass the Dixieland Entrance Examination given to all Yankees moving South at the South Carolina immigration station.

"It was rough," he said. "I spent three days at a motel near Dillon, South of the Border I think it's called, and took a refresher course called 'Southern Is As Southern Does' in an abandoned warehouse in Hamer, South Carolina, not far from Dillon. I told 'em at the immigration station that I had a great uncle from Sumter who fought on the side of the South, and a great-grandfather who was born, raised, and died in Waycross, Georgia, and who was for years a Justice of the Peace. That didn't make no difference. I still had to take the immigration test, and pass it, before being cleared to go further South."

So, in order to make things easy for those planning to retire and head South, let me clue you in on some of the basics that you should at least have a talking knowledge of before arriving at the Dillon immigration station and sitting down to take "the test."

- You should know the basic differences between Missionary Baptists, Free Will Baptists, Hard Shell Baptists, Primitive Baptists, and Foot-Washing Baptists. (And it wouldn't hurt none to brush up on what is Pentecostal and what ain't.)

- You should know the difference between a hissie fit and a conniption fit.

- You should know the difference between a tick and a blue tick.

- You should know the difference between a second cousin and a first cousin once removed.

- You should know where Rock City is.

- You should know at least the first verse of "Dixie."

- You should know the hometown of Flannery O'Conner.

- You should know the difference between "seerup" and "sirrup."

- You should know approximately how many fish are in a mess.

- You should know the difference between sour mash and bourbon.

- You should know at least one place where a fella' can buy a Moon Pie and an RC Cola in the same store.

- You should know approximately how long boiled peanuts should be boiled.

- You should know the price that Number One hogs and soybeans brought yesterday.

- You should know the difference between a bottom plow and a middle buster.

- You should be able to explain just exactly what "catty-cornered" and "cattywampus" mean.

- You should be able to name the entire cast of "The Andy Griffith Show."

- You should know these dates: when Lee surrendered at Appomattox; when the Grand Ole Opry was founded; when and where *Gone with the Wind* premiered; when Atlanta sold out to the North; when the Georgia-Florida game will be played this year; when the South rejoined the Union.

- You should know at least two recipes for biscuits, one for sweet potato pie, one for chicken and dumplings, one for hoecake, one for banana pudding, and none for chitlins.

- You should know the approximate location of Ludowici, Georgia, and you should know to slow down when you drive through.

- You should know the name of one Southerner who lives at Sea Island and one who lives at Hilton Head. If you have difficulty, make a long distance call to the chambers of commerce in each place. They might know if such a rarity exists.

- You should know what "stump juice" is.

- You should know what "pot likker" is.

- You should know the difference between a "boar" and a "sow." And between a "heifer," a "bull," and a "steer." (You can bet your passport they do.)

- You should know the sum total of forty 'leven dozen.

- You should know what a "bush bond" is.

- You should know the difference between "prefab" and "double-wide."

If you reach the point where you have at least a working knowledge of the above, you should have no difficulty passing the immigration test and proceeding on to your southern destination.

Good luck, and rest assured that you will be welcomed with open arms in Dixie.

DO'S AND DON'TS
FOR YOUSE

RELOCATING TO THE SOUTH CAN BE AS FRUS-
trating for Yankees as heading north often is for sons and
daughters of the South. Like Southerners, some Yankees
make permanent moves while others merely go for a look-
see and return home to tell their neighbors what happened. Like their southern counterparts, traveling
Yankees need to know these many things relating to culture and lifestyles that just should and shouldn't be done
once they've arrived at their destination. It isn't enough to
know how they do it in Boston or Chicago. When in
Rome . . . You know the rest.

To those who plan to move south from the frigid north
country after donating your snow shovel and mittens to the
children, bear this in mind: If your ultimate destination is
Atlanta, Georgia, and your plan is to live there permanently,

then forget or completely disregard everything suggested for your group that is designated for Yankees. It won't apply, because upon your arrival in Atlanta from New York City you won't be able to tell the difference (with the possible exception of the weather). Atlanta is a little warmer in winter but about the same in summer.

Atlanta, you see, was once a southern city. But that was before the northern industry with its northern money discovered it sometime in the mid-1950s. You will no doubt feel right at home in the Atlanta traffic, especially during rush hours. Natives of the South avoid it like the plague and wherever possible enlist sharecroppers and other underlings to travel to Atlanta and do their bidding. Reports abound of some who have made the trip and never returned, the contention being that they are still circling the city on Interstate 285, the 67-mile monster that encompasses the city under the guise of being a bypass.

It is documented that one Major League baseball pitcher, Pasqual Perez, failed to show up and take the mound for the Atlanta Braves at Atlanta–Fulton County Stadium because of a major difficulty on I-285. The young man simply couldn't figure a way to exit the monster and, coupled with the fact the Dominican Republic native spoke no English, missed his turn on the mound. In fact, he missed the entire game and earned the nickname "I-285," which sympathetic baseball fans familiar with the bypass had embroidered on the back of a Braves warmup jacket and presented to him in pre-game ceremonies later in the season.

"I-285" Perez is no longer with the Atlanta Braves, and the last account anyone had of his whereabouts was that he was on the monster somewhere in the vicinity of Marietta. Residents there say he drives by about every hour-and-a-half, with some handing food and drink to him as he passes.

You will also feel right at home with the Atlanta restaurants and the menus they offer. Such delicacies as quiche, chicken teriyaki, beef stroganoff, tuna Rockefeller, guacamole, spanakopita, shrimp scampi, chicken cacciatore, rice pilaf, vitello tonnato, moo goo gai pan, paella de Manhattan, oysters Rockefeller, chicken Kiev, and pasta have long since replaced such Southern standards as fried chicken, pork chops, chicken and dumplings, tripe, country ham, pickled pig's feet, chitterlings (chitlins), streak-o-lean, mullet, and grits. And waiters with cute names like Keith, Ralph, Pierre, Jordan, and Kirk have replaced such "How y'all" waitresses with born-again names like Mary Nell, Robbie Sue, Johnnie Faye, Emmy Lou, Ellie Mae, and Lawsy Me. Plus, most Atlanta restaurants now accept credit cards and take reservations—two real dyed-in-the-wool innovations.

The language? Don't sweat it. You could possibly go for months and never hear a southern accent, unless you make an appointment with one of the many "Suthen spoke by 'pointment" parlors where young ladies of the South will recite selected portions of *Gone with the Wind* and *Tobacco Road* for "a nominal fee, Honey Chile."

There you have it. If you're from "up yonder" and are moving to Atlanta, disregard what's coming next. But if by chance you have seen the light and plan to migrate further down south to roost forever more, take heed.

By keeping the following do's and don'ts in mind, you will enhance the quality of life once you've settled into your own place in heaven—Dixie:

Do

- Learn to say "Howdy" as soon as possible after relocating. "Hoi" just won't get the message across, and there are some who will think you are making reference to some Chinese political leader.

• Buy a shotgun, even if you can't shoot it and never load it. It's status in Dixie, bottom line status.

• Purchase some make of pickup truck with a gun rack in the back window and hang the shotgun there. Not only will it complete the picture of a previously barren back window but will also brand you in most circles as "O.K."

• Hide all your bowling trophies. One deer head mounted on the wall in your den will overshadow all your bowling trophies. There are stores available where deer heads can be bought or rented. Besides, you can take pictures of it and send it back to the boys in the shop. They will be amazed inasmuch as the only deer they ever saw was probably in "Wild Kingdom."

- Learn to stick a little snuff in your cheek, and maybe a wad of Levi Garrett now and again. The first week or two your wife will have to launder your shirts a lot, but once you get the hang of spitting you'll be able to clear a parking meter or drown a fly from six paces. You can easily learn to spit by observing the natives, and should you progress to the point where you are able to dip snuff or chew tobacco and eat boiled peanuts at the same time, you qualify to give lessons. But remember, *always* spit downwind.

- Learn to eat boiled peanuts. Eating chitlins is not a prerequisite to acceptance in the South, contrary to what you may have heard. Boiled peanuts are a staple; chitlins are not. Most men of the South have never tasted one and never will. It is the one thing that, when being cooked, will cause the flies to make every effort to get *out* of the house. I heard it said that some years ago a man in deep South Georgia dropped one on the kitchen floor, and his cat spent the better part of an hour trying to cover it up.

- Give all your knickers to the Salvation Army before moving South. Also your plaid and argyle socks that go along with them. While they might have been "the things" to wear on the links at prestigious and exclusive golf courses in Westchester and Ann Arbor, they are as out of place in Waycross and Alma as would be the Grand Dragon of the Ku Klux Klan at an NAACP convention.

- Remove all the polish from your nails before leaving for God's country. It just wouldn't look right for a fella' to be frog gigging, skinning rabbits, and cleaning catfish with manicured nails.

- Learn to change the oil in your car, put a new tailpipe and muffler on a pickup, and fix a stopped-up drainpipe. Dixie men pride themselves on being able to fix things for themselves, and the ones who aren't adept at such things have wives who are. Heck, there are ten-year-old girls in the South who can overhaul a tractor, lay brick, and butcher a cow with the best of 'em.

- Learn to play poker if you don't already know how. This alone will ensure that you receive many invitations to fish camps, deer hunting camp houses, and oceanfront condos owned by the local doctors and shifty bootleggers. I know many men who go to fish camps, deer hunting camp houses, and oceanfront condos with regularity and never take a fishing pole, deer rifle, or bathing suit with them. But then, thanks to enterprising shopkeepers, there are adequate establishments and roadside stands where a mess of fish, a deer head, and a tanning parlor suntan can be purchased—credit cards accepted, even for Bicycle and Ace playing cards.

- Invest in a bass boat and park it where it can be easily seen in your yard. And join the local sportsmen's club. The boat will provide visible evidence that you are a good ole boy, and membership in the sportsmen's club will assure you of hearing the best and most current lies.

- Come up with a nickname before or soon after your arrival. Initials are acceptable. *Buster* and *Bubba* are used with such regularity that I suggest you try others on for size, you know, one that fits your personality. *Buddy* and *Slick* are popular, but neither is presently in use to the point of saturation. So are *Dude* and *Cuz*. There are people in my hometown who've known each other for more than forty years and still don't know each other's name. They go with nicknames. *Sloppy* is another one that has some character to it, but then I don't know how you dress or eat. Bear in mind that a nickname says an awful lot about a feller.

- Find yourself a morning coffee group and apply for membership. After all, how else are you going to know what's going on in Washington and Moscow? The coffee table is where you get the straight skinny, right from the horse's mouth as we say in the South. It will help if you are a veteran because most coffee tables fight the wars every morning, primarily World War II and Vietnam. Nothing has changed. We're still the winner in World War II, and nobody's real sure how Vietnam came out yet.

- Buy a pocket knife if you don't already have one. I'm not talking about a pen-knife for trimming the cuticle, opening letters, or cutting errant threads from a well-worn coat sleeve or a sweater damaged by your runaway cat. I'm talking about a knife that will clean a fish, sharpen a pencil, neuter a boar hog, or slit a deer's throat. A knife is as much standard equipment in the South as jumper cables.

Do Not

- Order Cream of Wheat in any cafe south of Macon.

- Order hot tea at Mel's Juke, located about a six-pack north of Broxton and two Willie Nelson tapes south of Macon.

- Turn down an invitation from your new neighbor to go coon hunting with him. The very fact that he invited you is one of the highest compliments you could receive; it means you've been accepted.

- Accept the offer from any owner of a pecan stand to roll the dice or draw high card to see if you pay double or nothing for the bag of pecans you purchased. A few years back a steel worker from Pittsburgh took the bait, and when the con artist finished with him he had been divested of his money orders, two diamond rings, a gold bracelet, and his wife's pearls. The word drifted back that the poor guy ended up going to a Christmas party back home wearing a seersucker suit and perforated shoes. Plus the fact he had to hitch-hike to the party.

- Go snipe hunting with the boys unless you are prepared to spend the night alone in an isolated ditch far removed from civilization.

- Partake of any liquid that is clear as water that is stored in a gallon jug or quart jar. While it appears harmless, novice sippers of the white stuff have been known to do strange things after partaking, like the retired banker from Buffalo who overindulged, climbed the town water tank and proceeded to remove all his clothes and bark at an imaginary moon. He eventually descended from his lofty perch and ran through town buck naked, stopping only momentarily when he found himself the center of attraction at the monthly meeting of the local garden club before continuing to sprint to his home. His fiasco wasn't a complete disaster, however, as he was notified later that he had won first prize for "best dried arrangement."

- Shoot pool with any man who asks, "Wanna' shoot f'r five dollars? I ain't very good at it but I like to

shoot." There is a good possibility that he is the town hustler who has sent two kids to college and bought a small farm with his winnings over the past five years.

- Put sugar on your grits or make an attempt to eat fried chicken or fish with a knife and fork.

- Ask the sheriff for directions to the union hall or wear your pinky ring in public. The absence of unions is the primary reason so much industry has moved in, and pinky rings flat won't get it in Dixie. In fact, legend has it that a New Yorker holed up in a small South Georgia town back in the late 1940s and began trying to sell pinky rings from the trunk of his Buick, only to be run out of town in less than 48 hours by the local sheriff and two burly deputies, both veterans of the Big War. "You in patrotick country heah, boy. We ain't got no room for Commonists," the sheriff told him.

- Order anything to eat that has a name with foreign connotations. Chances are your neighbors are convinced that no food item forced to go through immigration can compare favorably with the "grown down home variety."

- Eat collards or liver just to try and impress the natives. A vast majority would touch neither with a galvanized tongue and a cast iron stomach, and will talk about you if you do.

- Play poker with any man named "Doc" or eat in any establishment named "Mom's."

- Flash your credit cards around indiscriminately. They are gradually catching on in the rural South, but cold hard cash is still the way to go for now.

- Ask any woman at the church supper if her pie is a frozen one. This is the ultimate insult to southern women, and you might well end up wearing the pie instead of eating it. They're dead serious about their cooking.

- Ask for milk or bread by those designations only. You should specify "sweet" milk and "white" bread. And never ask for pumpernickel. Waitresses and cafe owners don't cotton to being insulted.

- Propose to a woman unless you're dead serious. They are, and so are their big ole mean Daddies. And remember this: In many areas of Dixie a formal wedding is one at which the father of the bride carries a white shotgun.

- *Ever* fail to stand when "Dixie" is played. Southerners are just as serious about "Dixie" as Daddies are about proposals to their daughters.

- Play poker or shoot craps with any man who wears long sleeves. It will greatly increase your chances of at least breaking even.

- Walk on the sidewalk without keeping your head down. Not only is tobacco juice nasty, it's also very slippery. What could be worse than for your friends in Yankeeland to read in the local tabloid that your demise came as a result of a broken neck from having slipped in a puddle of tobacco juice? Ice and snow they might understand. Tobacco juice? I doubt it.

- Curb your dog in a neighbor's yard. While he probably won't say anything to you about it, just remember that most folks in the South have cows. And wouldn't that make for an interesting obituary back home? Ice and snow they might understand. Cow dung? I doubt it.

- Take it for granted that just because an oncoming car is signaling for a left turn with his turn signal that he will actually make one. Somehow, it just doesn't always work out that way in the Southland.

- Act surprised if everyone you meet on the street signals a greeting to you, even though you don't know the sender of said greeting. Even drivers do this by lifting the right forefinger off the steering wheel and waving it back and forth. I realize that natives of Detroit, Chicago, New York, Philadelphia, and Newark do this also, but the big difference is that they use a different finger.

- Decline an invitation to visit a neighbor's garden. It is probably his pride and joy, and the main reason he

has one is so he can raise delicious fresh vegetables—
and then give them away.

- Ask a southern girl under the age of fourteen for a
  date, unless you are absolutely certain that her
  divorce is final.

RELOCATION BASICS

BELIEVE ME, IT WOULD BE AN ABSOLUTE DISASTER for virgin travelers or transplants to go South without at least making some basic preparations. Nothing he's experienced in life will have prepared the unsuspecting Yankee for what he or she is about to experience.

I have some suggestions that should help in making the adjustment easier and could spare untold embarrassment. And bear in mind that the helpful suggestions offered here are only the basics.

Suggestions for Yankees Moving South

- Don't, I repeat, *don't* make any attempt to learn to say, "How y'all" with the idea that it will make acceptance in the South easier. Forget it! A true Rebel can detect a counterfeit "How y'all" as quick as he can a "How's y'r mommer 'n 'em?"

- If your plan is to become a permanent resident of Dixie, at least get on a first name basis with such country music legends as Willie Nelson, Randy Travis, Roy Acuff, Ricky Skaggs, Loretta Lynn, "Alabama," Barbara Mandrell, and Little Jimmy Dickens. Invest in a few cassette tapes and listen to them while commuting to and from work every day. And it would help if you knew that the Grand Ole Opry is located in Nashville, Tennessee, and not in North Bergen, New Jersey:

- Practice walking slow.

- Learn to chew tobacco. Get yourself a pack of Levi Garrett, pop a wad in your mouth, stand on the George Washington Bridge, and practice spitting in the Hudson River. And don't worry about polluting it. Somebody already beat you to it.

- Wear long-sleeve white shirts, but roll the sleeves up as far as you can.

- If you want to go the second mile, try your hand at drinking buttermilk. And contrary to what you might think, I have it on good authority that your insides won't resemble the glass from which you drank the buttermilk when it dries.

- Go ahead and make a small investment in at least two pairs of white socks, one for weekly wear and one for Sunday, weddings, and funerals.

- Do not invest in a pink plastic flamingo for the front yard or a Confederate flag for the den. You will see an ample supply of both at hundreds of roadside stands once you cross the state line into South Carolina.

- Try and wean yourself away from quiche and hot tea before heading South. One is nonexistent in Dixie, and the other is in short supply due to a lack of demand for it.

- Once you hit Georgia, buy some boiled peanuts and a Coca-Cola (Cocoler) and practice eating and talking while driving. It is established practice in the Peach State. (Fear not the inability to locate boiled peanuts and a Coca-Cola. Both are readily available in the same type Georgia roadside stands as the ones in South Carolina featuring pink plastic flamingos and Confederate flags.)

- Never make reference in the South to the fact that you would really love to have a bagel. You do, and when you wake up the next morning your yard will be overflowing with cute little hound dogs.

- Go to your local library and read up on cotton, soybeans, peanuts, grits, cornmeal, hushpuppies, cane syrup, dove hunting, bass fishing, barbecue, overalls, collards, and chitterlings (chitlins). A general knowledge of these items will open many doors for you; in the case of chitlins, it will close many.

- You may want to consider dropping your first and middle names and use only the initials. Initials are big down South, and nobody questions what they stand for. They are just accepted.

- A few weeks before actually pulling up and heading south, practice "hanging out" a lot. Find a gas station, a pool room, a coffee shop, or a vacant lot and just stand around. Jingle the change in your pocket, tie and untie a piece of string, make marks and lines in the dirt with the toe of your shoe—then rub them out and repeat, using the heel. While it won't be too good for your shoes, it will say a lot for your lifestyle and will eliminate many questions by others hanging out with you down here.

- It might be well for you to brush up on the stock market. A lot of folks where you'll be moving to are pretty well into it and have been for many years. Now then, when I make reference to the stock market I ain't talkin' 'bout IBM, Xerox, Polaroid, GM, Ford, Texaco, AT&T, or Dow-Jones. I'm talkin' 'bout hogs (number ones and number twos), cows, wheat, corn, soybeans, peanuts, oats, and pork bellies.

DIETING UNDER STRESS . . . IN THE NORTH AND THE SOUTH

SOMETIMES I GET THE FEELING THAT EVERYBODY from "Fatty" Arbuckle to Jack Spratt's wife has come up with some sort of diet. Well, I have yet another one for you. It's called "Dieting Under Stress," and was sent to two friends of mine by their son who lives and works in Atlanta. Near as I can tell, it works equally well for Yankees as Southerners. It's called "The Stress Diet." The way I figure, the diet is what causes the stress!

This diet is designed to help you cope with the stress that builds up during the day.

BREAKFAST:
  ½ Grapefruit
  1 Slice Whole Wheat Toast, Dry
  8 oz. Skim Milk

LUNCH:

4 oz. Lean Broiled Chicken Breast

1 Cup Steamed Spinach

1 Cup Herb Tea

1 Oreo Cookie

MIDAFTERNOON SNACK:

Rest of the Oreos in the package

2 Pints Rocky Road Ice Cream

1 Jar Hot Fudge Sauce

Nuts, Cherries, Whipped Cream

DINNER:

2 Loaves Garlic Bread with Cheese

Large Sausage, Mushroom and Cheese Pizza

4 Cans or 1 large Pitcher of Beer

3 Milky Way Candy Bars

LATE EVENING NEWS SNACK:

Entire Frozen Cheesecake, Eaten Directly from Freezer

Rules for This Diet

1. If you eat something and no one sees it, it has no calories.

2. If you drink a diet drink with a candy bar, the calories in the candy bar are canceled out by the diet drink.

3. When you eat with someone else, calories don't count if you don't eat more than they do.

4. Food used for medicinal purposes **never** counts, like hot chocolate, brandy, toast and Sara Lee Cheesecake.

5. If you fatten up everyone else around you, you look thinner.

6. Movie-related foods do not have additional calories because they are part of the entire entertainment package and not part of one's personal fuel, like Milk Duds, but-

tered popcorn, Hershey Bars (with or without almonds), Junior Mints, Red Hots and Tootsie Rolls.

7. Cookie pieces contain no calories. The process of breaking causes calorie drainage.

8. Things licked off knives and spoons have no calories provided you are in the process of preparing something. Examples are peanut butter on a knife while making a peanut butter and jelly sandwich and ice cream on a spoon while making a sundae.

9. Foods that have the same color have the same number of calories. Examples are spinach and pistachio ice cream, cottage cheese and banana cream pie, mushrooms and white chocolate. (**Note:** Chocolate is a universal color and may be substituted for any other food color.)

10. For every burp, subtract 25 calories.

WE DO IT A LITTLE SLOWER IN THE SOUTH

I'LL BE THE FIRST TO ADMIT THAT THOSE OF US IN the South are pretty much laid back, like if it don't get done today—maybe tomorrow. And if it don't get done tomorrow—to hell with it.

"The road to hell is paved with good intentions." I've heard that all my life, but its true meaning didn't really come home to roost until I was returning home from a trip to Florida. It was almost dark when I pulled into a driveway at a house just south of Callahan, Florida, on U.S. Highway 1, to ask directions.

The house had a porch and a swing, along with a rocking chair. The man I presumed to be the head of the house occupied the swing, and the woman I presumed to be his wife was rocking back and forth in the rocker. Had Norman Rockwell painted a picture of what I saw, he would have drawn in a hound dog stretched out underneath the big oak tree in the yard and a few cats and kittens on one end of the porch.

Had I chosen a name for the man of the house, I couldn't have made a more fitting selection than did his Mama and Daddy years ago. His name is Silas. And I learned that his wife is Nellie, also appropriate for the rural setting.

I got out of my car, approached the front steps, and called out the customary greeting, "Howdy!"

"Howdy," Silas said in return. "Come on in."

I continued walking toward the steps and upon reaching them, stepped on the lower one—not in the middle mind you, but on one end. The step was not nailed down and the other end shot up like a jumping board. I caught myself with both hands as I went down but my right shin bears the loose-board battle scar, about five inches long. And as I was crouched there in an Olympic sprinter's position, Silas called out a word of warning that no doubt he's repeated many times to unsuspecting, and uninvited, visitors: "Watch aout for that first step! It ain't nailed down!"

I swallowed the reply that immediately came to mind, got up, and busied myself rubbing my right shin as I balanced on my left leg.

"Been meanin' to fix that step," he said. "The thing's been loose for nigh on to three years now, but ever'time I get set to fix it the fish seem to be bitin' or somethin' else comes up."

"More lak five or six," Nellie countered without looking up, still rocking.

"Well, it *is* a little dangerous," I said. "Somebody could get hurt bad."

"Yep, I reckon so," Silas agreed. "Don't never step on it, m'sef. Course, me an' Nellie both know 'bout it an' we don't have much comp'ny. But I'm gonna fix it one o' these days."

"Yeah? When?" asked Nellie, still rocking, but at a noticeably slower tempo.

"Oh, one o' these days. I'll git 'round to it," Silas promised, but didn't sign nothing binding.

"Yeah, I bet ya' will," said Nellie, who had stopped rocking.

I got my directions and left, figuring the loose-step argument fuse had been lit, and it was probably a short one.

As I drove home I pondered Silas's statement, "I'm gonna' fix it one o' those days," and the old quotation, "The road to hell is paved with good intentions." I rubbed my sore shin and almost became angry with Silas. But by the time I arrived at my house some six hours later, I had changed my mind about him and his loose board. Here's why.

We are so quick to criticize the inaction of others while things that need attention around our own houses go wanting. Take my house for instance:

- I've lived in it for almost seven years, and out back there is a piece of pipe sticking up out of the ground about four inches. It represents the remains of a clothesline erected by the previous owner who took the clothesline with him but left the pipe behind. I can't recall *ever* going in my backyard that I didn't stumble over that piece of pipe, and every time I do it I blame the previous owner, direct a few choice words his way, and vow to "fix it one of these days."

- I have a navy blue blazer with the top front button missing. The button is in the left pocket and has been resting in there since 1982. Every time I wear it I gaze down repeatedly and tell myself, "I'm gonna' get that button sewed on one o' these days."

- My kitchen stove hasn't worked since 1983. Something about a fuse or a relay, or somethin'. I only think about it when I get ready to boil some corn on the cob or have a cravin' f'r grits. But "I'm gonna' get it fixed one o' these days."

- I have a window fan in my bedroom. The breeze feels so good when it blows across my bed late at night and early in the morning. Something happened to it in the summer of '84, so I've been sleepin' on the sofa in the lobby at the radio station across the street ever since then. It really don't sleep bad, but "I'm gonna' get that darn fan fixed one o' these days."

- The margins on my typewriter don't work—haven't for years. Can't set 'em, and the result is that I get carried away sometimes and type a line all the way into my carport. But you can bet your correction tape that "I'm gonna' get the thing fixed one o' these days."

- I also have a favorite pair of gray slacks that I like to wear with my one-button navy blue blazer. It seems that I only reach for them when I have but a few minutes to get dressed, get to a speech commitment, a funeral, or to my Sunday school when it's fourth Sunday and my turn to teach. The problem is that for the past couple of years the zipper has been stuck—down! I'll tell you, its downright uncomfortable to walk around all day in a crouched position like maybe your back's broken or you're looking for the first available keyhole. But one thing for sure, "I'm gonna' get that zipper fixed . . . one o' these days."

Silas, I'll make you a deal. I'll step over your bottom step if you'll overlook that land mine in my backyard, my navy blue blazer, my inoperative kitchen stove, my broken bedroom window fan, the injured margin setter on my typewriter, and the busted zipper on my gray slacks.

Or maybe, just maybe, I could work out a deal with Nellie to fix my zipper in exchange for a repair job on that bottom step.

WE SOUTHERNERS VALUE OUR PRIVACY

ONE COUPLE WHO HAD RETIRED TO THE SOUTH from Cleveland, Ohio, after purchasing a small farm in South Alabama learned quickly the independence, out-spokenness, and conservative ways of at least two of their new neighbors shortly after arriving in Alabama. Both concluded that it would be a good idea to get out on a Sunday afternoon and visit some of their neighbors, exchange greetings, and generally get to know them.

This they did, and they made their first stop at a mod-est farm home featuring a porch. It was mid-afternoon on a hot Alabama July day, and the man and wife of the house were both sitting in high-back rocking chairs, the only chairs on the porch. The old man was chewing tobacco while his wife was dipping snuff. Both held and waved funeral home handheld fans, primarily to ward off the pesty gnats common to South Alabama.

The newly settled-in couple just-arrived-from-Cleveland got out of their automobile and approached the house, stepping around one hound dog and over two others. They stopped at the bottom of the front porch steps, and the Cleveland man opened what would be a short conversation with, "Hello there! My wife and I just moved in about two days ago. We moved from Cleveland and drove down this afternoon to speak with you, visit and become acquainted."

"Howdy," replied the old man in the rocking chair as he drenched a dead petunia with tobacco juice just to the left of a broken syrup bottle in the yard.

The old lady never looked up, continuing to rock and sew on what appeared to be a napkin. Like her husband, she took a snuff juice shot at a geranium just off the end of

the porch near a lazy cat. She missed the geranium but scored a bull's-eye on the cat's back.

The visitor, still standing with his wife, made another attempt at familiarity with, "Sure is warm this afternoon, isn't it?"

The old man saturated a fern this time before answering with, "Yep, always is this time o' year."

Becoming increasingly impatient, and a little bit perturbed at the reception he and his wife were receiving, the visitor remarked, "Seems to me like you don't have enough chairs."

"Got plenty o' chairs," the old man said, "just got too much dadblamed comp'ny."

IS THERE NO CULTURE IN THE SOUTH?

IT HAPPENED TO ME AGAIN LAST WEEK, AT A cocktail party. I was backed into a corner by a pair of New Jersey American transplants, now enjoying the good life in Middle Georgia after serving a near-life sentence in the Garden State. I served a seven-year sentence there, myself, before being paroled to Georgia in August, 1965.

The whole thing started after I sat down at what I thought was an unoccupied table, bent on enjoying a cup of coffee. No way.

I had no more than sipped when they appeared at the table, took their seats, and introduced themselves. It seems that they were there before me but left to go wherever Yankee transplants go when they up and leave their table at a cocktail party.

Following the introductions, we engaged in the usual chatter that goes on at cocktail parties—the state of the weather, the state of the nation, high prices, the quality of the hors d'oeuvres, and family backgrounds—to establish the proper pedigree, you know.

I learned, among other things, that they migrated south from New Jersey after retirement. No surprise. I mean, after all, have you ever heard of anyone retiring to the North?

And they learned that I'd spent a few years in New Jersey, 1960-67, an eternity for a Georgia boy.

The conversation was rocking along smoothly until the female rubbed salt in my redneck wound with this observation: "I enjoy living down here in the South, except for one thing," she said, baiting me.

I took the bait and asked, "Yes? And what's that?"

"No culture. I miss the culture that I enjoyed in New Jersey and New York," she said.

I gritted my teeth real hard, gulped down what was left of my coffee, and counted to ten. I'd been in this corner before and really had no intention of making a scene. Finally, I asked her, "And what culture is that you enjoyed up there that you miss so much down here?"

"Oh, things like the theater, art galleries, museums, excellent restaurants," she said. "Always something to do. But down here, nothing. Don't you find that to be true?"

"No, not really," I said. "It was my observation that of the eight million people in New York, about all 98 percent of them did was talk about the culture—the theater, and such—but they never went."

"Well, at least it was there if you wanted it," she said.

I just had to ask the next question, and did.

"By the way, what prompted you two to move to Georgia? Do you have relatives here?"

"Oh, no. I just told Frank that the day he his job in Brooklyn we were moving sou Florida or Georgia," she said. "We looked a decided on Georgia, Middle Georgia."

"A wise choice," I said, "but why leave all that culture in New York?"

"Well, the last year we lived up there we were robbed twice and mugged once," she said. "That did it. I decided to get out."

While establishing our individual pedigrees, I learned that they had lived in Oradell, New Jersey. I recalled that Oradell was also the hometown of one of our astronauts, Walter Shirra, who went into space in 1962. (I was living there at the time and would gladly have gone with him to get out of New Jersey.)

"Yes, we're very proud of Wally Shirra," said the husband.

"And understandably so," I said. "But he sure picked a heck of a way to get out of New Jersey, didn't he?"

"How's that?" the man asked.

"Took a space ship, Mercury 8. Talk about desperate," I said.

The female sipped her coffee, raised her painted eyebrows, and said, "Well, I still miss the culture in New York."

"Yeah, I reckon so. But you don't miss them robbers and muggers a whole helluva' lot, do you, ma'am?" I asked.

"Well, let me put it this way, we're not planning to move back," she said.

I thought about 'em all the way home. I'm gonna have to invite 'em to a cane grindin' or a peanut boilin', I reckon. It's a shame they're not takin' advantage of what culture we do have here, right?

TEST YOURSELF:
ARE YOU A
REDNECK?

ARE YOU A REDNECK? WANT A SURE-FIRE GUIDE to find out? Take a look.

You're a redneck if:

- You harbor a continuing urge to slap somebody, stomp on somethin', or spit.

- You still wear a burr haircut, chew on kitchen matches, and constantly hope some long-hair will make fun of your white socks so you can break his fingers as sort of an in-house joke.

- You're certain that anybody who drives an old VW with a Solar Power or Anti-Nuke bumper sticker is a Commie pinko.

- You hope some guy from New Jersey will honk at you when the light turns green so you can crawl out of your pickup, give him a Confederate talkin' to, and embarrass him in front of his old lady.

- You think the only people who shouldn't wear boots are women.

- The only people you're afraid to sass are your mama and daddy and the only people your daddy is afraid to sass are his mama and daddy.

- You wonder why all them people in coats and ties are going into Katz's Deli when the beer joint is right across the street.

- You wear white shirts, with snaps instead of buttons, with a little embroidery on them, and your bellybutton shows.

- You think all bars should have pickled eggs instead of hanging plants and you've boozed it up at Scoot Inn, the Horseshoe Lounge, the Manchaca Bar and Dry Gulch Watering Hole but couldn't find the Veranda, Wylie's, or the Inn Place with a Rand-McNally guide.

- You think the president should stop busing, nuke Iran, reinstate the draft, eliminate welfare, and reactivate CCC camps to try and make things as miserable as they were when you were a kid so children these days can develop some character.

- You can't stand Shakespeare, poetry, ballet, or plays, but love the chase scenes on HBO and enjoy it when the sheriff in the movie swears a lot.

- You only watch the Indy 500 to see the wrecks and cars blowing up.

- You think Bella Abzug and Jane Fonda ought to "jest shut the hell up," but Dolly Parton, bless her little ol' pea-pickin' heart, can say anything she wants to as far as you're concerned.

- The only time you hold a woman's chair is to keep from falling down at the Dry Gulch on Saturday night.

- You sign up for the draft and take your own mug with you only to learn they ain't signin' up for free beer.

- You never miss a civil rights rally and stand across the street and sing "Dixie" at the top of your voice.

- You swallow tobacco juice as a joke and can spit over an eight rail fence.

- You wouldn't own a shirt that didn't have two pockets.

- You can strike a match on your britches or with your thumbnail, can whistle through your teeth, and have your name burned on your belt.

- You prop your foot in the booth at the diner, dump cigarette ashes in the saucer, and wouldn't look at a menu if your life depended on it, preferring to tell the waitress, "jus' bring me two aigs done hard an' some o' them sausages. Lots o' grits."

- You ain't no golfer but "par for the course" is a blonde, a redhead, and a brunette over the weekend.

- The last newspaper you read was the one in which you advertised your four-wheel drive pickup for sale with "call for Bubba at the Dry Gulch Watering Hole between 9:00 P.M. and 3:00 A.M., Friday and Saturday."

- You've done a little time in Reidsville for "salt and battry" and still carry a teaspoon in your belt.

- You can roll a cigarette in the back of a pickup going sixty miles per hour between Brewton and Minter.

So? What's the verdict?

LIFE IS GETTIN'
CONFUSING

A Few Things
I Don't
Understand

I'M READY TO CONCEDE THAT I REALLY DON'T know very much. I once thought I knew a little bit about a lot of things, but no more.

It seems that the more I contemplate life around me, the less I know about it. There are just so many things I don't understand. Like . . .

- I don't understand blood pressure readings. What does it *really* mean if it's 130/80? Is that the time to call in the family and a priest or a preacher, or is it merely the odds on the Notre Dame–Penn State game? Nobody has ever explained blood pressure readings to me, although my blood pressure has been taken repeatedly for years.

- I don't understand the metric system. And furthermore, I don't give a hoot about it. I don't really care to have some sportscaster tell me that the slotback ran eighty-five meters for a touchdown or that my favorite stock car driver is in the sixty-sixth lap of a 500 kilometer race.

- I don't understand what Celsius means. I do understand that when—in mid-August—I hear a weather person say that the temperature is 104 degrees, I momentarily suffocate until I hear that it is 72 degrees Celsius. I'm comfortable with 40 degrees in January until some spoilsport meteorologist follows with " . . . but it's 8 degrees Celsius." I'll take Celsius in August and Fahrenheit in January, thank you.

- I don't understand what you do with math after graduation, unless you go on to teach it to others who won't understand what to do with it after graduation either. I can truthfully say that since I graduated from high school, not one person has approached me on the street and asked, "Excuse me, sir, but could you tell me the value of X or Y?" And postulates and axioms? Forget 'em. As best I can recall from having worked for years in Michigan on the Canadian border, postulates are ladies of the evening who sneak across the border after dark to entertain men for a fee . . . if the men approach them and axiom.

- I don't understand ice hockey or what particular significance the blue line has. And what the heck is "icing"? Down here in Dixie it has always had to do with cake making, the final touch so to speak.

- I don't understand what "proof" means to a bottle of whiskey or "octane" to a gallon of gasoline. But I think I do understand that it would be disastrous if the whiskey distilleries and the oil refineries somehow got them mixed up, resulting in my automobile weaving from one side of the highway to the other and a blue flame emitting from my mouth after having downed a Scotch and water and lit up a cigarette.

- I don't understand how, after all these years, I still can't make syrup and biscuits come out even. There's always a little of one remaining after the other runs out. For anyone who is a native of any place north of Richmond (and therefore not educated in the fine art of "sopping"), disregard the foregoing and concentrate your thoughts on the blue line and "icing." But should you have an insatiable desire to learn, remember that proper sopping etiquette dictates that you sop from left to right, making gentle and rhythmic swipes around your plate and through the sugar cane—*always* sugar cane—syrup with a cathead biscuit. Anybody who would dare to sop maple syrup would eat cream of wheat. *Cathead* biscuits? That's another ball game entirely and too delicate to get into at this juncture. I will tell you that cathead biscuits are the best biscuits in the world, especially if cooked in a woodstove. Trust me.

- I don't understand why anyone would want to live north of Nashville. I'm convinced that God has a mansion in the Belle Meade section of the Music City and embraces country music.

- I don't understand where clouds go.

- I don't understand why all of a sudden America is about out of pennies. Does Oliver North have them all stashed in that little metal box on the floor of his clothes closet into which he said he dropped all his change at night and came up with $15,000? At least that's where he said it came from.

- I don't understand how anybody could like Jane Fonda or dislike her daddy.

- I don't understand how instant replays work. A guy runs ninety-two yards for a touchdown, and before I can flip my Bic, danged if he don't do it again. I saw the same fella score four times in twelve seconds on successive fifty-four-yard runs during a recent telecast, but the score remained 6–0. How could that happen? Four times six is still twenty-four, ain't it?

- I don't understand how Jesse Jackson makes a living.

- I don't understand what the U. N. does, but I know who pays for whatever it is it does.

- I don't understand automobile sticker prices. Has anybody *ever* paid the sticker price for a car?

- I don't understand what "last" has to do with my shoe size. Why not "first"?

- I don't understand how spies know when they've run out of invisible ink. I mean, a spy could write a fifty-page espionage report, have the last twenty-seven pages come out blank, and get his tail shipped off to Siberia in winter . . . and never really know why.

- I don't understand what sort of container Styrofoam is shipped in.

- I don't understand why Ybor City, Florida, is pronounced "Ebo City" or why Thibodeaux, Louisiana, is pronounced "Tippydoe."

- I don't understand how a kaleidoscope works or how broken glass can make such pretty pictures.

- I don't understand how Ralph Nader makes a living.

- I don't understand Reaganomics and never have. Of course I never understood Carternomics, Fordonomics, Nixonomics, Johnsonomics, or Kennedynomics either. The best I have been able to figure out is that you just send all you can to Washington and hope to get a little in return.

- I don't understand why we drive on parkways and park in driveways. Try explaining that to someone who just arrived from Haiti.

- I don't understand why store prices are never even money. Why not an even $2.00 for crackers, $1.25 for peanut butter, and $15,000 for a new car? Why $1.99, $1.19, $14,999?

- I don't understand why cats bathe so much. They don't do a heck of a lot to get dirty just sitting around on the backs of sofas and automobile hoods with their motor running, staring at you like they know what you're thinking. I don't own a cat. I've never owned one. I don't want nothin' in my house that bathes more than I do, eats rats, and thinks like a psychiatrist.

- I don't understand why cars are engineered to go 120 when the speed limit is 55 or 65. Just asking for trouble, I think.

- I don't understand how cruise control works. And what if it gets stuck on eighty-five in the mountains of Tennessee? I guess that's when you really find out what those "runaway truck" ramps are for.

- I don't understand how a microwave oven gets the soup hot enough to take the hide off a hog without heating the bowl.

- I don't understand how a convicted murderer can be sentenced to life imprisonment plus forty years in 1984 and be back out on the street in 1991.

- I don't understand what *habeas corpus* is, or a *corpus delicti*, but both sound morbid. I just know that I don't want to own or be either.

- I don't understand why some people drink hot tea when they have a refrigerator full of ice.

- I don't understand disco dancing or how it ever got started. Did some guy and gal drop concrete blocks on their toes?

- I don't understand banks, but I do understand that the person who does the commercials ain't the one who makes the loans.

- I don't understand which is the opposite sex.

- I don't understand what holds up a strapless evening gown. I *think* I do, but I've always been afraid to ask.

- I don't understand where seedless oranges and grapes come from.

- I don't understand why telephone information operators are always in such a hurry. Don't they have to stay until the end of their eight-hour shifts?

- I don't understand why, if we are going to have No Smoking sections, we can't have No Jukebox and No Cheap Perfume sections.

- I don't understand why a church will build a new sanctuary to seat only 600 when it has a membership of 1,185.

• And finally, I don't understand why we don't pray more when we don't need anything and everything's running along smoothly. You know, just to say, "Thank you, Lord. I appreciate all you've done for me."

No, sir. I just don't understand why I don't understand.

MORE THINGS
I DON'T
UNDERSTAND

WILL ROGERS ONCE SAID, "WE ARE ALL IGNO-
rant, only on different subjects." The more I think about
it, the more I realize that Will Rogers was right, especially in my case.

I already listed some things I don't understand. Here's
an update, more things I don't understand.

- I don't understand why some men wear both a belt
  and suspenders, unless they subscribe to the theory
  "better safe than sorry."

- I don't understand divestiture or telephone bills. But
  then, does anybody? And who gets my money?
  Looks to me like it is divided about ten ways so that
  everybody gets a slice of the divestiture pie.

- I don't understand what a doctor means when he walks into the examining room and tells you to "strip to the waist." Do you remove your shirt or pants? Remove either and you've complied, right?

- I don't understand why possums keep trying to cross the road after seeing what happened to their predecessors when they tried.

- I don't understand why ants never take a break or demand overtime pay.

- I don't understand why glove compartments are so named when most of them have everything but gloves in them.

- I don't understand why shoelaces never break until you're running five minutes late for work.

- I don't understand what the STP stands for on a can of oil treatment.

- I don't understand why some 7–Eleven stores stay open twenty-four hours a day. If they insist on doing it, shouldn't they be renamed twenty-four-hour stores?

- I don't understand VCRs, but I don't concern myself with it. Most people don't understand VCRs.

- I don't understand people who say, "I just don't have the time." Don't we all have the same amount, twenty-four hours a day?

- I don't understand the meaning of "safety" matches. Any match capable of burning a building to the ground or destroying thousands of acres of timberland doesn't sound very safe to me.

- I don't understand people who take up two parking spaces with one car.

- I don't understand why most public restrooms have hot-air hand dryers instead of paper towels. My hands always get dry before the thing stops blowing. Not being a wasteful person, I just stand there with my dry hands under it until it stops. Actually, I'd rather use my shirttail—and have.

- I don't understand it when I hear somebody yell, "Sit down in front!" When God made us, he never intended that we sit down in front. In the first place, it is an impossible feat to accomplish. In the second place, try it and you'll dang near break your back.

- I don't understand why, when giving a speech, I'm always introduced by someone I've never met.

- I don't understand why, when I do my laundry, I always come up one sock short. There must be thousands of bureau drawers containing thousands of mismatched socks.

- I don't understand where the fat goes when somebody loses thirty pounds on a diet.

- I don't understand how a brown cow can eat green grass and give white milk and yellow butter.

- I don't understand how a 67,000-ton passenger ship keeps from sinking.

- I don't understand why nothing "tears along the dotted line."

- I don't understand why the sole of my left shoe always gets a hole in it before the sole of my right one. Don't they take the same number of steps?

- I don't understand why, during the course of a year, I receive hundreds of letters with the announcement in bold print on the outside of the envelope, "You may have won a million dollars!" or "Congratulations! You are a sweepstakes winner," but I never receive anything.

- I don't understand how I can spill an eight-ounce glass of iced tea and have two gallons drench the tablecloth.

- I don't understand why, when I drop a coin or a cuff link, it seeks refuge in the darkest corner of the room or underneath the bed.

- I don't understand why zippers always get stuck in the "down" position.

- I don't understand how fishing lines, garden hoses, extension cords, paper clips, and wire coat-hangers can become so tangled and twisted when nobody's touched them.

- I don't understand why coin machines never malfunction when you have a pocketful of change, but invariably will if you possess but two quarters and there's no place nearby to get change for a dollar.

- I don't understand what hermits do with their spare time.

- I don't understand why the one book I need from the library is always checked out.

- I don't understand why blisters always appear on the fingers we use most.

- I don't understand why, when I sneeze, folks up North immediately say, "Gesundheit!" In the South they always say "Bless you!" And it's always the same, no matter how many successive sneezes I manage.

- I don't understand why it is that when a batter is being intentionally walked by a pitcher, the pitcher still delivers the four required pitches, way outside, before the batter can move along to first base with a base on balls. Why not just tell the umpire to move him along and bring on the next batter?

- I don't understand why men's coat buttons are on the right side but women's are on the left. There has to be an explanation, but I have no idea what it is. Just another example of something I never learned in school or wasn't paying attention to when it was being discussed.

And if it will serve as any consolation to you, let me assure you that you aren't the only one who doesn't understand what's going on in the Middle East.

A FEW THINGS I DON'T KNOW

FACT IS FACT, AND IT'S A FACT THAT THERE ARE some things that I just don't know. My lack of knowledge surfaces primarily when driving on America's interstate highways, usually in Dixieland.

Other than listening to zillions of radio talk shows, there is little else to do other than dodge flattened possums and beer cans, or maybe catch an occasional tourist from New Jersey changing a flat tire.

Radio talk shows keep me awake, trying to anticipate the next stupid question and the next stupid answer. Psychologist hosts are the worst, the bottom of the talk-show barrel. They know everything, from how to burp a baby to how to get squirrels out of the attic. Put a psychologist on the radio, and it makes my forefinger twitch wanting to stop at the next pay phone and call in. Psychologists become experts when the microphone is turned on.

While I've never called a radio talk show, here are some of the questions I would pose if I did call. I know the answers would be forthcoming:

- What's the difference between beer and ale?

- What is *perestroika* as opposed to *glasnost*?

- What's the difference between a traverse and a petit jury?

- What's the difference between a speedometer and an odometer?

- What do barometric readings mean?

- What exactly is ground clutter?

- What's the difference between nylon, rayon, and Dacron?

- Where is polyester raised? And how is it harvested?

- What's the difference between a first cousin and a second cousin once removed? And how does one come up with a double first cousin?

- What's the difference between a bagel, a bugle, and a bungle?

- Does a falling tree make noise if there's no one within a hundred miles to hear it?

- What does AM stand for in radio parlance? Or FM?

- What does WD stand for in WD-40? Is there a WD-30? Or WD-50? If so, is WD-30 less expensive? Is WD-50 more expensive?

- What's the difference between an abridged and an unabridged dictionary?

- What does the term *bare facts* mean to a nudist?

- What's the difference between fluorescent, incandescent, and iridescent lighting? Any similarity to adolescent?

- I know about dry-cell batteries. Are there any wet-cell batteries?

- When does a kitten become a cat? Or a puppy a dog?

- Where is the Left Bank? Is it opposite the Right Bank?

- What is the Gaza Strip? Is it a dance of some sort? Or maybe a race track?

- What size shoe does Big Foot wear?

- Does the Loch Ness monster throw a Halloween party?

- How deep is a fathom?

- How long is a furlong?

- Can you "back up and go ahead"?

- Is it possible for one to actually be "beside himself"?

- Do owls ever have cataracts?

I really don't know the answers. Maybe you do.

I *Really* Don't Understand Hospitals

IF I WERE GIVEN THE ASSIGNMENT OF RANKING all the things I don't understand, there is no doubt that hospitals would be at or very near the top of the list. I have nothing against hospitals; it's just that I don't understand them.

I've been very fortunate in that I've required hospitalization only one-and-a-half times. I'll explain the half before I finish this report.

I was hospitalized in July 1981. Diagnosis: massive heart attack, in lay terms. On my doctor's chart and the volumes of insurance papers, it gets a little more technical: myocardial infarction. Had it happened to the right rear tire on my automobile, it would have been called a blowout.

I didn't mess around when I went in. I went the whole nine yards: emergency room, CPR, electric chest stimulation to "bring me back" four times, ICU for six days, followed by two weeks in a regular room and nine more at home before returning to my typewriter. The whole thing was about as much fun as midnight-to-eight guard duty.

I vowed that when I returned to whatever is considered normal and got back in the swing of things, I would not bore people by talking about my heart attack. And I haven't. Honest, except to answer questions asked by friends who really cared.

It is impossible to spend three weeks in any hospital without making certain observations. That is what I'll write about here, not the gory details of having experienced, and survived, a massive heart attack.

Mine was not your normal hospital admission. I went to the head of the line. I've never gone through a normal admission, but having admitted my dear mother on several occasions, I can report what happens.

First, it is necessary to survive the admitting office. A lady sits behind a desk with papers everywhere and asks questions. Her job is to get background information, and you can believe me when I tell you she is going to get it. You can have one foot in the grave and the other on a banana peel, it makes no difference. You don't go nowhere until she's filled in all the blanks on the form on her desk pertaining to you.

Most of her questions I don't understand. Like your mother's maiden name, the identity of all uncles and cousins on her father's side of the family, a listing of all her childhood diseases, Social Security number, and the most important question of all, the name of her insurance carrier. And you must produce the insurance card. She makes a photocopy.

After having survived the admitting office, you are assigned a room. But you don't walk to the elevator to go to it. Not on your life! An orderly puts you in a wheelchair and rolls you to it.

Once in your room, the fun starts. Also the confusion and a lot of things you don't understand.

First, a nurse's aide hands you a thing that bears a strong resemblance to a wrinkled gray bedsheet. Maybe Rip Van Winkle slept on it for forty years. It is technically identified as a hospital gown. You immediately have a question: Why in the heck would they put you in a four-hundred-dollar-a-day room and then dress you out in a forty-five-cent nightgown? You have trouble understanding that.

The hospital gown was undoubtedly designed by Houdini. It has three "ties" in the back. You have to be either a contortionist or an escape artist to tie even one of them. Oh, you can tie the one at the top and occasionally the one at the bottom. The one in the middle? A physical impossibility. It has never been tied. It will never be tied. And you wonder what hospitals have against zippers or why the ties aren't in the front? Is there a law against either?

Resigned to the fact that you will never secure the middle tie, you crawl in bed with your bottom as bare as the day you were born. Within minutes you doze off. You are sleeping as soundly as Rip Van Winkle did when the hospital cheerleader bursts through the door and calls out, "Wake up, Mr. Whaley! Wake up!" And can you possibly imagine why she wakes you? Are you ready for this? To give you a sleeping pill!

You take the sleeping pill without voicing those thoughts in your mind that are just itching to escape your lips. Of course, while she's there she "hooks you up." This is a layman's phrase for "connecting you to the intravenous apparatus" that injects a solution, usually glucose, directly into one of your selected veins.

A word here about glucose: Obviously hospital purchasing agents overbuy on glucose because every patient,
no matter the malady, gets glucose. Personally, I would
just as soon they cut back on glucose purchases and
spring for a little better grade hospital gown. I think there
is a strong possibility that glucose is administered to give
the patient something to do while waiting for the sleeping
pill to take effect. He can count as the stuff drops, one
drop at a time, from the little clear plastic glucose bag into
a clear plastic tube leading to his vein. In the hospital you
don't count sheep. You count glucose drops, at roughly a
dollar a drop.

You try to sleep, but your sleep is interrupted at fifteen-
minute intervals when another nurse's aide awakens you
to the tune of "Vital signs! Time for temp and pressure!"
which, of course, means temperature and blood pressure.
The fact that a nurse's aide is going to take your temp and
pressure at fifteen-minute intervals is as certain as the fact
that the IRS will come calling on April 15. Given a choice,
I'll choose temp and pressure every time.

All goes fairly well until the next morning, just before
daylight, when the cheerleader appears from out of
nowhere and yells, "Wake up! It's X-ray time!"

A word here about X-rays. In the first place, why are X-
rays always taken before daylight? Won't the camera
work in the daytime? You don't understand it, but you
also don't question it. All is not lost, you think. At least
you will be "unhooked" from the glucose contraption for
a little while, right? Wrong! Some fool came along years
ago and attached wheels to the contraption so that it could
go with you to X-ray. So you roll along. . . .

The elevator is always at the other end of the hall from
your room. You're on the sixth floor, and X-ray is always
on the first. Accompanied by the cheerleader and the glucose contraption, you begin the trek to the elevator. You're

dressed out in your forty-five-cent hospital gown with the center tie waving in the wind, untied. You are acutely aware that the gap in back is as wide open as the Grand Canyon as you shuffle slowly past the other rooms, with their doors open. Your right arm is held high, your right hand gripping the glucose contraption. You bear a strong resemblance to either the Statue of Liberty or the late Adolph Hitler. As you roll past each room, you hear snickers and not-so-muffled giggles. You are acutely aware that the gap in the back of your forty-five-cent hospital gown is what prompted the snickers and giggles. Also, you come to realize the real meaning of what it means when doctors note on your chart, "Hold For Observation."

Finally, twelve giggles later, you make it to X-ray where a little girl tells you to get up on a big, black table that has been in cold storage for three weeks and is as hard as granite. Does she put you on your stomach? No way. On your back, and as you ease down on the frozen slab of granite wearing the gaping forty-five-cent hospital gown with your backside exposed, you come to know the true meaning of "ICU."

As you lie there, the little technician—and X-ray technicians are always little—pushes a button and out on a railroad track comes a camera the size of a freight car. She pushes another button, and the freight car drops to within an inch of your chest, scaring you within an inch of your life. For the first time since leaving your room, you completely forget about the gaping backside of your forty-five-cent hospital gown. She turns some little knobs, makes some adjustments, and all is in readiness. But just listen to what she tells you:

"OK, now there is nothing to worry about. It won't hurt you. Just lie still for a minute."

Nothing to worry about? It won't hurt you? Who does she think she's kidding? Know what she does next? She runs like the devil and hides behind a lead shield before pulling the trigger!

All finished, you make the return trip. More snickers, more giggles, more sleeping pills, more vital signs . . .

SAME-DAY SURGERY
IS CONFUSING

NOW, FOR A REPORT AND OBSERVATIONS ON MY half-day hospital stay in the new kid on the block, same-day surgery. But let me first synopsize what took me there.

It was my right knee. I could be dramatic and say that the condition was due to an old football injury when I was tackled in the end zone after scoring the winning touchdown in the conference championship game. Not so. I could say that I damaged the knee when I slid into home plate with the winning run in the College World Series. Not so. I could say that the knee was damaged in the early 1960s while chasing a bank robber in New Jersey. Not so. Or I could say that Miss America's boyfriend was very jealous and hit my knee with a chair after spotting the young lady and myself in a McDonald's just outside Atlantic City in September 1961. Not true.

The truth is I damaged the knee while crawling into a very small bathtub in a very large hotel in Birmingham, Alabama, and couldn't get out. I heard the "rrrriiipp" when it happened. A kindly maid heard my plea for help and summoned the male desk clerk, who pulled me out and took me to the emergency room. Diagnosis? Torn ligaments. Treatment? Arthroscopic surgery. Where? Same-day surgery. When? Two days later.

I went into the same-day surgery building at 9:30 A.M. My knee was arthroscopized an hour and a half later. I arrived back home at 3:30 P.M. There was a bill from the hospital in my mailbox—$2,700 and change—when I arrived. I guess the policy is same-day surgery/same-day billing. But what got my attention was this notation in big red letters on the bottom of the bill: OVERDUE!

I did make some observations while at same-day surgery, the first one being the parking facilities. There are two parking lots in front of the building, one for doctors and one for patients. Now get this: The doctors' parking lot, designated with a big sign that reads Restricted. Same-Day Surgery Doctors' Parking Only! is thirteen steps, or approximately thirty-nine feet, from the front door. Behind it, and well removed, is the parking lot for patients, with a small sign that reads simply, Same-Day Surgery Patient Parking. It is eighty-eight steps, or approximately 264 feet from the front door. I know these measurements are correct. I went back after I recuperated, stepped off the distances, and recorded them. I failed to understand the parking arrangements. Here's why:

I didn't understand, and still don't understand to this day, why patients with busted knees, hips, ankles, and so forth are forced to hobble seventy-five steps more than the doctor who would operate on them. Ever seen a fella with ripped and torn ligaments trying to walk? He looks like a pit bulldog has a death grip on his trousers and is being dragged along. You don't walk on a leg with ripped and torn ligaments. You drag it.

So much for the parking situation. Let's take a look at the bill. I didn't understand it, and I still don't understand it. For instance, can you believe that I was charged $4.50 for the Bic throwaway razor, which sells for no more than thirty-five cents in any discount drugstore, that the nurse used to shave my knee? True. And I didn't even get the razor!

Remember the worrisome gray and wrinkled forty-five-cent hospital gown I wore in my previous hospital stay? They gave it to me again in same-day surgery, and at a charge of fourteen dollars. I didn't get it either, not that I wanted it. But I could have worn it Halloween night and won the twenty-five-dollar first prize for ugliest costume at the Halloween costume contest and made a net profit of eleven dollars. Or I could have used it to wash my car.

I was in the same-day surgery building for a total of five hours, and my itemized bill covered four pages of computer printouts. I think I paid for everything from the water used by the doctor to wash his hands before operating to the towel he used to dry them. Four pages! I couldn't even pronounce most of the charges itemized, much less read them.

The only plus is that my same-day surgery bill didn't arrive postage due.

But now, two years later, I'm walking without a limp. And bear in mind that I never said I didn't appreciate same-day surgery. I only said that I didn't understand it. Actually, as a patient, I don't think I'm supposed to.

THE (NOT SO) WONDERFUL WORLD OF BIFOCALS

I REALIZE THAT MANY OF YOU MAY NOT UNDER-stand this chapter and hope that you never have the opportunity to experience what it is all about—the world of bifocals. As a member of the bifocal club for the past sixteen years, I feel that I can speak (write) with some authority about them.

My initial experience with bifocals came as a lad when I would put on my grandfather's and play like I was in the fun house at the county fair where all those crazy-shaped mirrors make everything, including yourself, appear either ten times too fat or ten times too tall and your face looks like it got caught in an elevator door. It was fun back then because I could take the darn things off and still see. Today, it is quite different.

First, you notice little telltale signs when you hop over the forty mark that indicate you might need to have your eyes examined.

The first big decision is what kind of eye doctor to go to: do you go to an optometrist, an oculist, an optician, an ophthalmologist, or maybe an optimist? After discussing the problem with all your friends and neighbors (who don't know either), you decide on one or the other and get your trusty old telephone book.

Trying to find telephone numbers therein is the prime reason you made the decision to take the plunge anyway. You found out that your arms were about nine inches too short when you extended your arms as far as they would reach while staying attached to your shoulders:

D. Tatched Retina, Optometrist

315 Iris Street : : : 272-1234

By Appointment Only

So, what do you do? You do the same thing that any normal, red-blooded American male would do! You get either one of your 20-20-visioned children or your wife with the x-ray eyes to look it up. You're not about to admit that you're over forty and need a little eye help. No, sir! Not the All-American boy who could spot a miniskirt at five hundred yards and tell right away if she was wearing a wedding ring or not.

With the appointment made and the examination finished (and having failed to read that little Russian's name—RZNFCBOG—that your friend, the optometrist flashed on the wall), you get the word from him in about three weeks when you return to his office to get the glasses:

"Welcome to the world of *bifocals*!"

You leave his office and step (or *try* to step) out into a new world that you never knew existed before, the not so wonderful world of *bifocals*! And, as you stand there on his front steps and prepare to descend from the top of the Washington Monument, you feel certain that everybody is watching you. You cautiously slide your lead foot to the edge of the top step with all the caution of the Great Wallendas on their high wire or a wandering husband trying to negotiate a strange and dark stairway in a hostile neighborhood at five martinis after midnight. Well, you successfully negotiate the first step, and the second and the third fall into place. But then, it feels like the sidewalk just jumped up and met the bottom of your shoe about three feet too soon! And that cotton pickin' line won't vanish from the bottom of your lens! You can wipe, rub, and squint all you please, but the only thing that will erase that line is time, and a lot of stumbles and stumped toes.

Now that you have safely negotiated the steps without breaking the glasses or your neck, it is time to try to learn something over again that you first learned about thirty-nine years before: *How to Walk!* So you just throw caution to the wind and strike out down Jackson Street to your office, or somewhere—anywhere. You give the appearance of a drunken ostrich, wearing skis as you lift one foot and then the other high in the air to step over all those cracks in the sidewalk that look so much like the Grand Canyon. You actually feel, and look, like a forty-year-old fool playing hopscotch on Main Street. Some smart aleck city engineer has raised the curb from seven inches to a disastrous three feet! (The marred and scuffed toes of your previously bright, shiny loafers are evidence of this.) Somehow, by the grace of God you make it to your car and safely home. That's another story.

Later in the evening, while seated with the family for dinner, you try to remain calm and composed as you reach for the salt shaker and ram your thumb and forefinger two inches into the mashed potatoes and then drag your coat sleeve through the gravy as you withdraw your fingers. Of course, you succeed in overturning your water glass with your elbow in the process!

At this point you are sorely tempted to pull off those bifocals and deposit them with your high school class ring, your Second Class Boy Scout badge, and the tassel from your high school graduation cap that hung so prominently from the rearview mirror of your 1947 Ford for years. But you finally settle down and actually succeed in reaching for and getting a roll without turning over your iced tea, or your daughter's who is seated next to you. It seemed that things were going to be all right until your sweet wife becomes enemy number one when she calmly asks:

"Would you please carve the turkey, dear?"

Carve it? Man, you can't even find it! But, you try. Through the bifocals the thing won't be still, and you aren't real sure that it's dead. You reach out to carve a leg for your starving son and succeed only in snipping off the end of your left index finger. In the meantime, your wife has busied herself in the kitchen; she has no desire to witness the explosion she knows is coming, and does!

With dinner out of the way and having stumbled over two chairs, a toy fire truck, a Persian cat, and an end table, you seat yourself in your favorite chair with the newspaper, ready to reap some of the benefits from those bifocal monsters. You hold your head back and try to adjust it and the paper so that both fit into those little inserts called bifocals. It doesn't work. Either your head is too far back, or you are holding the paper too low. It doesn't help at all when your son makes his ill-timed statement, "What's the matter, Daddy? You got a crick in your neck?"

You don't answer, but the look you flash back at him would melt an Alaskan iceberg! Mama knows better. She just takes her time doing the dishes while your daughter cleans the tablecloth.

You finally give up on the paper and opt for a little TV before retiring. No sale, Big Daddy! You again rear your head back as you squat in front of the tube and try to find Channel 5 only to find that 5, 2, 7, and 4 all look alike through the bifocals. So off you go to bed. Your prayer that night will surely be that should you dream, you might be spared the agony of dreaming through bifocals!

How to Spot New Bifocal Victims

1. Observe the earlobes; they will be nicked and scraped from shaving.

2. Check the area around the gas tank nozzle on his car trunk lid. You will notice numerous dents and scratches in a circle about ten inches in circumference (since the advent of self-service gas).

3. Watch him try to read his watch . . . and then turn to the first person available and ask, "You got the time? I think my watch has stopped." (It did, the day he slapped on the bifocals!)

4. Observe him closely as he attempts to unlock the car door or put the key in the ignition. It is during those trying times that old Dad reverts to his boyhood days at grandfather's house and the pin the tail on the donkey game.

He will receive one instant benefit from his newly acquired bifocals, though. When he gets the bill from his eye doctor, he won't be able to read it!

I'll Never Understand Insurance Companies

I DON'T USUALLY GIVE UP EASILY. IT TAKES A LOT to convince me that the ball game is over, that the ship is sinking, or that I'm really overdrawn at the bank. Heck, I was still putting milk and cookies by the fireplace on Christmas Eve when I was forty-two years old. Last year I broke a tooth off my upper plate. Know where it went? Right under my pillow. The fact that I live alone made no difference. I guess the Tooth Fairy was on vacation or had gone to a rock concert, but I will try again.

I have given up completely on one thing, however: insurance companies. I don't understand insurance companies and never have. Although I've been paying health and life premiums for nigh on to forty-five years, for some reason I have never met the deductible. I doubt that Methuselah *ever* met the deductible in all his 900-plus years. But I must admit that my insurance company is very reliable. In all the forty-five years I've been insured with them, they never missed sending me a bill.

If by chance you've ever tried to decipher an "Explanation of Benefits" computer printout, you might just as well be reading a Russian newspaper.

Insurance companies, like lawyers, do not speak or write English. They write and/or speak Insurance. I have no bone to pick with the agents, it's the system and the home office that blow my mind. I'm convinced that the system was conceived by some government agency and programmed by another.

On my desk is a mountain of insurance forms, each plastered with terms that mean absolutely nothing to me. Like these:

- *Major Medical*: I have never been able to determine what is major and what is minor. To me, major is if I have the malady. Minor is if you have it.

- *Applied to the Deductible*: I never have been able to determine how insurance companies come up with how much to apply to the deductible. Judging from my insurance company's reluctance to pay off claims, I think my policy has a one-hundred-dollar debatable.

- *Out of Pocket*: I think I know what it means, but I have always been afraid to ask.

- *Co-insurance*: Does that mean somebody is sharing my insurance with me? If so, why doesn't he spring for half the monthly premium?

- *Uninsured Motorists*: What? I was under the impression that the law required that every motorist be insured.

- *Applicable Discounts*: I have no earthly idea what this means, but I would sure as heck like to get some. Do I write in for 'em, stand in line, or what?

- *Subrogation*: If this means what I think it means, maybe I need to avail myself of the services of a competent attorney. But if his fee is too high, maybe I'll settle for an incompetent one.

- *Death Benefits*: This is an oxymoron if I ever saw one. I guess it means that when I die, I don't have to pay any more premiums.

The main thing I don't understand is the payment of claims provision. If your payment is thirty minutes past due, the insurance company sends you a threatening letter that says in no uncertain terms, "Unless payment is received in this office immediately, we will notify your ex-mother-in-law, your neighbors, your preacher, your librarian, your bank, and your employer that you are a bad credit risk. So there!"

However, submit a claim and see what happens. Nine times out of ten, in about two months you will receive a notice stating, "Send more detailed information in order for us to evaluate your claim. Based on information previously received, we are unable to make a determination."

Always remember this: The fellow who sold you the policy ain't the one who pays the claims.

I submit few claims, but I did submit one on January 7, 1991, on behalf of my mother for reimbursement of prescription drug purchases. Chronologically, this is what happened, and it is documented as fact:

- *January 7*: Claim form submitted for drugs purchased from August through December.

• *February 9*: Letter received from insurance company advising that home office was moving from Atlanta, Georgia, to Illinois, effective February 15. (A toll-free 800 number was furnished).

• *February 28*: I dialed the toll-free 800 number probably twenty times. Busy . . .

• *March 6*: I dialed the 800 number several times, finally got through, and heard this: "All our service representatives are busy. Please hold and one will be with you shortly."

Shortly? I listened to "Autumn Leaves," "Moonlight Serenade," "Stardust," "A String of Pearls," and most of "Theme from *A Summer Place*" before hearing a voice say, "This is Crystal. May I help you?"

"This is Bo. Yes, you may."

I repeated the claim information and asked, "What has happened to the claim?"

I was put on hold again. I wanted very much to hear the rest of "Theme from *A Summer Place*" but was forced to settle for "Mack the Knife" and "King of the Road."

Crystal eventually returned and said, "The computer has no record of your mother's claim. Is she a new policy-holder?"

"Relatively," I said. "About forty-five years, since 1946."

(I could almost hear Crystal say, "Smart ass.")

Standard procedure is, if you can't blame it on the computer, blame it on the move.

"Due to our recent relocation, some of our files are still in Atlanta. Your mother's may still be there. I suggest you call back in about three weeks."

I also had a suggestion. I didn't make it. I'm still surprised at myself that I didn't.

• *April 26*: I called the 800 number again. My luck was getting better. I got an answer on the fifth try. There was no music. I was lucky again. Rock music could have been on, and I could have been placed on hold for hours. This time I talked to Ginger. I had to repeat everything I'd told Crystal. "I suggest you talk to my supervisor, Catherine Miller," Ginger said.

"Put her on."

"I can't. She's gone to a conference in Chicago and won't be back in the office until April 29th."

• *April 29th*: Catherine Miller told me two checks were mailed February 20. I told her they were never received. She said she would stop payment and reissue them, but it would take about three weeks to "cut" them.

"Why is that?" I asked. "It only takes about forty-five seconds when I 'cut' one to pay you."

(I'm pretty sure that then and there I was again labeled a smart ass).

• *June 29*: I called to advise the insurance company that my mother had died that day.

• *July 29*: Two checks arrived, for 17 percent of the amount claimed. There was this note: "Remaining checks being processed." Also, in a separate envelope, this love note: "Premium payment past due since July 1. Unless payment is received on or before August 1, this policy will be canceled effective at 12:01 A.M., August 1, 1991."

Somehow I don't think my mother is really worried about that.

I went back and looked at the notification again that the company headquarters was being moved from Atlanta to Illinois. I couldn't believe the reason: "To better serve you."

Insurance Interpreters Are in Large Demand

WHEN I AM IGNORANT ON A SUBJECT, I WILL readily admit it. Realizing that I was totally ignorant in the field of insurance, I persuaded a good friend in the business to allow me to accompany him to a four-hour seminar on the subject.

"I just want to listen and learn," I assured him.

The next day we traveled to Cordele, Georgia, where the seminar would be held in the Holiday Inn. I went armed with pad and pencil, prepared to absorb and record the four hours of wisdom that was to make me an insurance whiz kid.

"Participation is important," my friend told me on the way to Cordele. "The more you participate, the more you'll get out of the seminar. I'm registering you as my employee so you'll have the same status as everyone else in attendance."

I did participate, and well, but only during the coffee and doughnut hour prior to the beginning of the seminar. I elaborated on the Persian Gulf War, the baseball season, inflation, the forthcoming 1992 election, the 1988 election, all sorts of pertinent stuff. I was, in all probability, the number one participator in the group.

But then the coffee and doughnut hour ended, and the seminar began. From that point on, I was as mute as a Mafia boss appearing before the Jimmy Hoffa grand jury. The conversation had switched abruptly from the English language to the foreign language of Insurance. Oh, how I longed for an interpreter or an Insurance language dictionary.

There were thirty-seven of us present. The other thirty-six each had at least twenty years' experience in the insurance business. I had at most, eyeing the wall clock at 9:07 A.M., a total of seven minutes.

I listened as the others asked questions, super-intelligent questions. The answers furnished by the instructor had to have come straight from Princeton, Harvard, Yale, or the Brookings Institute. I desperately wanted to participate and came real close once to asking a question, but fortunately I recalled the quotation from some wise philosopher: "It is better to sit there and be thought a fool than to open your mouth and remove all doubt."

My only real contributions to the seminar were turning off the air conditioner once at the request of the instructor, inasmuch as the thermostat was located on the wall adjacent to my right shoulder, and picking up the sheet we all signed to record our presence and walking it to the front of the room.

I really strutted as I walked back to my seat in the back of the room. I could just imagine what the others must have been thinking: *He must own his own agency.* Nonchalant? Poised? Calm? Self-confident? Ha! Perry Como would have looked like a nervous wreck compared to me.

I was asked but one question during the four-hour session and answered it correctly. The question came early, about ten minutes into the seminar, when the instructor asked, "Can everyone in the back of the room hear all right?"

I responded with a loud "Yessir!"

One question; one correct answer. Having scored 100, I sat back, relaxed, listened, and made copious notes for the remainder of the session.

After lunch, my friend and I headed home. I drove and he slept the entire seventy-four miles. As I drove, I thought about all the insurance terms I'd heard that morning. Most were confusing to me, and I began to wonder how an individual might comprehend them upon hearing them for the first time—an individual who was buying his first insurance policy.

This imaginary conversation went through my head:

Picture, if you will, Mr. Jack Lapse, Route 3, Premium, Georgia, who has been caught up in the no-fault law. He is fifty-three years old, married to Jane Coverage, and has never had insurance of any kind on his house or automobile. "I'll take my chances," he would always say.

Lapse is seated at the desk of Slick Talker, owner of the Clippum Quick Insurance Agency in downtown Premium. He has two children—a son, seventeen, and a daughter, nineteen—living at home. The conversation could have gone like this:

"Mornin', Mr. Talker," Lapse says. "Th' lady over at th' tag office told me I can't buy my tag 'til I git some insurance."

"That's right, Lapse. I'll be glad to take care of you," Talker assured him as he reached for pad, pencil, and a rate book. "Hmmmmm . . . let's see now. Have you had any tickets in the past two years?"

"Well . . . yeah. I had two dang good 'uns to a Braves-Pirates game back in May, but it got rained out in th' fourth inning. Doggone good game too, Talker. Them Braves was . . ."

"No, Lapse. I mean speeding tickets."

"Speedin' tickets? Shoot naw! I don't speed."

"Good, very good," said Talker. "Now, as to your limits of liability. Would 10/25 limits be satisfactory?"

"Well, no, not quite. Might be all right for my wife, Talker, but sometimes I drive a little faster than that. Like I said, I don't speed. But I do go more than ten and twenty-five," Lapse advised.

"I see. Well, what about 50/100? That should take care of it, shouldn't it?" Talker asked.

"Ought to, unless my boy is drivin'."

Talker said nothing. He just frowned and gritted his teeth. Lapse lit his pipe.

"All right, 50/100 will take care of your BI and PDL along with BI for UM and we can also add PD for a nominal fee," Talker rattled off in Insurancese. "You will also want PIP and Medpay along with Comp and Collision with a deductible of a hundred on collision and ACV on the comp, right?"

Lapse took his time and relit his pipe before answering. "Sounds 'bout right to me, Talker."

"Good. Now, now let me see . . . your car falls in Group Three and you and your wife are both Class One . . ."

"Ya got that right, Talker," Lapse said proudly. "Just ask anybody in Premium. They'll tell you that both me an' my ole lady are first class."

Talker didn't bother to reply. He merely shifted in his chair and frowned again as he reached for and opened his little blue rate book. "I see here that you are in Territory Nineteen . . . "

"Nope. You're wrong there, Talker. I'm in the Eighth District, and me and my ole lady both voted for Jack Brookins. He oughta won, too. Doggone good man, that Brookins. Th' way I figure it, he'd a won easy if it hadn't been for . . . "

"Right. OK, Lapse. But I'm talking about Territory Nineteen for rating purposes; not about Mr. Brookins so . . . "

"Whadda ya mean for rating purposes? I rate Brookins right up there with the best of 'em. And let me tell you another thing, young feller . . . " Lapse blurted out as he got up to leave.

"Hold it! Wait a minute, Mr. Lapse. I'm all for Jack Brookins. I voted for him. I was just trying to explain how your car is rated so I can determine the cost of your premium," Talker assured him.

"Well, as long as you put it that way . . . "

Talker turned to his calculator and fingered it like a concert pianist, coming up with a figure of $312.60.

"Sounds a little high to me, Talker," Lapse said, frowning, as he removed his fat wallet from his left rear pants pocket. "Let me think about it f'r a few minutes. Now then, how 'bout givin' me some figures on my house and b'longings, not includin' my bird dogs. You see, Talker, I've 'bout quit huntin' since I got drunk las' year and run my pickup through the gymnasium an' broke my lef' leg an' back. Too bad, too. We was ahead by eight points in the fourth quarter, but they had to call the game off after I knocked the goal down and . . . "

At this point, Talker's mouth got real dry, and he felt a strange emptiness in the pit of his stomach. He merely shook his head as he placed the cover over the calculator and replaced the pencil in his shirt pocket. He leaned way back in his chair, looked Lapse straight in the eye, and, speaking Insurancese, said:

"Well, Mr. lapse, it appears to me that as far as your Homeowner's policy is concerned, you will need at least an HO-2, and possibly an HO-3, with limited deductions and exclusions, some of which can be handled by endorsements and inasmuch as you are in Fire Class Six you may get a break there. The contents can be handled at ACV and you can schedule your wife's jewelry and your guns. The deductibles can be handled at a flat minimum with an inflation guard for a small 2 percent, quarterly. You are a Code 42, and if you choose to go with an HO-6 Plan for Loss Assessment Coverage or Optional Deductibles with a premium modification you may qualify for a Preferred Option. Also, you would certainly want to consider the Theft Coverage Extension or Endorsement HO-34 covering other structures. Then you can utilize Basic Forms FR-1, FR-2, and FR-4. Coverage can then be modified and revised to clarify the intent to exclude certain devices covered under FR-8 and FR-10, with certain premium modifications and adjustments, of course. Certain named perils are not identified specifically but can be added by endorsements and . . . "

Talker looked up from his desk just in time to see Lapse putting his hat on his head and his fat wallet back in his pocket as he headed for the door.

"Hey! Mr. Lapse! Wait a minute! I haven't finished explaining your coverage. Where are you going?"

"To see my friend, Jack Brookins, over at his law office and find out if he can get me an interpreter to translate what you're saying," Lapse yelled back over his shoulder as he opened the door on the driver's side to his much-damaged and dented pickup.

SOME THINGS ARE JUST HARD TO DO

I HAVE LONG MAINTAINED THAT THERE ARE three things that can't be done: Climb a fence leaning toward you, kiss a girl leaning away from you, and spit into the wind without getting tobacco juice in your face.

There are other things that aren't impossible, just extremely hard to do. Like trying to trim an unruly lock of hair behind your *right* ear with an oversized pair of scissors while looking in the bathroom mirror. I tried it once and almost cut off my *left* ear. My *left* ear!

If you are right-handed, as I am, the mirror immediately reverses that and you become left-handed. Your ears exchange places with each other. So do your eyes and eyebrows. Your nose stays put, but the nostrils swap sides.

After whacking a hunk out of my ear, I managed somehow to stick one blade of the scissors in my right nostril, or was it my left? Only my bathroom mirror knows for sure.

Here are some other things that come to mind that are hard, if not impossible, to do:

- Get in your car when someone has parked too close to it on the driver's side.

- Carry a sofa upstairs (or downstairs) if you're the one walking backward.

- Draw a circle freehand that doesn't resemble an egg.

- Tie a necktie so it comes out even on the first attempt.

- Put the ice trays in the freezer without spilling water.

- Trim the fingernails of your right hand with your left hand if you're right-handed, or vice versa.

- Turn a mattress over alone.

- Change a pillowcase without holding the pillow under your chin.

- Open the door when you're carrying two bags of groceries and a six-pack of Cokes, or whatever.

- Remove anything from your pocket when you have your seat belt fastened.

- Back your car out of your driveway with a utility trailer attached, using only the rear-view mirror for viewing.

- Throw a piece of Scotch tape away with one hand.

- Unscrew a regular screw with a Phillips-head screwdriver.

- Get the color right again on your television set once you've messed it up.

- Remove some foreign object from your eye without having your glasses on, which you had to remove in the first place to get at whatever's in your eye.

- Walk with a full cup of coffee without spilling it.

- Get rid of the toothpick after you've eaten an hors d'oeuvre at a cocktail party or wedding reception.

- Button the collar of a heavily starched shirt.

- Tie a bow tie so that it is straight.

- Go straight home from the office on Friday night.

- Write in a straight line on a blackboard.

- Wrap a package without using Scotch tape.

- Make notes in a telephone book.

- Thread a needle while wearing your first pair of new bifocals.

- Get all the peanut butter out of the jar.

- Make eggs, bacon, grits, and toast come out even.

- Parallel park and, should you succeed, un-parallel park.

- Locate the section of a week-old newspaper that contains the news story you partially read before putting the newspaper aside to go to the golf course.

- Make the gas pump at a self-service gas station stop on even money, say ten dollars, when that is all the money you have with you. The pump will jump to $10.07, at least.

- Remain silent while standing in the "Express, Six Items Or Less, Checkout" line holding but a quart of milk and a loaf of bread while the jerk in front of you has his cart overflowing with seventeen items and the cashier says nothing to him.

In any of these situations, it might help to remember this: No problem is so big or complicated that it cannot be run away from.

IT WAS SEW
SIMPLE WHEN
MAMA DID IT

I'M CONVINCED THAT MOST MEN, INCLUDING this one, are more or less helpless when there's no woman in the house to do the things that women do best, like sewing a button on a shirt. Take it from one who knows. It ain't easy.

I've seen my mother sew on hundreds of shirt buttons. There's an art to it. First, she would roll just enough thread off the spool and either bite it or break it with two fingers. I've tried it. Thread will cut your fingers. I have the scar to verify that. Then she would pop one end of the thread in her mouth and moisten it before twisting it, again with two fingers (thumb and forefinger) to a fine point before threading the needle. Next, she would tilt her head back, twist her lips together tightly, and pop the thread through the eye of the needle on the first try.

She would then stretch the thread to its full length and tie a one-handed knot at the end to keep the end of the thread from following the needle through the hole it would make.

Next, she would push the needle and thread alternately through the four holes in the button with her thimble-covered right index finger until she was satisfied it was secured. Finally, she would sneak the needle underneath and sew crossways for a few stitches before biting the thread.

She would then check to see if the button was properly aligned with the corresponding buttonhole.

Job completed.

I tried it while getting dressed to go to a wedding. My admiration for button sewers skyrocketed.

I removed the lone clean white shirt from my closet and began buttoning up. I buttoned the right collar button. The left one was missing. Surely, I thought, there is a machine at the laundry that pulls the buttons off my shirts and shoots them through the toes of my socks.

The time was 6:35 P.M. The stores had been closed for thirty-five minutes, and the wedding was at seven o'clock. I had to make a decision. I made a bad one. I would sew a button on my white shirt, but first I had to find one, along with a needle and thread.

I raided an innocent pink shirt and, because I couldn't find my scissors, snipped the bottom button off with a pair of toenail clippers. I prayed that the bride would never know about the toenail clippers. "Something old, something new, something borrowed, something blue" is traditional, but a shirt button removed by toenail clippers ain't part of the tradition.

Next, I had to find the little utility kit that Delta Airlines gave me on a flight from Atlanta to New York. I recalled that included in it was needle and thread. By some miracle, I found it.

Delta was ready, but I wasn't. I had to try to thread the needle while wearing bifocals. I soon began swearing at Delta for having given me an eyeless needle. I saw no hole, and then suddenly I saw two. By some miracle I got the thread through one of them.

Next, the button. It had four holes. I missed several times, pricked my finger twice, dropped the button and watched it disappear under the sofa never to be seen again. I ended up with two little splotches of blood on my collar.

I gave up and went to the wedding decked out in a one-button collar looking like a pigeon with a broken wing. I sat in the back of the church and no one noticed. The reception was another spool of thread.

From the time I signed the bride's book with the traditional feather until I left, I walked around with my head cocked conspicuously to the left, feigning a pulled neck muscle in an attempt to conceal the fact that I was wearing a one-collar-button shirt. I lied repeatedly, telling interested sympathizers that "I must have pulled it while swinging a golf club."

No problem until one observant female approached me from the blind side, touched my collar, and whispered, "Are you aware that there's a button missing from your shirt?"

I never flinched and whispered back, "Oh, thank you! It must have come off when I kissed the bride."

That's when she spotted the two little splotches of dried blood, and asked, "What happened? Did she bite you, too?"

I left it at that.

My Kitchen Speaks a Foreign Language

MY LITTLE HOUSE IS A SIMPLE PLACE, WITH A couple of bedrooms, a bathroom, a den, a living room, scattered clothes closets, and the monster: the kitchen. My kitchen and I aren't on the same (micro)wave length. I speak what can best be termed regional (southern) English. My kitchen speaks a foreign language, which one I do not know. I only know it doesn't understand me, and I don't understand it. I live alone, so it goes without saying there's no interpreter.

I spent a week in my kitchen one day after receiving an invitation to attend a party at the home of friends. There was a request at the bottom of the invitation—just below the RSVP—that presented a problem for me. The notation sounded simple and would have been for most folks. Not for me. "Please bring a covered dish," it said.

I've received many such invitations with similar notations in the past. No problem. I simply had a restaurant prepare a covered dish, paid for it, and went to the party with covered dish in hand. Or I would go to the grocery store and pick up something at the last minute, cover it, and arrive at the party à la Betty Crocker. But for this party, I was determined to prepare my own covered dish. That presented a problem for this old single man who has extreme difficulty heating hot dogs or making toast without directions.

I had a reason for deciding to prepare my own covered dish. I get sick and tired of other guests whispering behind my back, "Well, I see Bo Whaley has arrived with his usual Vienna sausages and saltine crackers." I would remedy that by preparing an exotic dish that would knock their hats in the creek.

The day after receiving the invitation, I trucked over to the library and checked out *The Bachelor's Cookbook*. On the way back home with cookbook in hand, the thought flitted through my mind that I might even consider dismissing my personal chefs—Boy-R-Dee, Sara Lee, Colonel Sanders—who have kept me alive for years.

Once home, I eagerly began reading the cookbook. It contained fifty-two menus and, according to the inside cover, "Even the rankest amateur can put together a meal that will draw the astonished applause of friends and family." There was only one thing correct in that statement: rankest amateur. Astonished? Definitely. Applause? No way.

I chose menu twenty-six, an exotic-sounding concoction called Spanakopita (Spinach Pie). That was my first mistake, because I live by the rule, "Never eat anything you can't pronounce."

According to the cookbook, "Every cook has one favorite dish, the one you wheel out for special occasions.

It should look sensational when brought to the table, and the first bite should melt in your mouth. During the meal, the dish should be the main topic of conversation." The main topic of conversation? Absolutely right.

The cookbook goes on to say that the first bite should prompt the question, "Mmmmmmm, what's this?" The second bite: "Hey, what *is* this?" By the third bite, people should be asking for a second helping. And by the fourth bite, they should be begging for the recipe. In my case I guess two—the first two—out of four ain't bad.

Here is the recipe for Spanakopita that I tried to follow:

The Staples: Eggs, salt, pepper, oregano, rosemary, garlic, lemons, olive oil, sugar.

The Shopping List: Two pounds of feta cheese, one pound of filo dough, two pounds of spinach, two large onions, one pound of butter.

The Preparation: First, use a pastry brush to spread butter over the thin sheets of dough. Then melt a large chunk of butter—three or four tablespoons—in a frying pan over medium heat. Add an onion, chopped fine, and one clove of garlic, minced. Cook until the onions are softened.

Now for the spinach. Rinse several times in a pot of cold water. Dry it with paper towels, chop it fine, and add it to the onions. Add salt, pepper, a large pinch of oregano, and a large pinch of rosemary.

Separate half a dozen eggs, putting the yolks in one bowl and the whites in another. Beat the yolks for a few minutes, and blend in one pound of feta cheese, crumbled. Stir in the spinach mixture. Finally, beat the egg whites until they are stiff, and fold them into the rest of the pie filling.

Preheat oven to 350 degrees. Melt half a pound of butter in a saucepan over low heat. Carefully unroll the filo dough, and use a pastry brush to paint the bottom of a rectangular nine-by-thirteen-inch baking dish with melted butter. Lay a single sheet of filo dough over the pan, and brush butter on the dough. Repeat until you have ten sheets of dough. Spoon in spinach mixture and cover with another sheet of dough. Repeat until you have used up the filo. Butter top with pastry brush. Place in oven and bake for 50 mintues.

It all sounds so simple, right? Wrong! Complications immediately.

I had no pastry brush, so I used an old paint brush that had been simmering in turpentine in a coffee can for almost seven years since I painted some concrete blocks. I also had no rosemary, so I called a bachelor friend who is a self-proclaimed expert chef and radio announcer.

"You got rosemary at your house?" I asked.

"Rosemary? Heck no. I don't even know the girl! Why?"

"Because I'm making Spanakopita and . . ." I said.

"Shhhhhhhh! Watch your language, boy! I'm on the air!" he cautioned.

"Well, I need rosemary real bad," I pleaded.

"Oh, yeah? Good luck. How 'bout Margie, Lucy, or Irene? Want their phone numbers?" he asked.

"No, thanks. Got to have rosemary."

My next problem surfaced when I realized I had no paper towels with which to dry the spinach. I used three old newspapers.

I also couldn't find any filo dough. I substituted several slices of white bread, thin sliced. Also, no feta cheese, but the partial can of parmesan left over from a spaghetti dinner a few months back worked fine.

Also, I've never been able to remember the difference between a teaspoon and a tablespoon. Which is larger? I just dropped in three or four of each filled with butter. And inasmuch as I had no "large pinch of oregano," whatever that is, I just pinched rosemary twice and let it go at that, doubled the salt and pepper ingredients, and added half a bottle of Louisiana Hot Sauce on my own, just for good measure.

Finished, I placed the Spanakopita in the oven for the required fifty minutes, or so I thought. But would you believe that my oven conked out in thirteen minutes? No doubt from lack of use.

I removed my Spanakopita, covered the dish with what was left of the newspapers (no aluminum foil or Saran wrap in the house), and took it to the party. I figured that my dish would probably be the star of the buffet table. But just in case, I stuck a couple of cans of Vienna sausages and a box of saltines in my pockets—for Rosemary, if she happened to be there.

As predicted in the cookbook, the first bite produced a chorus of "What's this?" The second bite—right on cue—produced a second chorus of "What *is* this?"

I said nothing, but I can tell you that the Vienna sausages and saltines were delicious.

Rosemary? She never showed up. I figured she was probably at my radio announcer friend's house.

You Don't Need a Cart for Just a Few Items

I GET OFF TO A BAD START IN SUPERMARKETS BY never taking a shopping cart from the stack. This probably dates back to my early bachelor days when I reached for one, got one with ruptured wheels that wouldn't go straight on an AA pledge, and nearly demolished the store by knocking down a mountain of apple sauce, hitting the bread rack head-on, and almost sideswiping a senior citizen.

I always say to myself as I eye the carts, "Only gonna' pick up a couple of items. I don't need one." Have you ever tried to "pick up a couple of items" in a supermarket?

Hear me, friends and neighbors. You can hitchhike to Forsyth, take in a movie, have an ice cream cone at Howard Johnson's, hitchhike back to Me-Ma's for country ham, syrup, and biscuits in Allentown and hoof it on back to Dublin before you can negotiate the check-out with a "couple of items" at the supermarket. They just ain't programmed for bachelors and other singles.

You want to put a halt to supermarket shoplifting? Simple as ABC. Just put a guy on a stool near the front door, give him a cigar box, change for a ten, and a sign, "Single Men Only—No Carts Allowed."

And you won't even need to give Green Stamps. All the poor guy wants is out with his Vienna sausage, saltines, six-pack, and a couple of rolls of Charmin without a lot of hassle.

It is always my avowed intention when entering the supermarket to pick up something like two cans of soup and a loaf of bread. Hah! The road to the check-out is paved with good intentions.

What I usually end up with (sans the cart) is this: six cans of soup (on sale), Cheer, bread, four cans of apple sauce (the store buyer went ape over apple sauce and you run into mountains of it at every turn)—and I don't even like apple sauce—three cans of Vienna sausage, three bananas, two rolls of Charmin, a tube of toothpaste, one can of sliced peaches, a pound of ground beef, two cans of Hungry Jack biscuits, and a package of cheese, my weakness.

And, remember, no cart. I *never* have a cart.

So here I come, all the way from the meat counter in the back, the most distant point in the store from the cash registers.

Please don't ask me why I didn't *start* at the meat counter. If I was smart enough to answer that, I'd be rolling a shopping cart instead of going into my juggling act up aisle five. And here's the way it works:

First, the toothpaste—shirt pocket; Vienna sausage—two cans in right front pocket, one can in left rear pants pocket; cheese—crammed in pants at the waist near the navel area; one loaf of thick-sliced bread, soon destined to become one loaf of thin-sliced bread—under right armpit;

(three bananas join the bread); Charmin, two rolls—under left armpit; ground beef goes between the Charmin; six cans of soup, four cans of unwanted apple sauce, and a can of sliced peaches—you're right, stacked like stovewood from my Timex to my Izod alligator.

Aha! You thought I forgot the Cheer, didn't you? No way. Where does it fit in the scheme of things? Right up there, all snuggy like, under my chin.

All set, I begin my advance toward check-out, walking with all the poise and dignity of a lobster with a double hernia and a broken neck. I approach a doctor and his wife but manage to hide behind an apple sauce mountain to avoid explanations.

As I creep past the crackers and cookies on aisle five, I slip up on the saltines and reach for a box. I grasp it but in so doing a restless can of apple sauce, sensing it's not wanted, escapes, drops to the floor and rolls to aisle six. While I'm trying to capture the wayward sauce a discontented can of Beef Chunky defects to aisle three and eight ounces of mild cheddar slides down my left pants leg. An escapee from the juvenile detention home, riding a shopping cart à la Evel Knievel, runs over it.

I finally limp on to the check-out counter and stand there, a member of the walking wounded, while a sweet little lady proceeds to drop her handbag, thereby dumping an assortment on the counter matched only by grandma's sewing machine drawers.

I was all set to unload when I heard the little guy behind me say, "Excuse me, do you mind if I go ahead? I only have two cans of soup and a box of Cheer."

"Be my guest," I said. "You don't even have a cart, do you?"

"Naaa, never use 'em. I just pick up a couple of items at the time," he said. "Try to avoid the hassle."

"Yeah, I know 'bout them hassles," I mumbled as he left and fourteen "thin" slices of bread dropped at my feet.

WHERE ARE ALL THE COKES IN SIX-OUNCE BOTTLES?

IT WAS ABOUT A MONTH AGO THAT I DROVE TO Swainsboro for graduation exercises at Emanuel County Junior College (ECJC). Naturally, it was a hot and sultry day. But then, aren't ALL graduation exercises held on a hot day?

But this column isn't about graduation exercises . . . it's about the world's number one soft drink—Coca-Cola—and the difficulty I experienced in locating one following the ECJC graduation.

I visited every Coke machine on campus, but came away empty-handed. Oh, the machines had Cokes all right—but in cans. And I steadfastly refuse to drink Coke from a can. Call me hard-headed, stubborn, picky, or whatever . . . but I don't drink Coke from a can.

I grew up on Cokes in six-ounce bottles and I won't compromise. I also don't want a king size Coke, a Coke in a plastic bottle, or any part of one that is measured in liters. Just a plain Coke in a six-ounce bottle suits me fine.

I also don't particularly care to have a Coke machine talk to me. I approach the box to make a purchase, not to have it wish me a good day. I well remember the first talking Coke machine I ever saw. I felt like a fool standing there carrying on a conversation with a machine.

" . . . And how's your mama 'n 'em?" I kept asking.

And all the big red machine had to say was "Thank you. Have a good day."

Six-Ounce Bottles Almost Extinct

After leaving ECJC, I drove to several service stations where I bought Cokes in six-ounce bottles in the sixties. Oh, they still sold Cokes, but in cans. Needless to say, I made no purchase.

I visited the local pool room in search of a Coke. My redneck research has determined that pool rooms provide one of the few remaining sanctuaries for Cokes in six-ounce bottles.

The pool room was closed . . .

There are four drug stores in downtown Swainsboro. I went to each one. Do any stock Cokes in six-ounce bottles? Negative.

My next stop was the bus station. No luck . . .

I gave up and started home, but for some reason decided to make one more stop—at Thompson's Minit-Mart on Highway 80. There I found my Coke in a six-ounce bottle.

It made no difference to me that I paid exactly twice as much for the deposit on the bottle as I paid for the Coke as a boy.

Coke Drinking Is a Lost Art

As I drove toward Dublin, drinking my Coke, I pondered the way it was back in the late 30s and early 40s when, as a boy in Oglethorpe, I drank Cokes as fast and as often as I could muster up a nickel.

Mr. Dan Kleckley, who owned Kleckley's Grocery in Oglethorpe, always had the coldest Cokes in town. He kept them in an ice box . . . a real ice box. He iced those gems down with real ice and anybody who wanted to buy one had to reach down in the box up to his arm pit to get it. I'd venture to say that on Saturdays, most 12-year-olds in Oglethorpe walked around with a frozen arm, clean but frozen.

My Coke-drinking hero was an Oglethorpe lawyer, Col. Jarred J. Bull. I never figured why everybody called him "Colonel," but never questioned it. After all, Col. Bull had hair down over his ears even back in the 30s, smoked Home Run cigarettes, and always carried a pistol in his back pocket. Who's gonna' question a man like that?

Col. Bull's office was directly across the street from Mr. Kleckley's store and he started his day with three things: his morning mail, a Home Run cigarette, and a Coke in a six-ounce bottle. (Heck, that's all there was.) And he ALWAYS checked the bottom of the bottle to see where it was made. Of course, I was to learn that this determined who paid for the Coke. If six men drank 'em the one with the nearest city paid for everybody.

It took exactly four "bluggles" for Col. Bull to down a Coke. And within seconds after finishing it he sounded like Mount Vesuvius erupting. I'm sure people in Montezuma, two miles away, could hear him, and he must have rattled grave markers in houses in Andersonville, nine miles off distant.

Col. Bull flat knew how to enjoy a Coke.

Then, I thought about Lawrence Mashburn. Lawrence was a unique Coke drinker. He wouldn't drink one unless he had a package of Tom's toasted peanuts to pour in the bottle. He'd let 'em soak for a spell and then go at it. And he always had to beat on the bottom of the bottle to get that last peanut. We all figured that's why he had two chipped front teeth.

Bobby Jack Coogle was another one worth watching. He never uncapped the bottle. Nope, he'd simply take his knife and make a little hole in the cap and drink from that. Folks who knew Bobby Jack well claimed he was so stingy that he did that to make it last longer.

Jimmy Parker may have been the most unusual Coke drinker I ever saw. What Jimmy did was uncap the bottle, put his thumb over the top of the bottle, and shake with all his might—like he was getting ready to shoot dice or something. Then, he would stick thumb and bottle in his mouth and turn her loose. I'm amazed that Jimmy didn't blow his brains out.

Finally, there was Harold Bartholomew, a real cute little fella' who grew marigolds and painted pictures nobody understood. Harold was the only boy in Oglethorpe who drank Cokes through a straw.

Lawrence Mashburn ended up working as a fireman for the railroad; Bobby Jack Coogle went into the Marines; Jimmy Parker bought his very own bulldozer; but I sort of lost track of Harold Bartholomew.

Seems like I did hear a few years back though that Harold wound up in San Francisco. Anyway, I watched on TV all during the Democractic National Convention but never once saw anybody in the street crowd drinking Coke through a straw.

And every time I hear a clap of thunder I think of Oglethorpe, Cokes in six-ounce bottles . . . and Col. Jarred J. Bull.

Vending Machine
Frustration

For years I've been fighting vending machines that refuse to do what they're supposed to do. Half the time they don't work, and when they do they don't deliver what I paid for.

Here's what happens to me. I insert my coins and pull the lever for a candy bar and get cheese crackers. I pull the lever for chewing gum and get potato chips or pork skins. More often than not I drop four dimes and a nickel in the slot, pull the lever designated for a Hershey bar, and nothing happens. I jiggle the coin return thingamajig and get back two dimes and a nickel. The other two dimes? Where they go I'll never know. And just try and find somebody who will take the responsibility for the foul-up and see what happens.

"We don't know nothing about it," says the girl behind the counter. "We just lease the space to the vending company. You'll have to speak to the manager, Mr. Johnson, about it."

"Fine. Would you tell Mr. Johnson I'd like to speak to him?"

"Can't. He's on a cruise and won't be back for three weeks."

You stand the same chance of getting your money back from Johnson as you would from a television evangelist or a flim-flam artist.

Here's another thing that prompts an urge to go on a break-and-destroy mission: After depositing my coins and pulling the lever for the item I want, always up top, it falls off the Empire State Building and gets caught in a mass of twisted wire about the eighth floor or ends up crossways at the exit chute. No matter how much shaking and kicking I do, it won't budge, and a hand won't go up into the chute far enough to grab it. Trust me. I know this to be a fact.

Coin-operated vending machines offer an endless variety of items, from stamps to nail clippers, soft drinks to peanuts, cigarettes to self-portraits, combs and newspapers.

Ahhhhh . . . newspapers. Not only do the darn machines play tricks, but some of the folks who fill them are a day or two late now and then, the large dailies I'm talking about. This happens to me with alarming regularity, especially late at night when I really want a newspaper before retiring.

What happens is this: I approach the newspaper machine in pitch-black darkness. I insert my coins, remove a newspaper, and drive home where I settle down in my favorite chair with a reading lamp over my shoulder. Somewhere along about page seven, section C, what I'm reading has a familiar ring to it, and well it should. There I sit on a Thursday night reading the same newspaper I bought and read on Monday! There's nothing more aggravating to a newspaper addict than to deposit money in the machine and end up reading Monday's paper on Thursday.

Now, a word about coin-operated coffee machines. I'm convinced they're programmed at the factory to tilt the cup at forty-five degrees when it falls into place. What happens is you put your forty cents in the slot, select the desired combination of cream and sugar—black, black with sugar, extra sugar, cream, extra cream, and so on—and then stand back and watch. The little cup, about the size of a thimble, falls from outer space and sits sideways at the pre-programmed forty-five-degree angle. Then, half your coffee goes into the cup and the other half disappears down a drainage system installed for just such an occasion.

OK, try to slide the glass covering up and remove the half-thimble full of coffee at the same time. Two will get you one that the hot stuff will saturate your wristwatch or shoes should you succeed in removing it from the machine.

I've been fighting coin-operated vending machines, and losing. I think I know why. The darn things are made by the government.

GREAT TRAIN
MISCOMMUNICATIONS

I HAD AN UNCLE, COMER JERNIGAN, WHO WAS A
conductor on the Central of Georgia Railroad for thirty-
five years before his retirement. Long after retirement,
railroading was still in his blood.

According to my grandfather, Wes Whaley, every time
Uncle Comer heard a train whistle, he would instinctively reach for his official railroad watch, glance at it,
and put it back in his watch pocket. But if somebody
asked him the time, he would immediately reach for his
watch again and check.

Uncle Comer would sit and tell railroad stories by the
hour, and while these didn't originate with him, they have
been around for many years. You may have heard them,
but that's all right. So have I.

*   *   *

237

It seems that many years ago a man and his five-year-old son were passengers on a train. As the train roared through the countryside, the man would periodically turn and slap the youngster with the back of his hand.

Finally, after several such wallops, a well-dressed and obviously affluent woman sitting across the aisle reprimanded the man with this statement:

"Excuse me, but I must ask you to stop hitting that child. I am burdened with problems, plus I have a terrible headache. Somebody stole my mink coat, I ran my Rolls-Royce into a fire hydrant, my French poodle is ill, and four of my blue chip stocks dropped four points yesterday," she said. "With all these problems, surely you can understand why I am upset. And your repeated slapping of that youngster simply complicates my dilemma. I must ask that you stop."

The man hesitated, then turned and walloped the youngster again before addressing the woman.

"Problems? You say *you've* got problems? Lady, you don't know what problems are. Let me point out my problems to you," he said. "I'm on my way to the state prison to visit my oldest son who is being executed in the morning for murder. My wife ran off with the leader of a rock band last week and took my guitar and Ernest Tubb records with her. My youngest daughter is in a home for unwed mothers expecting a child in three weeks. On top of that, my IRS refund check bounced. I've got ingrown toenails, and my undershorts are too tight. I've got an abscessed wisdom tooth, and my brother-in-law is suing me for wrecking his pickup truck. Plus, this young 'un has messed up his pants, eaten the tickets, and on top of all that I'm on the wrong train! And you say *you* have problems?"

An exchange of letters between a nervous man who lived next to a railroad yard and the local railroad agent:

Gentlemen,

Why is it that your engine has to ding and dong and fizz and spit and bang and hiss and pant and grate and grind and puff and hump and chug and hoot and whistle and snarl and growl and boom and crash and jolt and screech and throb and roar and rattle and grunt and strain and tug and tear and stop and start all night long when I'm trying to sleep?

After due deliberation the local railroad agent penned these words in the form of a reply to the complaining resident:

Dear Sir,

In reply to your recent letter regarding noise made by our trains:

Sorry, but if you are to get vital needs including meats and sweets and breads and spreads and guns and buns and beans and jeans and shirts and skirts and shirts and blouses and socks and locks and booze and shoes and dippers and slippers and lotions and notions and candy bars and nuts in jars and sugar and spice and everything nice to make you happy all your life and satisfy the fancy of your devoted wife . . . you really shouldn't criticize the noise made by our trains.

Making fun of the slowness of trains has long been an American tradition. Like the story of the woman and her husband who boarded the train in Atlanta en route to Washington, D.C.

En route, the woman gave birth to a baby just outside Richmond, Virginia. When the ordeal was over, the obviously annoyed conductor castigated the new mother, saying: "Young lady, you never should have boarded this train knowing you were in that condition."

The young mother retorted, "Well, when my husband and I boarded this train, I wasn't in that condition."

The old gentleman had never before ridden a train. He approached the ticket window at the Jacksonville, Florida, station and said, "I'd like a round-trip ticket, please."

"Where to?" grunted the ticket agent.

"Back here."

The little old lady had never before ridden a train. She boarded and took a seat by the window.

Shortly, the conductor came by taking up tickets. The little old lady searched diligently in her handbag for hers. In the process, she dropped an apple and a banana, broke a bottle of Milk of Magnesia that saturated the conductor's trousers, watched a ball of yarn roll from one end of the railroad car to the other, dropped $2.45 in change under the seat, stabbed the conductor in the groin with a knitting needle while trying to recover the money, and spilled a bottle of aspirin in the aisle. Still, no ticket.

Feeling that she should offer some explanation, she said to the conductor, "You know, I've never ridden the train before."

"Yes, ma'am," the conductor agreed. "We ain't missed you, either."

TREASURES OF

BOTCHED

COMMUNICATION

I KEEP ON MY DESK A LITTLE BOX. I CALL IT MY trivia box. It contains written reminders of stories either sent or related to me. Here are a few of my favorite treasures.

A Matter of Survival

A woman from South Georgia went to Atlanta to see the governor about getting her husband out of prison.

"What's he in for?" asked the governor.

"For stealin' a ham."

"That doesn't seem too bad. Is he a good worker?"

"No, suh. To tell ya th' truth, he's purty lazy."

"Oh. Well, he's good to you and the children, isn't he?"

"Not really. He's purty mean to us."

"How many children do you have?"

"Eight, with 'nother 'un due in two months."

"Is he a steady worker?"

"Nope. He don't work."

"Then why would you want a man like that out of prison and back home?"

"Well, Governor, it's like this. We've done run outta ham."

Some People Talk Funny

Highlands, North Carolina, is the summer home of thousands of Yankees who migrate there each June from New Jersey and New York by way of West Palm Beach, Florida, and stay until mid-October, then return to West Palm Beach.

One afternoon late in October, a man from Massachusetts stopped at a service station in Highlands on his way to Florida for the winter. It was his first time ever in the South.

"Tell me, young man," he said to the station attendant, "Where can I find some of those people around here who talk so funny?"

"You're too late, mister," the attendant replied. "They ain't none heah now."

"None here? Why not?"

"They done all went back to Florida f'r th' winter."

Everybody's Gotta' Be Somewhere

She left him on the sofa when the telephone rang and was back in a few seconds.

"Who was it?" he asked nervously.

"My husband," she replied calmly.

"Your husband! Where was he calling from?" he shouted in a near-panic tone.

"Relax," she said, patting him on the hand. "He won't be home for another three or four hours."

"How can you be so sure?"

"Because he's at the club . . . playing poker with you."

A Party Argument

A Republican husband and his Democrat wife rode in silence for hours following a heated political argument. Neither would budge. Finally, the husband pointed to a jackass in a pasture.

"Relative of yours?" he asked sarcastically.

"Yes," she replied. "By marriage."

Prelude to Manslaughter

The scrawny little fellow walked into a bar, ordered a margarita, and asked the burly bartender if he enjoyed dumb-jock jokes.

"Listen, shrimp," the bartender growled. "See them two big guys at the end of the bar? Them's both defensive line-men for the Atlanta Falcons. See the fella at th' pinball machine? He's a professional 'rassler. An' th' one by the jukebox readin' a comic book is a world champion weight lifter. An' 'nother thing. I played tackle f'r th' Pittsburgh Steelers f'r nine years. Now then, you still wanna' tell your dumb-jock joke here?"

"Nah, I guess not."

"No guts, eh?"

"Oh, it's not that."

"No? What then?"

"I just wouldn't want to have to explain it five times."

Yuppies Are Indeed Different

A yuppie was driving his new BMW convertible around Atlanta with his left arm hanging over the side and his tape player going full blast. A garbage truck pulled around him, sideswiped his BMW, and kept going.

The yuppie pulled to a stop, observed the damage to the side of his BMW, and in a frantic rage cried out, "My car! My beautiful car!"

Shortly, a policeman came by and the yuppie told him about the accident.

"Look! My beautiful BMW is a wreck!" he shouted.

"You've got more than your car to worry about, buddy," the policeman said. "You need an ambulance. Look at your left arm."

The yuppie looked at his badly injured and bleeding left arm and cried out, "My Rolex! My beautiful Rolex!"

Being a Conversation Captive Is No Fun

WHILE I DON'T UNDERSTAND IT, THERE ARE those who are convinced that engaging another in conversation when both are in captive surroundings is a required activity. What are captive surroundings? They are places where you happen to be and can't escape, such as elevators, airplanes, lunch counters, waiting rooms, stadium bleachers, rest rooms, and bank teller lines.

Being caught in captive surroundings happens to me with alarming regularity. I can think of several instances right off the bat:

• *Coffee Shops:* Recently I was seated on a stool at a lunch counter in a coffee shop in a strange town. A man came in, chose the stool next to me, sat down, and ordered coffee. Before he had put cream and sugar in it, he proceeded to tell me in no uncertain terms what was wrong with the Social Security system in America.

I was a captive, with the choice of abandoning my fresh cup of coffee, leaving and finding another coffee shop, or staying to listen to a lengthy discourse as an unwilling student in his Social Security 101 class. I chose the latter but flunked the course when I finally disagreed with his theories on the subject.

• *Elevators*: You are in the basement of a sixteen-story office building and push the button for the fifteenth floor. One other person steps on and pushes the button for the twelfth floor. Know how he starts the conversation? And bear in mind that you are in the basement.

"Goin' up?" he asks.

If he were going to the fifteenth floor, too, do you know what he'd do right after you push 15? Right, he'd follow suit and push it, too. Why? Would that make the elevator go twice as fast?

• *Airplanes*: I doubt that there is any more captive surrounding than being a passenger on a commercial airline. Let's assume I'm flying from Atlanta to New York. This is how it usually goes with me:

I select seat number C-27, which is the center seat in a cluster of three. I really want W-27 (window) or A-27 (aisle), but inasmuch as these are spoken for by the time I arrive at the loading gate because I lost over an hour trying to find the Atlanta airport exit off I-285, I settle for C-27, a loser.

So, there I sit in C-27, seat belt fastened as required and newspaper in my lap as desired, when W-27 and A-27 arrive. W-27 is a recently paroled former rock band cocaine junkie turned born-again Christian on his way to New York to team up with a TV evangelist for a crusade. He will serve his apprenticeship en route to having his own TV ministry and spread the message from pillar to post: send money. He chooses to practice his spiel on me, but the cross—approximating the size of the *Queen Mary's* anchor—hanging on a chain around his neck keeps getting in the way.

A-27 is heading home to mama in Brooklyn after throwing in the towel on a twelve-year marriage that produced seven kids, "because he gave me very little attention and made me feel neglected." (What? Seven kids . . . twelve-year marriage . . . very little attention . . . neglected. Hmmmmmm.)

Our flight isn't three minutes off the runway before I become—unwillingly—her marriage counselor. I listen to her and nod all the way to Richmond, Virginia, before W-27 relieves me. From Richmond to New York neither W-27 or A-27 speaks to me. They speak *across* me. Being a victim caught in captive surroundings, I'm forced to listen to all the gory details of an unhappy marriage and the pitfalls of cocaine addiction.

I think A-27 and W-27 were engaged when the airplane touched down at LaGuardia Airport. I wished them both well and breathed a sigh of relief.

• *Waiting rooms*: How do you handle it when you're seated in a filled-to-capacity waiting room at your dentist's office with a right jaw that looks like you're chewing on a grapefruit, and the guy seated next to you wants to talk? All you really want is to die or get relief. He comes on with, "Whatsa matter? You got a toothache?" and you're in so much pain it hurts to grunt.

And what about the character that comes in and sits next to you while you're waiting to see your doctor? Your right arm is in a cast up to your right armpit. What does he ask? You got it: "Didja hurt y'r arm?"

• *Football stadiums*: Here's one you can count on. There you sit in the south stands, Section 135, Aisle 66, Row Z, Seat 50, so far removed from what's going on down on the football field that the game is nothing more than a rumor. And here *he* comes, the holder of the ticket to Seat 49.

He's decked out in black trousers with a miniature Bulldog emblazoned on the left front pocket, a red shirt with the dog's twin brother sitting over the pocket, a red-and-black cap flashing "Go Dawgs" on the front, and carrying a red and black umbrella, a portable radio, and a container of liquid. The guy is so much a Bulldog he doesn't, when introduced to you, shake hands. He runs around back and sniffs the seat of your pants.

Even before taking his seat, he declares his loyalty, saying, "I'm for them Dawgs, buddy. How 'bout choo?" He then makes three circles, takes his seat, and proceeds to explain in detail the game plan, including why the coach should have run for the U. S. Senate and the pedigree of every Bulldog on the field. The entire litter, all ninety-five of 'em!

From the initial kickoff to the final gun at game's end, he's one step ahead of the Bulldog cheerleaders. He may be the only person among the 85,000 in attendance who knows all the words to the alma mater.

When the game is over, he'll follow you all the way out of the stadium and across the parking lot telling you how and why the Bulldogs won, or lost.

• *Restrooms*: This situation always presents a problem for me. I never know just what to say when standing shoulder to waistline with "The Incredible Hulk." Like when he glances over and asks, "You fum Chicago, buddy?"

"No, sir." I answered weakly. "But I'll move there if you want me to."

I've always enjoyed the story about the stranger who attempted to initiate a conversation with a junkie standing on a Los Angeles street corner.

The stranger stopped, pointed to the sky, and said, "Say, fella, is that the sun or the moon up there?"

Without bothering to raise his head, the junkie replied: "I don't know, man. I don't live around here."

JUST ASK THE GUY IN THE NEXT SEAT

ONLY ONE PERSON CAN SOLVE ALL THE WORLD'S problems, and wherever you sit, he's usually in the chair right next to you.

I read that on the wall of my doctor's office one day, and it set me to thinking about the many times I've been forced to listen to the unsolicited comments of some blowhard in a restaurant, at a ball game, or in a doctor's office.

How many times have you walked into your favorite breakfast spot, newspaper in hand, and selected a seat way back in the back booth, only to be confronted by some character at a nearby table who isn't hungry, can't read, and is "mad as hell with Reagan"?

"Country's in bad shape, ain't it buddy? That damn Reagan's gonna' have us all in the bread line 'fore he's through. But what does he care? He's got that big ranch out in California and a wife who wears $5,000 dresses and buys china like a drunk antique dealer with seven credit cards and her husband's check book. And who the devil ever heard of payin' $250,000 for a set of dishes? I remember when fillin' stations gave dishes away, don't you?" he bellows.

"Yeah, right," you grunt.

"Remember when a man could buy a dang good breakfast for 75 cents? Now look—two eggs, grits, sausage, toast, and coffee, $2.83. It's a doggone shame, I say," he gripes.

"I guess so, friend," you say, turning the page.

"And how 'bout Lebanon, the PLO, the Israelites, the Gaza Strip, an' all that mess? All they know is fightin', they was raised on it. I tell you what I'd do if I was Reagan. I'd get me a bunch of Marines, call Wesley Gore, M. O. Darsey, and Bud Higgins back to active duty and . . . " he rambles on.

"Right," you say with all the enthusiasm of Leonard Bernstein at a Rolling Stones concert, or Mick Jagger at a Bernstein symphony performance.

You finally give up on the newspaper, fold it away, and concentrate on your two over easy, with chatter—unsolicited chatter.

It almost never fails when I go to Athens to see the Dogs play. I climb and climb and climb and finally reach Section XX, Aisle YY, Row ZZ, Seat 11. One more row up and I'd be dodging birds and airplanes.

I'm still trying to catch my breath when the holder of the ticket for Seat ZZ-12 arrives. Squeezing him into one seat is like trying to stuff a size forty-six into a pair of size thirty-two knickers.

And he's a football expert, a big-mouthed football expert who guzzles vodka and smokes stinky cigars.

"Dogs ain't gonna' do it today," he announces to one and all.

"Why not?" I ask, wishing immediately that I hadn't.

"Simple. 'Cause Dooley ain't usin' his big yard dog right, that's why," he says authoritatively.

"His big yard dog?"

"Right. Herschel Walker. Dooley jus' ain't makin' the best use of the boy."

"What do you mean?"

"Jus' wait til' the game starts an' I'll show you," he says.

Meanwhile, he finishes off a fifth of vodka, lights up a stale rope, and succeeds in insulting the sweet thing in YY-13 twice.

"I knew thirteen would be an unlucky seat for me this year, Harry," she whimpers to her husband. (But Harry doesn't hear her. He has the cheerleaders zeroed in with his binoculars. You see, Harry's "game" always begins thirty minutes before kickoff.)

The kickoff finally comes, fatso in ZZ-12 goes into his coaching routine, and Harry in YY-14 has isolated the third cheerleader from the left in his lenses.

"See there! Tha's what I'm talkin' 'bout. Dooley's got Herschel runnin' straight ahead. Dumb! Jus' plain dog-gone dumb!" he yells.

"But he gained eighteen yards," I say in defense of Dooley.

"Don't make no difference. Oughta' run the big dog wide ever' time he ain't a flanker goin' out for a pass," he says.

This continues for the entire first half and everybody hopes for a breather at halftime. Not so!

"O. K., now let me tell you what Dooley oughta' do in the second half. First, try an onside kick an' then put the big yard dog at quarterback and . . . " he rambled.

YY-13 and 14 got up and left. Everybody within earshot understood why, except the vodka guzzler and rope smoker.

I have the same luck in doctors' offices that I have in restaurants and at ball games. I no sooner sign in and take my seat and start reading a 1959 issue of *Field and Stream* than the guy in the next chair starts in.

"Did I ever tell you about my days in the Peace Corps? Well, I went to South America and . . . "

He can also tell you how to curb inflation, cure the common cold, solve Rubik's cube, stop unemployment, how to tune up a 1965 Mercury, solve the Atlanta traffic problem, and why gold is so high.

If you sit and listen long enough, he'll explain the situation in Lebanon, tell you how to make a million in the stock market, and what caused Carter's defeat—all unsolicited.

DID ST. PATRICK DRIVE THE SNAKES TO CLAXTON?

LEGEND HAS IT THAT ST. PATRICK, THE 5TH CENtury Christian missionary, drove all the snakes from Ireland. That's what my friend at *The Soperton News*, Jim Windsor, says and when Jim Windsor talks, I listen; when he writes, I read.

If the legend is true, Jim, and St. Patrick did indeed drive all the snakes from Ireland, I have news for you. After 1,500 years I've found 'em. At least I found 346 of 'em last Saturday.

I found them in Claxton, Ga., at The Fourteenth Annual Evans County Rattlesnake Roundup, along with some 15,000 snake enthusiasts.

Here I am on the shady side of 50 and thought I had seen about all there was to see in the way of spectaculars. I mean, what else could an old country boy hope for? I'd seen a soap box derby, a cock fight in the Philippine Islands, the World Skeet Shooting Championships in Pontiac, Mich., the Olympic ski jump trials in Ishpeming, Mich., the Indianapolis 500, the Super Bowl in Miami, Mardi Gras in New Orleans, two World Series, the Kentucky Derby and the Masters Water Ski Championships at Callaway Gardens. What's left?

A Rattlesnake Roundup? I've spent all my life running from 'em, but last Saturday I went to find them in Claxton. I wasn't exactly overjoyed at the signs I saw once I hit the city limits. First one said "Hospital," with an arrow pointing straight ahead. The next one was on the lawn of the First United Methodist Church, "Welcome to Rattlesnake Country."

Ever heard of such a thing? A church advertising snakes? My book tells me that man's troubles all started in the first place because of a snake in the Garden of Eden. While my book doesn't say the serpent was a rattlesnake, it doesn't say it wasn't, either.

I drove on to Rattlesnake Roundup headquarters at the Claxton Tobacco Warehouse and entered. That was my first mistake. Within minutes I was ushered through the assembled thousands to the center ring known as the snake pit. Before I knew it, I was inside the snake pit with my trusty camera.

I looked around at the more than 300 rattlesnakes. I watched them coil and listened to them hiss and rattle. I watched grown men reach down and pick up rattlesnakes nearly six feet long and milk venom from their mouths. I was on my knees less than 12 inches away snapping pictures of the pit vipers.

Suddenly, a thought occurred to me. I wondered where all the other columnists were. I didn't see Lewis Grizzard, Doug Hall, Bill Boyd, Bush Perry, Furman Bisher, Harley Bowers, Daryl Gay, Tom Coffee, Ron Hudspeth, Bill

Rogers, Jim Windsor, Bill Ricks, Dahlia Wren; nobody there but me. I figured out why, but prefer to keep it to myself. (Another fruitcake in Claxton?)

I Won Two Trophies in Absentia

I wasn't even entered in the roundup competition but won two trophies. I presume they'll be mailed to me because I wasn't around when the awards were presented. It happened this way:

I was crouched next to a flimsy pen holding about 100 rattlesnakes trying to take a picture of one with his head up about 10 inches and flipping his (or her) forked tongue out. A guy was simultaneously taking snakes from a nearby flimsy pen and milking them. Well, sir, he dropped one and it fell on the concrete floor not more than three feet from yours truly. Right then is when I won my first trophy for "Jumping the Highest When a Rattlesnake Is Dropped Nearby."

My second first-place trophy, which I hope will arrive in this week's mail, was for "Running Fastest While Wearing Wet Pants With a Nikkormat Camera Strapped Around Your Neck." (I darn near ran over a fella, in a wheelchair. Would have, too, if I could have caught up with him.)

Which reminds me of the story of the rural youngster who was sent to the spring by his mother to fetch a pail of water. He returned shortly, as white as the proverbial sheet, holding an empty bucket.

"Where's the water, boy?" his mother questioned.

"Didn't git no water," he puffed.

"Why not?"

"Because there'a a big ol' snake in that spring," he said.

"Aw, come on now. You just remember this. That snake is just as scared of you as you are of him," his mother assured him.

"Are you sure about that?" asked the boy.

"Positive," she said.

"Then there ain't no use to go git no water out of that spring."

"Why not?"

"Because it ain't fit to drink!"

Then there's the one about the traveling salesman who pulled into a dry South Georgia county one hot July day and inquired of the hotel clerk where he might get a drink of whiskey.

"Can't. This here's a dry county. Only whiskey in town is at Doc Lunsford's office. He keeps it for snake bites. Course you can go on down to Doc's office, but it's mighty late in the afternoon," the clerk told him.

"What do you mean?" asked the salesman.

"Well, Doc ain't got but one snake, and by this time of the day he's plumb tuckered out what with all the salesmen we get in this town."

MAKE SURE IT'S CLEAR, HEAR?

I GUESS IT MATTERS NOT HOW YOU WRITE IT AS long as you get your message across. Like the little girl in the third grade geography class explaining on a test how much she likes her state: "I think we have the most beautiful state in the whole world. Of course, I may be a little pregnant."

Then there was the sixth grader who replied to the question, "What is a will and what purpose does it serve?" with this answer: "A will is a written document in which a dead person tells how he wants his property divided among his errors."

Youngsters have no monopoly on making errors while writing or speaking . . . or spelling. Like the husband and wife who decided that it was time to start spelling out words to each other that they didn't want their daughter, age three, to hear.

Shortly after initiating their devious little scheme, the father came home from his office one hot July day and paused in the doorway where he was greeted by his wife and their three-year-old daughter.

"Hi dear—what kind of a day did you have?" asked the wife.

"Boy! I had one hell of a D-A-Y!" he replied.

One more?

A little six-year-old girl who lived in a very wealthy suburb was asked to write a story about a poor family. She took out pencil and paper and proceeded to write: "This family was very poor. The mommy was poor. The daddy was poor. The brothers and sisters were poor. The upstairs maid was poor. The nurse was poor. The cook was poor. The butler was poor. The yardman was poor. The gardener was poor. The chauffeur was poor . . . "

Examples of Unclear Writing

The following sentences were reportedly excerpted from actual correspondence received by one of the social service departments in a large American metropolis:

- "I want my money as quick as I can get it. I've been in bed with the doctor for two weeks and he hasn't done me any good. If things don't improve, I'll have to send for another doctor."

- "I have no children as my husband is a truck driver and works day and night."

- "In accordance with your instructions, I have given birth to twins in the enclosed envelope."

- "My husband is unable to work and I have Affa Davis to prove it."

- "Why do you say I appear to be Oblivious when my forms clearly say I'm a Baptist?"

- "Please send my money at once because I have left town and have no forwarding address."

- "Enclosed find my files which I have lost. Can you find them for me?"

- "My sister and her seven children live with me and I can prove it if you will just come by my house and listen."

- "I am forwarding my marriage certificate and six children, all of whom were baptized on half a sheet of paper."

- "I am writing to say that my baby was born two years old. When do I get my money?"

- "Mrs. Wilson has not had any clothes for nearly a year and as a result is being visited regularly by members of the clergy."

- "I am happy to report that my husband who is missing, is dead."

- "This is my eighth child. What are you going to do about it?"

- "Please let me know for certain if my husband is alive. I am living with my boyfriend and he can't eat or do nothing until he knows."

- "I am very much annoyed that you have branded my son illiterate. That's a dirty lie as I was married a week before he was born!"

- "In answer to your letter, I have given birth to a 10-pound boy. I hope this meets your requirements."

- "I am forwarding my marriage certificate and three children, one of which you can see was a mistake."

- "You changed my little boy to a little girl. Will this make any difference?"

- "Unless I get my husband's money pretty soon, I will be forced to live an immortal life."

THINGS I DO
UNDERSTAND

I'M VERY FORTUNATE. THANK GOD, I KNOW THAT. I live the good life. I enjoy good health, have great friends, two fine children, two fine grandchildren, an outstanding son-in-law and daughter-in-law, a comfortable house, a little backyard, and a swing. I spend lots of time in my swing. I'm convinced that if there were more backyard swings, we would need fewer psychiatrists.

I have an abundance of money, unless of course I decide to buy something. I'm privileged to do what I enjoy most, write and travel. And I also think a lot, both while traveling the countryside and sitting in my backyard swing. That's where this chapter came from, the front seat of my car and my backyard swing. As I rode for a few days and swung for a few nights, it occurred to me that in working on the manuscript for this book I had listed a number of things I didn't understand, but there are so many things that I do understand.

Here, then, are a few things that I understand—and appreciate:

- The music of children's laughter.
- Good, old-fashioned patriotism.
- Good books, old leather, and libraries.
- Woodstoves.
- The smell of bakeries and good coffee—just ground.
- Fridays and Sundays—but I prefer Sundays.
- Good conversation.
- Classroom teachers.
- Recess.
- Short sermons when you're hungry.
- Seven-layer chocolate cake.
- Fireplaces, and Perry Como singing it slow and easy.
- Touching and being touched.
- The leaves of October and the beautiful pictures they paint.
- Thin cornbread and thick biscuits.
- Looking at old photographs and making new ones.
- Banana sandwiches.
- Tomato sandwiches, but only with homegrown tomatoes.

- Turkey sandwiches the weeks after Thanksgiving and Christmas.

- Mama. (She's gone now, but I understood her and loved her so much.)

- The smell of bacon cooking.

- Flowers.

- Senior citizens with all their wisdom.

- Parades.

- Pretty little girls and pretty big girls.

- A pat on the back, deserved or not.

- Vienna sausages, saltine crackers, and an ice-cold Coke.

- Good barbecue, like Jack Sweat cooks at Sweat's Barbeque in Soperton, Georgia, and the nice ladies who serve it.

- A car that starts in winter and doesn't overheat in summer.

- Rainy Saturday mornings and broken alarm clocks.

- Country music.

- Hershey bars, with or without almonds.

- Prayer, between just God and me—anywhere at anytime.

- Preachers, regardless of denomination.

- Small towns with courthouse squares.

- Broken parking meters.

- Front porches, rocking chairs, and lazy dogs.
- Trains.
- Paid bills.
- Refunds.
- A long touchdown run by the kid who never expected to get in the game.
- The Citizenship Award at graduations.
- The Best Sportsmanship Award at sports banquets.
- Clean jokes.
- Driving 53 and smiling as I pass a state trooper in a 55 m.p.h. zone.
- Excellent waitresses, like Sylvia.
- Great cooks like Dot, Eddie Mae, and Inez at Ma Hawkins Restaurant in Dublin, Georgia; and Liza at the Elks Club. If there is ever a Cook's Hall of Fame, they'll be charter members.
- The innocence of a child and the wisdom of a senior citizen.
- Scoutmasters, like Joe Wilson and Kelly Canady.
- Promptness.
- The privilege of living.
- The memory of a great father.
- Solitude.

And more . . . much more.

SOUTHERN BELLES

TRAITS OF A TRUE SOUTHERN BELLE

THE TRUE SOUTHERN BELLE IS AS IDENTIFIABLE AS magnolia trees and kudzu. In addition to her soft and warm southern accent, she is recognizable by scores of traits and traditions handed down to her by her mama and daddy, their mama and daddy, and their mama and daddy, and so on. . . .

Here are some to watch and listen for.

A true southern belle:

- Must know who all her *real* cousins are, even if her mama and daddy won't allow her to discuss them outside the confines of the house or when company comes.

- Must know what turnip greens are. She may hate them and become nauseated by their smell, but she needs to know just in case her northern cousins visit and ask about them. She would never want to appear ignorant regarding southern delicacies.

- Must know that the things [turnip greens] are actually green.

- Must know the difference between turnip greens, mustard greens, and collard greens.

- Keeps a dictionary close at hand for spelling and looking up words that her northern cousins use.

- Always wears a dress to church and never sneaks out during the closing hymn or opens her eyes during the prayer.

- Always appears to have an IQ larger than her waist size. It's nice to have a small Scarlett O'Hara waist, but she must never let on that her IQ is smaller.

- Never wears a corset or a girdle. She attains the desired waist measurement through dieting, aerobics, or prolonged breath holding.

- Doesn't waste hours engrossed in soap operas. She much prefers living out her own fantasies, which have more excitement and intrigue than is ever shown on television.

- Knows that a Blue Plate Special does not mean that mayonnaise is on sale.

- Would never ride a horse sidesaddle.

- If talented, can take a bubble bath and read *Cosmopolitan* at the same time.

- Always takes her cordless telephone with her to the bathtub when the time comes for a long bubble bath.

- Can shoot a hook-shot and dribble with both hands.

- Always prays that the IRS agent who does her audit is single.

- Loves to shag.

- Knows where the old home place is and where all her ancestors for generations are buried, and what they died from.

- Can say "No!" while smiling sweetly.

- Knows how to pump her own gas, but usually doesn't have to.

- Thinks silicone is Baskin-Robbins' thirty-second flavor.

- Displays the correct technique when kicking her tires so everyone watching will conclude that she knows mechanics and can change her own oil, install new spark plugs, and set the idle on her carburetor.

- Stands nearby and watches every move when a mechanic is repairing her car.

- Does not call her brother Bubba or her cousins Cuz.

- Makes no effort to keep up with the Joneses but gloats at their efforts to keep up with her, not necessarily with regard to material things.

- Does not wear black bobby pins with blonde hair.

- Knows that blondes are supposed to have more fun but scoffs at the idea, realizing that down in Dixieland all shades of hair color have a ball.

- Will go to a wrestling match, hide underneath a scarf, and forever deny having been there.

- Knows the difference between a wide receiver and a cornerback, a safety and a field goal, and can explain a two-minute drill or a down-and-out in detail.

- Never goes to bed in rollers, or any place outside of the house with her hair in rollers.

- Never drives the kids to school while wearing her robe and bedroom shoes.

- Can drive a car, drink a Coke, smoke a cigarette, adjust the radio, and watch the baby all at the same time.

- Can parallel park.

- Loves to eat out.

- Is always looking for a new low-calorie salad to go with her Shoney's hot fudge cake.

- Believes that to go "all the way" really does mean with mustard, catsup, and onions.

- Knows that stoned ground crackers are not good ole Georgia boys that have smoked too much marijuana.

- Always has a quarter in her pocket or purse to make a telephone call if necessary.

- Never pops chewing gum in public.

- Keeps in touch with her mama regularly, even though at times she would just as soon not.

More Traits of a True Southern Belle . . .

A TRUE SOUTHERN BELLE:

- Speaks to everyone she passes, whether she knows them or not.

- Attends the family reunion every year and knows and kisses everyone there.

- Expects a man to remove his hat (or cap) indoors and won't hesitate to tell him.

- Doesn't expect people to call before dropping by. Friends are always welcome.

- Never returns a pie plate or a casserole dish to a friend empty.

- Says "ma'am" and "sir" to her elders no matter how old *she* gets.

- Starts cooking the minute she hears there's been a death in town.

- Fits in as well at a formal dinner party as she does at an outdoor barbecue and can be ready for either in less than an hour.

- Never says "No" to just one more for dinner, especially when it's one of her children's playmates.

- Talks as sweet as sugar until you mess with one of her young'uns. Then she'll let you have it with both barrels so quick you won't know what hit you.

- Won't live anywhere but in the South and can't understand for the life of her why anyone else would.

- Can bait a hook, load a gun, catch a fish, and kill a bird, but lets her husband clean the fish.

- Never has to measure anything when preparing one of her favorite recipes.

- Knows what pot likker is and that overindulgence in it won't put her over the .10 mark on the intoximeter.

- Knows how to make redeye gravy.

- Never shaves her legs above the knees, except in summer.

- Always goes to Daddy for money, married or not.

- Never notices cobwebs in her own house but can spot even the smallest in yours.

- Knows everyone's ancestors for at least three generations back and holds you responsible for your grandfather's wild ways.

- Would never allow her daughter to date your son.

- While shopping, will tell her best friend that the dress she's trying on is "really you" and "simply gawgeus" because it makes her look ten pounds heavier and five years older.

- Only gossips in the name of sympathy. "Poor Violet. I'm so concerned for her sanity. You know how bad Vernon is to drink an' all."

- Travels to the city to buy her expensive clothes with designer labels—at the Junior League's annual yard sale.

- Never admits her ineligibility for membership in the Daughters of the American Revolution or the United Daughters of the Confederacy. She just "doesn't have the time" for either, she says.

- Always leaves one important ingredient out of a recipe before she shares it and adds one visible ingredient to any recipe she borrows.

- Sheds genuine tears in private, preferably in a locked bathroom; public tears have an ulterior motive.

- Smiles sweetly but says nothing when she visits her Yankee in-laws with her husband and they make fun of her southern drawl.

- Hides the Visa bill from her husband. If she really becomes desperate, Daddy always come to her rescue; and she accepts both his check and the lecture.

- Has a family story for each piece of furniture, bric-a-brac, table linen, and wall hanging—all true in her mind.

- Keeps sheets draped over the best furniture until company comes. Local drop-ins get to view the sheets but sit elsewhere.

- Will serve a drop-in guest the last drop of soup or spoonful of grits and with her eyes dare the children to say they're hungry.

- Cleans out the accumulated gook in the bottom of the sink with her bare hands, but wouldn't touch a mousetrap on a dare—or a double-dare—or a double-dog-dare.

- Has her own monogrammed cue stick and carrying case that one would best not touch.

- Never sweats, even if the temperature is 105 degrees in the shade.

OOPS!

WRONG ZIP CODE!

NEVER UNDERESTIMATE THE FURY OF A WOMAN, especially a southern woman. She doesn't get mad; she gets even, as depicted in this story told to me by a good friend.

He says that a husband and wife down in Albany, Georgia, had a violent and prolonged argument, and both were still fuming when they went to bed, she in the bedroom and he on the sofa, the Siberia for errant husbands.

The next morning, they didn't speak. Both worked and were getting dressed when she put on her favorite dress but couldn't reach the zipper. Without saying a word, she backed up to her husband and pointed to the zipper.

He proceeded to zip it up. Then he zipped it down. Then up. Then down. He thought how funny that was, so he just stood there zipping it up and down until he broke the zipper—at half-mast. He then had to cut her out of her favorite dress, and you can imagine what that did for her disposition, which already was at the boiling point.

She was livid with rage and ran off to her bedroom crying, slipped on another dress, and left for work without saying a word.

All day she thought about two things: her favorite dress with the broken zipper . . . and *revenge!*

She arrived home late in the afternoon. Pulling into the driveway, she parked behind her husband's car. She saw two legs sticking out from underneath his car and knew then and there what her course of action would be.

She walked over to his car. Saying nothing, she reached underneath the car and got a firm hold on the zipper she found there. Zip! Zip! Zip! She ran it up and down repeatedly until it broke.

"There! That'll take care of him!" she thought to herself.

She then went on in the house, where, to her amazement, sitting at the kitchen table drinking coffee and reading the newspaper was her husband!

And this one was told to me by another good friend, a Georgia state patrolman who swore it was a true story. I'm in no position to refute it, so I'll just tell you what he told me and let you draw your own conclusions.

He said he was patrolling on a state road in a rural area of South Georgia on a cold and rainy night when he came upon a two-car accident about 1:30 A.M.

He then said he would have to go back a little ways, before the accident, for background purposes and explain that a girl named Sarah Taylor lived in the area not far from the accident scene. Sarah lived with her sister Irene, the driver of one of the cars involved in the accident.

Irene worked nights, and Sarah worked days. Sarah had been to the beauty parlor that afternoon and had her hair fixed. When she got ready to go to bed, she couldn't find her hair net. Not wanting to mess up her new hairdo, she had to improvise.

Sarah searched the house over from top to bottom, including all closets and boxes in the attic, but found no hair net. The closest she could come to duplicating one was a pair of nylon underpants. So she pulled them down over her hair. It felt just fine, so she turned out the light and went to sleep.

At two o'clock in the morning, the patrolman radioed the state patrol post and had the night man call Sarah to tell her that her sister had been in an automobile accident and needed her automobile insurance policy. Sarah immediately hung up the telephone without waiting to learn that Irene was not seriously injured. Not knowing if her sister was half dead, badly injured, or what, she was scared to death.

Sarah jumped out of bed, jerked on a housecoat, removed the insurance policy from a chest of drawers, and drove the short distance to the scene of the accident.

Then the trooper paused and chuckled.

"I'll tell you, that was the toughest job I ever had," he said, "standing there in the rain at two o'clock in the morning, looking poor Sarah in the eye, and trying to keep a straight face while relating to her what had happened to her sister . . . wondering to myself why she had her underpants on the wrong end!"

SOUTHERN WOMEN NEVER WALK ALONE

I HAVE NO IDEA AT WHAT STAGE IN LIFE LITTLE girls are cautioned to never go to the ladies' room alone. Maybe it starts in kindergarten or first grade when children are paired up to go everywhere, holding hands: to the lunchroom, to the gymnasium, on field trips, to the library.

Then again, maybe it all started in the Girl Scouts where the buddy system is employed for safety reasons when the girls go swimming or hiking.

I guess it could have started, too, at home in the country years ago when the ladies' room was way out behind the house in the dark, vulnerable to boogers and ghosts in the form of older brothers who would scare the daylights out of a little girl making her way after dark to the little outhouse with the half-moon cut in the door.

Wherever and whenever the tradition got its start, it has been sustained to this day. Women absolutely will not make the trip to the ladies' room alone.

I am convinced that deep, dark secrets are transmitted in ladies' rooms all over the South. Danger surely lurks behind those closed doors.

Does every mother caution her little girl at a very early age to "Never accept gifts from strangers, and *never* go to the ladies' room alone"? No doubt in my mind they do, because they don't. They go together, in coveys, like quail.

Here is a typical scene: Harriet, Lois, Marlene, Grace, Ramona, Virginia, and Margaret are at the club for dinner with their husbands. Less than three minutes after they arrive, Grace pops the question, "Would anybody like to go with me to the ladies' room?" And like quail, off they march—Harriet, Lois, Marlene, Ramona, Virginia, Margaret, and Grace—with Grace leading the march.

Once they enter the secret chamber, they stay longer than the NBA playoffs. Finally, they return to the table only to learn that John and Jane have arrived.

After greetings are exchanged all around, the girls take their seats. They're seated for no more than thirty seconds when Jane pops the welcomed question, "Would anybody like to go with me to the ladies' room?"

Right on cue, up stand Harriet, Lois, Marlene, Ramona, Virginia, Margaret, and Grace to join Jane for the trip. Do any of them really have to go to the ladies' room? Is nature calling? Certainly not! Each is afraid, but not of boogers, ghosts, or big brothers scaring the daylights out of them. Each is afraid of what might be said that she would miss if she stayed behind to sip the white wine and nibble on mixed nuts and didn't go.

A southern woman never passes up an opportunity to go to a ladies' room, and if she's alone in any establishment she'll approach a complete stranger and extend an invitation to join her. When they exit after an extended stay, they will be chatting like long-lost sisters.

No, a southern woman would no more pass up an opportunity to go to a ladies' room than an alcoholic would pass up a bar if it meant missing his plane.

Those of us who escort ladies to restaurants, clubs, and lounges can only guess as to what deep secrets are shared in ladies' rooms, because only the ladies know for sure.

And they never walk alone . . . At least not to the ladies' room.

Where There's a "Will" There's a Way

The ingenuity and determination of a southern woman should never be underestimated. Many men have, only to shake their heads in disbelief in the end.

Take the case of the South Alabama housewife and her no-good and inconsiderate husband:

Legend has it that the husband came home one afternoon to pick up his fishing tackle. His wife met him at the door and said, "Honey, I'm so glad you're home. I need your help. My car won't start, and I have to take little Jenny to the dentist in half an hour."

The husband stared at her briefly, then said, pointing to the area just above the pocket, "Woman, take a good look at my shirt. Do you see 'Mr. Goodwrench' there?" And with that he went on his way, fishing tackle in hand, leaving his wife to manage as best she could.

A few days later, he was again greeted by his wife when he arrived home from work to grab a bite to eat before going to his weekly poker game with the boys. "Herman, before you leave would you please take a look at the washing machine? I have a load of clothes in it, and it just stopped while in the middle of the wash cycle," she told him.

"Woman, take a good look at my shirt," he said, again pointing to the area above the pocket. "Do you by any chance see 'Maytag' there?" And with that he went on to the poker game, leaving her to manage as best she could.

The very next week, after arriving home, the wife approached ole Herman as he was changing clothes before heading to the golf course on a Wednesday afternoon. "Herman, I hate to bother you but the electricity is off in the kitchen and I can't cook supper. Could you please . . ."

"Woman, take a good look at this shirt," he said, again pointing to the area above the pocket. "Do you see 'Electrician' there?" And he left to go to the golf course, leaving her to manage as best she could.

The next afternoon, upon arriving home, Herman noticed that his wife's car was humming like a sewing machine in the driveway. Once inside the house, he heard the washing machine purring like a kitten. The lights were on in the kitchen, with supper cooking on the stove.

"Well, I see you managed to get the car, the washing machine, and the kitchen lights fixed," he said. "How'd you do that?"

"Oh, no problem, Herman. You know that nice new neighbor, Will, who moved in across the street last week?" she asked.

"You mean the ski instructor?"

"Right."

"Yeah, I know him. Why?"

"Well, he had the day off today, and he fixed them all this morning," she said.

"Oh? What'd he charge you?"

"Nothing," she said, smiling. "He just gave me a choice."

"A choice? What kind of choice?"

"Well, he told me that I could either go to bed with him or bake him a cake so . . ."

"Well? What kind of cake did you bake him?"

"Cake? What cake? Herman, take a good look at my blouse," she said, pointing to the area just below her left shoulder. "Now then, I ask you, do you see 'Betty Crocker' there?"

TO EVERY BOY
COMES THAT
MOMENT OF
AWARENESS

AT WHAT AGE DOES A BOY BECOME ACUTELY aware that girls are different and are something other than objects at which to hurl insults, make faces, ridicule, and generally ignore? While I really can't pinpoint it, I know that the time comes when he realizes that girls ain't really all that bad, that they smell better than he smells, and possess a magnetism that mystifies him no end.

The time also comes when he leafs through the Sears, Roebuck catalog at a much slower pace and isn't in as big a hurry to get to the bicycles and toys as he once was. Suddenly, the lingerie section fascinates him, and there are days when he never gets to the bicycles and toys.

I recall vividly just when the moment of truth came for me, and I was reminded of it a few years back while driving on Interstate Highway 16, near Macon, Georgia, as I pulled up behind a caravan of vans, motor homes, and tractor trailers. It didn't take me long to figure out where they were going; they were carnival vehicles headed for the Macon Fairgrounds to set up for the upcoming Middle Georgia Fair.

I laughed to myself as I followed the caravan for a few miles, purposely not passing it. I laughed because I thought of two stories, one fictional and one factual. I'll go with the fictional one first.

A young Tennessee lad of fourteen was getting ready to go to the Tennessee State Fair in Nashville many years ago and was being addressed by his mama.

"Now, Rodney, you go an' have a good time on them rides an' everthing. But I'm warnin' ya', don't you go in that ole girlie show they got out at th' fairgrounds 'cause I hear tell they's things a-goin' on in there whut you don't need to see," his mama told him.

"Like whut, Mama?" the boy asked.

"Never you mind 'bout that," she said, "You jus' don't go in there, ya' heah?"

"Yes'um."

The boy went to the fair, rode the rides, ate the cotton candy, and strolled along the midway. Shortly, he came to the tent that housed the girlie show and heard the band music issuing from inside. He also heard the sound of loud male voices yelling and urging, "Take it off! Go ahead, take it all off!"

Curiosity got the best of the youngster, and he eased up to the ticket seller, stood on his toes to appear as tall as possible, bought a ticket, and slipped inside where he took a back row seat. It was dark with the exception of the small stage on which a scantily clad girl was going through her routine, divesting herself of flimsy, transparent articles of clothing until there was nothing left to divest. She ended her act as naked as a hammer handle while the assembled men cheered and whistled, hooted and hollered.

The boy eased outside and walked home, his mind boggled by what he had seen inside the tent. His mama greeted him upon his return.

"Well, didja' hav' a good time at th' fair?"

"Yes'um, it wuz rail good."

"Ya' didn' go in that ole girlie show, didja'?"

He studied his hands and feet, then confessed. "Yes'um, I did. I know I done wrong, but I went."

"Whut! Ya' did!" his mama bellowed. "Ya orta' be 'shamed o' y'sef, ya' know that? An' atter I tol' ya' plain as day you'd see things in there ya' won't sposed ta' see. Well, didja'?"

"Yes'um, I did," the boy confessed. "When they turned the lights on at th' end o' th' show I seen—"

"Whut? Ya' seen whut, boy?"

"I seen Daddy standin' in a chair right down on th' front row jus' a-yellin' his head off!"

Now, for the factual.

I guess it was along about 1939 or 1940 when I went to the local fair in my hometown in South Georgia with several buddies one Saturday night. We were all about fourteen or fifteen, and, like the young boy from Tennessee, we were strolling along the midway when all of a sudden, out of nowhere, a girl sprang from a tent, stood on a small platform about the size of a medium pizza right in front of us, slung her flimsy dance dress up over her head and yelled, "Yaaaaahhhhh-hoooooo! It's showtime, boys!"

It was, too! It was *really* showtime. So we bought tickets and went inside to see our first girlie show. I can tell you this: we didn't ride another ride the rest of the time the fair was in town because at the precise moment that gal threw her dress over her head and yelled, we became acutely aware that there's something definitely different about girls.

We said goodbye to the ferris wheel and the merry-go-round forever!

Warning! Watch Out for Women in the Spring

FOR THE MAN OF THE HOUSE THE SUNSHINE AND gorgeous weather that come with spring usher in visions of long-awaited hours on the golf course or fishing in a favorite lake.

First, there are two major obstacles to overcome: the neighbor and the wife. How so? Let us take a look at the neighbor, and if any man has the misfortune of living next door to one like this, he's in big trouble.

It is a beautiful Saturday morning with bright sunshine beaming down, prompting the urge to take out the driver or two-iron, "really get into one" and hit the perfect shot that has been on hold all winter. Mentally, it soars some 260 yards "right down the middle," and the choice of the club for the second shot is a difficult one. He goes with a three-wood. Another perfect shot!

Then, you hear it! The sound is unmistakable. Handy Andy, who can do everything around the house, has cranked up his lawn mower! He's been up since dawn puttering around in the yard, and now he's going to mow the lawn.

Your wife snaps her eyes to the kitchen window with all the precision of the finest and most sophisticated radar detector, and her hair rollers almost unwind. She says nothing. She doesn't have to. Her silence is deafening, but her eyes speak loudly as they methodically snap to and fro, from the window to the golf glove you shift back and forth in your hands.

The look in her eyes causes instant guilt feelings as you steal a glance over the rim of your coffee cup and view your yard that strongly resembles the Okefenokee Swamp. Andy's lawn mower just whines away in the background.

You wonder why the guy couldn't have waited just ten more minutes to crank the darn thing up, and why his mower always starts on the first pull while you have to play tug-of-war with yours for half the morning to get it started—maybe.

You actually hate Andy, but all the neighborhood women love him. A regular Mr. Fixit. Besides, the guy couldn't hit a golf ball with a bulldozer!

No doubt about it, with the first sign of spring, the little lady wants her man out in the yard getting it done, like Handy Andy.

Remember when you moved into the neighborhood? You bought pesticides, insecticides, herbicides, phosphate, nitrate, peat moss, Vigoro—you name it. You also went to the Agriculture Extension Office and picked up every pamphlet ever printed about putting in lawns. In your yard you had sprigged, sodded, clumped, broadcast and sown, and sprinkled enough water to float the

Empire State Building. But did you get a lawn? No! Only a barely visible trace of green here and there.

What about Andy? When he moved in, he just poked a few holes in his yard, dropped in the sprigs, kicked a little dirt, and turned on the sprinkler for a few afternoons. What happened? His yard now looks like an exact replica of the sixteenth fairway at the Masters, and yours like the giant sand trap that dominates the middle of it.

Try and explain to the little woman why your yard looks like the aftermath of the great drought as she stares at you with that look, a look that says, "Ours might look like Andy's if you would stay off the golf course long enough to 'repair the green' in our yard."

You say nothing because you know she's right. But you fantasize. "Boy! Would I like to get that troublemaker on the golf course at a dollar a hole! I'd have him going to the Christmas party in a straw hat, seersucker suit, and perforated shoes."

The spring sunshine also brings other danger signs, like the great painting escapade. Why is it that women are happiest when they have their men up on a ladder juggling a paint can when the temperature is a perfect 72 degrees? And how do they get them up there in the first place? Simple. They use looks, and their favorite is the neglected look. It works like this:

You are out in the storage house pulling your rod and reel from underneath all the leftover Christmas wrapping paper and tinsel. She suspects as much instantly and comes out with the gallon of "outside white" she bought on special two years earlier. Again she says nothing, but puts on her best neglected look as you walk toward the back door pulling tinsel from your reel. The moment you see the paint can, you know that the old spring paint-up fever has struck. So, back goes the reel and rod to rest another day with its Christmas companions, and you accept the fact that you must paint the carport.

Now it's time to play the annual game of "find the paint brushes." You must have bought a thousand since you moved in. After moving two boxes of old clothes, a broken vacuum cleaner, two shovels, a broken lawn chair, and a lawn sprinkler that doesn't work, you find the brushes. They are in the same paint can that you left them in twelve months earlier when you painted the kitchen. They are as stiff as a celluloid collar and will forever be stuck to the bottom of the can. They're as hard as jawbreakers, and it would take a blowtorch or three well-placed sticks of dynamite to remove them.

You just shake your head as you drive to the hardware store to buy two more brushes and wonder why the women always say, "I'll paint the trim." No woman ever lived who didn't picture herself as a great trim painter, wearing one of your old shirts, of course.

I once saw a great cartoon. It was in five panels. The first showed two men—neighbors—on ladders with paint and brush. The second showed them looking at each other. In the third, one is saying to the other, "How much vacation you got?" In the fourth, he answers. "Only two weeks." In the fifth, the other fellow says, "You lucky devil. I've got three!"

Then there is the story of the husband who promised his wife faithfully that he would mow the lawn while she was at the local laundrymat doing the family wash for nine. He headed for the golf course as soon as she left, and after completing his round he confided to his golfing buddies what he had done.

"Boy! I'll bet your wife hits the ceiling when you get home!" one said.

"Yeah, I guess she will. But she always does. She's a lousy shot," he said.

Finally, there was the woman who tried repeatedly to get her husband to work in the yard, to no avail, as he spent his days off fishing. So she tried a new tactic.

Before leaving the house, she stuck a shovel in the yard with this note attached to it: "Henry. Start digging and see what satisfaction you will find. Helen."

When she returned home, she immediately saw the shovel and walked to it only to find this note scribbled on the back of hers: "Started digging. Found worms. Gone fishing. Henry."

Remember, the wife who drives from the back seat is no worse than the husband who cooks from the dining room table.

HALL OF FAME
HOUSEKEEPER

PROBABLY THE TWO MOST EXCITING AND MIND-boggling purchases young people make in a lifetime are their first automobile and their first house. My daughter, Lisa, purchased her first car in Dublin several years ago. She and her husband, Keith, purchased their first house, in Macon, not long ago.

It's a very nice house and I'm probably as excited about their purchase as they are, maybe more. I don't have to make the payments.

I waited for three weeks before visiting their new domicile. Why so long? Simple. Even with my favorite daughter and favorite son-in-law, I needed an invitation, and it wasn't forthcoming until everything was in shipshape order.

Lisa is a great housekeeper. The girl actually loves to clean, mop, and scrub. She could take a bottle of cleaner, a couple of rags, a mop, and a Dirt Devil and clean up the mess in Florida left in the wake of Hurricane Andrew in about three days.

My initial visit to the new house was revealing from the outset. I parked in the backyard and walked to a side door, only to find two pairs of thongs standing at attention at the top step. I opened the door only to hear a blood-curdling scream from the lady of the house, "Take your shoes off before you enter!"

A pair of black tassel loafers joined the two pairs of thongs, and I was careful to line them up "just so." Even as I did so I couldn't help but wonder if somewhere way back there might have been some Japanese ancestors in my past. I mean, after all, both Keith and Lisa drive Japanese cars—she a Honda Accord and he a Toyota pickup. I made a mental note to have Allen Thomas and June Adams, Dublin's resident genealogists, check that out. But then I thought about the fella I know who paid out $1,000 to have his family tree traced only to fork over another $1,500 to the genealogist when he finished to keep quiet about it.

I know Lisa is proud of her new house. But manicured (roofing) nails? Laminated door mats? Monogrammed dishrags? "Keith and Lisa" commode handles? I think that's a bit much, don't you?

Keith grilled steaks on my first visit. Delicious! After dinner Keith and I retired to the den to watch the Braves play the Reds. He was gracious enough to permit me to sit in his La-Z-Boy recliner, normally reserved for royalty— King Keith or Queen Lisa. Lisa was still outside Simonizing the barbecue grill and polishing the cooking fork.

Like I said, the girl is a great housekeeper. She joined us just after Terry Pendleton hit a home run.

Lisa is prone on occasion to light up a Virginia Slim. Her daddy will occasionally light up a Winston. In the den?

No way! She escorted me to the designated smoking area, the front porch. "When in Rome, do as the Romans do." I understand that. I also understand that "When in Macon, do as Lisa does."

She went back inside before I did, and I couldn't help but notice through a spotless window that she was standing behind the La-Z-Boy headrest, holding a large magnifying glass in her left hand and a Dirt Devil vacuum in her right. Later, during a moment when Keith and I were alone and Lisa was dusting the bottom side of the telephone with a cashmere dusting cloth in the foyer, I asked Keith, "What was Lisa doing with the magnifying glass and Dirt Devil?"

"Oh, she was just making a dandruff check," he said routinely. "She does it to me all the time. And if she finds the evidence, out on the porch you go!"

Like I said, Lisa is a great housekeeper . . . but washing the dishes with Perrier water is a bit unusual.

I was in Milledgeville on a rainy Friday night to watch Troup County High School (LaGrange) play Baldwin High. I was there because my oldest grandson, Jeremy Whaley, is on the Troup County team. A freshman who wears Number 20, he dressed out for his first game with no expectation of playing.

Also in attendance were his father, Joe, his mother, Cindy, his ten-year-old brother, Brett, Aunt Lisa, and Keith, one of his best buddies.

The rain started just before the opening kickoff and never stopped during the entire game. *Torrent* is the best word to describe it. Noah would have been wearing a raincoat and sporting an umbrella. His animals would have scurried to the nearest shelter on the ark. But not the Whaley clan. We were there for the duration. Two weeks later my wallet was still wet.

Now, for the big moment: Troup was leading 27-0 with 2:26 to play in the game. Several Troup substitutes sprinted on the field wearing unsoiled jerseys. And Number 20 was among them, weighing in at a strapping 140 pounds. Cindy spotted him first. Then she spotted a Baldwin player, Number 57, who weighed in at 295 and stood six feet, six inches. She made the inevitable comparison, bit her nails to just above her wrist, and offered up a wet prayer: "Oh, Lord! Please don't let him hurt my little boy!"

I said one, too, for the kid who just last year it seemed was sucking his thumb, talking in his sleep, and convinced that girls (cheerleaders) were a necessary evil.

All of us stood soaking wet at the fence surrounding the playing field. Baldwin had the ball. Number 20 was lined up at left defensive back. The Baldwin center snapped the ball to the quarterback, about six feet, one inch, and 185, who attempted to sweep right end. He didn't make it past the line of scrimmage. Enter Number 20 from Troup High, Jeremy. He charged, lowered his head, and plowed into the quarterback. The ball flew out of his arms and Troup recovered. Luckily, so did Jeremy. He had made his first tackle.

Was I proud? Shoot, I reckon! Rain? What rain? It was a perfect night. Cindy cheered. Joe cheered. Brett cheered. Lisa went into hysterics. Keith grinned a broad, proud smile. Granddaddy Bo dang near jumped the fence.

Then Lisa the housekeeper did her thing. Get the picture now: Her nephew had just moments before made his first tackle, causing the Baldwin quarterback to fumble and Troup recovered. Jeremy's teammates were congratulating him, patting him on the head and butt, and calling him by name. The cheerleaders were jumping up and down. The moment was as big for Jeremy as was the closing on her new house for his Aunt Lisa.

Above the crowd noise I heard Lisa's voice as she yelled to the entire Whaley clan, all of whom would return to her house in Macon to spend the night: "Remember, now! Everybody take your shoes off when we get to my house! And smoking *only* on the porch!"

Joe, who occasionally lights up a Vantage, turned to me and said, "I can tell you that I'm very familiar with that porch, Dad."

THIS AND THAT

THE PROS AND CONS OF LIVING ALONE

I WAS STROLLING THROUGH THE DUBLIN MALL A couple of weeks ago and encountered a lone soul who has recently embarked on the single life via the divorce route. I didn't understand it but I didn't question it. Question it? Heck, this day and time I wouldn't blink an eye if told that Roy Rogers and Dale Evans had split. Only, "who gets Trigger?"

She showed me a list of living alone facts she had received from a friend. I got quite a kick out of 'em and, being an expert on the subject, added a few of my own. Do you other singles relate to any of 'em?

The Nice Things about Living Alone

- You can start squeezing a new tube of toothpaste anyplace you want to.

- You can take an afternoon nap without feeling guilty.

- You can read a whodunit without anyone telling you who done it.

- You can stack up $20 worth of return-for-deposit bottles and nobody bugs you about it.

- You can make popcorn with your electric blanket.

- You don't have to own a bathrobe.

- You can always leave the bathroom door open.

- You don't have to change bed linens unless you have company coming.

- You don't have to race anyone for the Sunday papers.

- You can mix daiquiris in the washing machine.

- You never have to wait to use the telephone and it's never busy when you call home.

- When you open a can of mixed nuts you can eat ALL the cashews.

- You can heat your coffee roll with your hair dryer.

- Free samples that come addressed to "Occupant" are all yours.

- You can put your cigarette butt anyplace you like.

- There's no one to pick up after you and, better yet, no one to remind you they picked up after you.

- You can answer a midnight phone call, or make one, and not have to explain it.
- When you burp, you don't have to say "excuse me" to yourself.
- There's no wait to get in the bathroom in the morning.
- You can wash one dish at a time . . . as you need it.
- You don't have to hide magazines.
- You can cut the grass when YOU'RE ready.
- You can sing as loud as you please in the shower and there's no one to laugh at you.
- You can eat potato chips and crackers in bed without anybody glaring at you.
- You can run around the house with a half-pound of white cream on your face and no one calls you Marcel Marceau.
- You can drink orange juice right out of the bottle.
- You can park smack in the middle of a two-car garage.
- You can leave the stereo and all that rock junk turned off for months at a time.

The Tough Things about Living Alone

- There's nobody to sit on your feet when you do situps.
- If you get caught in a zipper, you stay caught.
- You're always the first to know when you're out of toilet paper.

- There's nobody around to hand you a towel when you shampoo and get soap in your eyes.

- When you have a nightmare, there's no one around to wake you until it's over.

- When the late, late show is on you have to watch "Psycho" all by yourself . . . and then shower.

- The toilet seat is hardly ever warm.

- All the funny jokes you tell yourself, you've heard before.

- If you forget your house key, there's no one to wake up to let you in.

- On your birthday all you can do is yell "Happy Birthday!" down the kitchen sink drain and listen to the echo.

- When you go on a diet, there's no one to tell you you look thinner. So, you lie to yourself.

- You talk to yourself, and even worse, you're the only one around to listen.

- It's impossible to defrost half a pizza or open half a can of soup.

- If your dress zips up the back, you have to put it on frontwards and jump around fast.

- There's no one to hold down the string when you wrap a package.

- You have to put away Christmas decorations all by yourself.

- When your bank account is overdrawn (or underdeposited) you know who done it.

- You always have to sniff the milk before you drink it.

- Supermarkets don't package groceries for one.

- The telephone always rings when you're in the tub.

- You have to clean up your own mess after cooking fish.

So, there they are, the Pros and Cons of living alone. Which outweighs the other? Take your pick. And, should you feel lonely and want someone to talk to?

You can always go to the Laundromat . . .

ONE CLEAN
FINGER AND
RAGGED BRITCHES

IT'S FUNNY HOW ONE SIMPLE ACT CAN BRING back so many memories. And while I don't live in the past, neither do I have any regrets for my childhood.

I was raised poor, I guess, but nobody bothered to tell me so I never really knew it. Of course, there are all kinds of ways to be poor. A family can have mountains of money, but no love, and wallow in the muck and mire of poverty. But I have great memories of a beautiful childhood, and a wonderful mother and father who did without so their little boy wouldn't know the pitfalls of poverty.

A little incident that happened in the obscure village of Register last week triggered my childhood memories, if for only a little while.

It was enroute to Savannah and stopped at a little country store to buy a Coke, some Vienna sausage and saltine crackers. There are times, you know, when only such delicacies will satisfy.

After making my purchases, I went outside to eat them off the hood of my car. While partaking, I heard one heck of an argument and turned to see three dirty little boys yelling at the top of their lungs. Being a nosey character, I ambled over to see what was going on.

I was amazed and very pleased to see what it was they were in such a heated argument about. Marbles! They were shooting marbles, something I hadn't seen done in years. The argument was incidental. I offered to buy them Cokes and that ended it anyway.

After leaving my outdoor restaurant I thought about the game all the way to Savannah. Marbles . . . funny how the meanings of words and phrases change with the years. Forty years ago if you had told my parents, "Bo has lost his marbles," their only concern would have been that the preacher's son had been playing "for keeps." (There were only two ways to play marbles; "for keeps" or "for fun." And the preacher's son just wasn't allowed to play "for keeps.")

Today, however, should you inform a mother that her son had "lost his marbles," she would immediately place an emergency call to the family shrink.

For those of you who may have been unfortunate enough to glide through adolescence without experiencing a good game of marbles, you may have just missed a bit of what America was all about in the '30s. Heck, in those days a 13-year-old boy without a sack full of marbles was as out of touch with reality as one today without a tape player. His prized possession? His agate, of course. (If you don't know what one is, ask your daddy. He'll know if he's over 50.)

The worst fight I ever saw was between Edward Coogle and Buttercup Hill, in Oglethorpe, over the ownership of an agate. I don't remember who won the fight but Doyce Ellis and myself won all the marbles. (When I got home I hid mine under the church steps next door to our house. Like I said, preachers' sons weren't allowed to play "for keeps.")

Marbles had no value. They were a status symbol. When I was in the sixth and seventh grades in Oglethorpe there was no way I was going to school without a pocket full of marbles. My morning routine was: eat breakfast, grab my books, reach under the church steps and load my pocket, walk to school looking like a wagon with a broken spring, and sounding like hail on a tin roof.

My best friend, Doyce Ellis, was the best marble shooter I ever saw. He only lived two doors from me and we shot marbles every day.

Two distinct signs identified the dedicated marble shooter . . . a hole in the right knee of his britches and dirty and raw knuckles on his right hand. No way to play marbles on the pro tour like Doyce and I did without ripped britches and raw knuckles.

When the marble game ended, Doyce and I always followed the same ritual, he'd go home with me or I'd go home with him—for "refreshments," which usually consisted of leftover biscuits, sweet potatoes, and sausage or ham. To this day I can't recall having eaten anything that tasted better.

Now then, we didn't just grab that cold biscuit and start eating. No, sir! First, we held it tightly with our dirty left hand cupped around it. Then, we slowly, and methodically, took our dirty right forefinger and poked a hole in it, being particularly careful that the forefinger went straight and true, about two-thirds of the way in.

Then, we took the syrup bottle and poured real cane syrup in the hole and waited for a minute to allow the syrup to saturate the inner regions of that biscuit. Experts, which we were, could do it and never spill a drop. Ummmm, syrup and biscuit, cold sweet potato, cold country ham or sausage. How're you gonna' top that? Especially if you're two cold and hungry professional marble shooters?

Many times, after I was grown, I heard my daddy say that Doyce and I had but one clean finger the entire time we lived in Oglethorpe—our right forefinger.

I still eat sausage, biscuit, and syrup for breakfast every morning. The difference now is that they aren't my mama's biscuits and I don't poke holes in them with my finger any more. I think I'll just change that in the morning, though, and poke me a good hole and pour in the syrup.

My good marble-shooting friend, Doyce, can't be with me because he died a few years ago. But, I can sit there, alone, and reflect on our good boyhood days together.

What the heck—I may even poke holes in two biscuits. I have the feeling Doyce would like that.

WHAT IS A GOLFER? A GUY WHO . . .

WHAT IS A GOLFER? A GOLFER IS A GUY WHO:

- Will ignore his wife, shun his secretary, hang up on his brother and lie to his boss—but will give undivided attention to his caddy.

- Will tread the muck and mire of creeks and ditches, and wade through briar and snake-infested swamps wearing $75 slacks and $90 shoes, looking for a $1.25 golf ball.

- Will walk across his lawn with grass and weeds two feet high to get to his car and drive to the golf course where he will methodically and meticulously survey, inspect, and remove every leaf, pine needle, blade of grass and insect on the green before putting.

317

- Will leave his lawn mower, boat, motorcycle, automobile and garden tractor out in the weather for months but immediately covers his golf clubs at the first hint of rain.

- Will take an hour to get dressed for church on Sunday morning but can change clothes quicker than Superman and be on the way to the golf course in less than three minutes after returning home.

- Balks like a stubborn mule at the thought of paying $12 to get the heat pump repaired but won't hesitate to shell out $115 for a new "miracle" driver that guarantees him that he will never "slice" again (or so the ad in his golf magazine says).

- Will approve a $50,000 loan, sell a house, transfer a deed, write a prescription (or fill one), write a newspaper column in a matter of a few minutes—but will study, ponder, examine and argue over a scorecard for the better part of an hour debating "things," "birdies" and "sandys" worth a quarter each.

- Will stand underneath his carport at 12:45 P.M. with Hurricane David blowing his lawn furniture, barbecue grill and kid's trampoline down the street at more than 90 miles per hour, and with water hubcap-deep in his driveway, and confidently yell to his wife through the kitchen window, "See ya' later, Dot! I don't think it's raining at the golf course."

- Will sit at his desk in the plant all week, surrounded by hundreds of tons of roaring machinery, but refuses to hit his tee shot on Number Three until the loud-mouth bird in the tree on Number Two stops his infernal chirping.

- Can't help his son with his third-grade arithmetic, but can stand on the first tee and figure handicaps and strokes with the accuracy of a bank computer.

- Will neglect the battery in his wife's car for months, and jump-start it with his 100 times, but will get up in the middle of the night and drive four miles in his pajamas, robe and slippers to plug in the battery charger to his golf cart.

- Will bump into and knock down little old ladies and children in the supermarket, plod right through a neighbor's freshly planted lawn and hop-scotch across a just-painted porch, but resembles The Great Wallenda as he carefully avoids stepping in his golfing companion's "putting line" on the green.

- Will sit at his office desk all morning talking golf, then go to the golf course and talk business all afternoon.

- Won't hold his wife's chair, light her cigarette, or open her car door—but never fails to "attend the pin" when his partner is putting.

- Won't buy his kid an extra Coke at the basketball game, but just let him break 80 for the first time and listen to him yell in the clubhouse, "OK, bartender . . . set 'em up! Drinks for everybody, on me! And pour yourself one!"

- Couldn't find his cuff links in his bureau drawer with a magnet and a magnifying glass, but can immediately put his hands on every tee, ball marker and spike wrench in his cart shed.

- Can't plow a straight row in his garden, has no idea where his property line is, and doesn't know a plumb bob from a crowbar, but can "read" a green and determine the "break" more accurately than a surveyor.

- Forgets with regularity his anniversary, daughter's birthday, son's graduation, dental appointment and church committee meetings—but is ALWAYS on time for his 1 P.M. tee time on Wednesday, Saturday and Sunday afternoons.

- Will take the time to repair a green or replace a divot while his front lawn has holes in it that Smokey the Bear could hibernate in.

- Won't take the wife and kids to the beach for the weekend because he can't stand the feel of all that sand, but will go to the golf course three afternoons a week and play in it for the better part of three hours.

- Won't bend over to pick up a sock or a dirty shirt, replace a loose tile or pick up the garbage can at home because of "that ol' back injury," but will do 36 deep knee bends during the course of a round of golf.

- Wouldn't read a good novel or a periodical if you offered to pay him double the minimum wage, but will sit for hours (on end) reading and re-reading an article by Bob Toski in *Golf Digest* on "The Absolute Sure Cure for Slicing and Shanking."

- Will lug 50 pounds of golf equipment several miles in 100-plus degree heat in July, but then come home and sit in his air-conditioned den and, while sipping his favorite drink and puffing on a cigarette, yell for his 10-year-old son to bring him an ashtray.

Finally . . . a word to the wives. Just remember this: When your husband arrives home from the golf course with beggar lice and sandspurs covering the bottom nine inches of his wet pant legs—that's not really the best time to ask him, "Did you have a good round today, dear?"

GOLF FROM A FISHERMAN'S POINT OF VIEW

GOLFERS AND FISHERMEN HAVE HAD A FRIENDLY argument going on for years as to which is best.

- Lawyers play golf.
  Gen. Norman Schwarzkopf fishes.

- Golfers wear silly orange and pink slacks with no belt loops and pro shop shirts that cost a fortune.
  K-Mart is the only clothier a fisherman needs.

- Golfers wear special shoes with kinky names like Foot Joy and Etonic.
  Fisherman wear battered sneakers and thongs. Some even go barefoot.

- Televised golf is thick with British accents and Cadillac ads.

Fishermen on TV talk like they're from Yulee, and the ads are for beer and chewing tobacco.

- Golf is hidebound by musty traditions, such as who has honors off the tee.
  When fishermen see a big swirl, there is no honor, only a scramble to be the first to cast.

- Golf is burdened by archaic rules drawn up in Scotland.
  Fishermen can learn the rules at Sleepy's Bait and Tackle.

- Golfers chew Doublemint.
  Fishermen chew Red Man.

- Golfers won't stoop to diving into a lake after a lost ball.
  A fisherman will step over cottonmouths to retrieve his favorite lure.

- Golfers complain that a 7:30 A.M. tee is too early.
  To a fisherman that's midmorning.

- Golfers go to a practice tee and practice before play begins.
  Fishermen don't need to practice. They're ready the minute they step out of the pickup.

- Golfers say it takes mental toughness to play golf, a demanding focus for eighteen holes, a cerebral analysis of each shot.
  All it takes to fish is a can of worms.

- Fast-track business types hit the golf courses to unwind, then verbally abuse each other, throw and break clubs, and curse the heavens. This is not relaxation.

Fishermen get so laid back they sometimes fall asleep waiting for the rod or pole to bend.

- To a golfer, "hazards" are small patches of sand, quiet ponds and—this one's really frightening—trees.
Fishing hazards include capsizing, man-eating sharks, and snapping barracuda. You haven't lived until you've shared the cockpit of a small boat with a fish that doesn't want to be there.

- Golfers have names like Chip, Lance, Steve, and Ian.
Fishermen are Bubba, Earl, Bo, and Slick. And if you don't know another fisherman's name, just say "Hey, Bud," and you'll have made a friend.

- Golfers kill time by cleaning little pieces of sod from their spikes with a tee. (They wouldn't dare use their fingers).
Fishermen kill time by probing for bits of Vienna sausage with a wooden match.

- The slightest disturbance—the click of a shutter or chirping of a bird—can upset a golfer's backswing, throwing him into a rage.
Fishermen sometimes bring radios with them.

- Golfers smell better, but fishermen hang out with other fishermen so it doesn't matter.

- Golfers yell "Fore" before beaning one of their own.
No such formality among fishermen. An errant cast is usually accompanied by "Watch out!" before the treble hooks lodge in your buddy's scalp.

- Fishermen come home with supper, a fresh seatrout or bass fillet.
A golfer's wife sends him to the supermarket for frozen cod from Newfoundland.

The Thin Line between Truth and Fiction

THERE IS A THIN LINE BETWEEN TRUTH AND FIC-
tion. A good example of this can be heard every year during the Masters golf tournament:

Fiction: "Nah, I decided not to go this year. You see one
Masters you've seen 'em all. I'd rather stay home and
watch it on television."

Truth: He had no tickets although he made 327 telephone calls trying to find some. He offered to drive to
New Jersey if necessary to come up with tickets. He ran an
ad in the newspaper and on the radio and would gladly
have paid $200 per ticket.

I've collected lots of other examples.

Fiction: "No way am I going to vote in this year's election with what we have to choose from."

Truth: At 7:05 A.M, he's at the polling place and can hardly wait to get into the voting booth. He would have been there earlier but he stopped to put a bumper sticker on his car that reads "Vote for Blowhard—A Proven Winner."

Fiction: "Who, Connie? Man, I wouldn't take her to the office Christmas party if you paid me to do it. I'll admit she looks good, but she ain't too smart. Know what I mean?"

Truth: He started in January asking Connie to go with him to the party. He asked every week, sent flowers and candy regularly. Connie turned him down every time.

Fiction: I'm thinking about cashing in all my CDs and putting the money in Treasury notes. The interest on the CDs is way too low. I can do better with my money."

Truth: The only notes he has are for two loans, both overdue. His checking account is getting close to the red border, and a deposit is needed immediately.

Fiction: "Yeah, I played professional baseball for five years. I quit when I wasn't brought up to the majors after having two great seasons in a row. I even led the league one year."

Truth: He played for five years. That's true. He neglected to point out that his batting averages were .139, .181, .202, .144, and .176. He did lead the league one year—in broken bats and stolen towels.

Fiction: "No, thank you. I wouldn't have one of those cars if you gave it to me. Nothing but trouble."

Truth: He has a 1965 Plymouth and a 1969 Chevrolet. It's a miracle when both are running on the same day. His most valuable accessory is a set of jumper cables.

Fiction: "Oh, yeah. I've already decided. This year I'm either gonna take the family to Panama City, the Bahamas, or Disney World. I may fly and take 'em to all three."

Truth: What he did was load the family up and take 'em to Jaybird Springs for a day and for a picnic on Turkey Creek. And he didn't fly, he drove.

Fiction: "Man, I've got the best fishing hole around. I caught sixteen there yesterday. I'd be glad to tell you where it is, but I promised the owner I wouldn't."

Truth: He caught sixteen all right—three stumps, two old shoes, three tin cans, two turtles, four limbs, and two fish about the size of a small pocketknife.

Fiction: "Did I eat 'em up? Man, I hadn't been in Las Vegas more than ten minutes when I hit a $1,000 jackpot on a slot machine. I went on to win $1,200 at blackjack and another $1,500 on the roulette wheel. That was just the first night. The next day I stuck with the craps tables and doubled my money. I started not to come home."

Truth: He started not to come home, that's for sure. He lost his return air fare and had to wire his mama to send him $350 to get home on.

HAVE YOU EVER NOTICED?

SOME THINGS WE SEE ARE ALMOST BEYOND belief.

I was returning to Dublin and stopped at a convenience store in Milledgeville for coffee. I get about eighteen miles to the cup on regular—twenty-two on decaffeinated.

As I was putting cream and sugar in my cup, a man walked in with a large Pepsi cup in his hand. He filled it with coffee. Then he repeatedly tore open little sugar packets and poured the contents into the coffee. Then, the nondairy creamers. I was amazed at the number of both he used.

I asked the clerk, "Do you have any idea how many sugars and creamers that fellow over there put in his coffee?"

Without hesitation, she said, "Yes, sixteen sugars and ten creamers. He comes in every morning and every afternoon for coffee. He always uses sixteen sugars and ten creamers."

I saw him do it. And I have a witness. She would verify it.

I'll bet he has a ball when he puts mustard and catsup on a hot dog or hamburger.

Have You Ever Noticed?

Many of us, myself included, often begin a statement with "Have you ever noticed?" Then we relate some observation we've made. Like these:

Have you ever noticed:

- One of the most difficult things in the world is to know how to do something and to watch, without comment, somebody else do it incorrectly.

- It doesn't start to get bumpy on an airplane until the flight attendant starts to serve the coffee.

- In America there are ten million laws to enforce the Ten Commandments.

- A man can say what he thinks in this country, provided he isn't afraid of his wife, his boss, his neighbors, his customers, or the government.

- You can complain because rose bushes have thorns, or you can rejoice because thorn bushes have roses. It all depends on how you look at things.

- "In most cases on the job, if you aren't fired with enthusiasm, you'll be fired with enthusiasm."—Vince Lombardi.

- "An autobiography usually reveals nothing bad about its writer except his memory."—Franklin P. Jones.

- A lot of drivers don't need seat belts as much as they need straitjackets.

- A joint checking account is never overdrawn by the wife. It is just underdeposited by the husband.

- The average girl would much rather have beauty than brains because the average man can see much better than he can think.

- Some people will believe anything, if you whisper it.

- School days can be the happiest days of your life, provided your children are old enough to go.

- Some women show a lot of style, and some styles show a lot of women.

- No conversation is more boring than one where everybody agrees.

I recall a great statement by the late Sen. Everett Dirksen on the subject of anger. He said he had the greatest and wisest secretary in the world. When he dictated a letter in anger, she would not type it for twenty-four hours. Then, she would ask him, "Do you still want me to send that letter to So-and-So that you dictated yesterday?"

In most cases, Dirksen said, he would tell her to tear it up.

Dirksen's admission underscores this quote by the great philosopher Seneca: "The greatest remedy for anger is delay."

WISDOM FROM
SOUTH GEORGIA

THE WELL NEVER SEEMS TO RUN DRY WHEN IT comes to xeroxed tidbits of humor and wisdom. Friends supply me with them.

The latest envelope, containing several, came last week from Adel. Dan Cowart, Cook County probate judge, sent them to me after I'd been there to speak at the first Founder's Day banquet of the Cook County Historical Society.

Dan Cowart collects humorous articles and items. These were among the ones he sent me:

What Is an American?

- He will work hard on the farm so he can move into town where he can make more money so he can move back to the farm.

- He may not be able to fight his way out of a paper bag, but spends twenty bucks for a ringside seat so he can tell the professionals how to fight.

- He is the fellow who yells for the government to balance the budget, then uses his last dollar to make a down payment on a car.

- He whips the enemy, then gives him the shirt off his back and tons of money to help him get back on his feet.

- He yells for speed laws that will curtail fast driving, but won't drive a car if it can't go one hundred miles per hour.

- He knows the line-up of every baseball team in the American and National leagues, but doesn't know half the words to "The Star-Spangled Banner."

- He'll spend half a day looking for vitamin pills to make him live longer, then drive ninety miles per hour on slick pavement to make up for lost time.

- He ties up his dog but lets his sixteen-year-old, wild-as-a-tiger son go whenever he pleases.

- He is proud of his backyard, the manicured lawn and beautiful flowers, but builds a high fence around it to keep others from seeing it.

- America has more food than any other country in the world and more diets to prevent its people from eating it.

- He will work hard and save to build an expensive house, then go on vacation and sleep in a tent in the mountains.

- Americans are the people whose eyes moisten when Old Glory passes in a parade, but just try and find a man who'll admit it.

THE HEIGHT OF FRUSTRATION

I'VE HEARD THE EXPRESSION "THE HEIGHT OF frustration" all my life. But what is the height of frustration? I'm not sure I know, but I think it varies depending on the individual.

I can think of many experiences, mostly little aggravating things, that when they happened I was sure it was the height of frustration. Here are a few that you may be able to relate to:

- You arrive at the supermarket checkout, your shopping cart filled to overflowing. The cashier enters each item in the cash register and, after the final item has been entered, she renders her verdict: "That comes to $63.87," she says.

And there you stand with $59.12, no checkbook, no food stamps, and six impatient shoppers in line behind you chomping at the bit.

- You're getting dressed to go to a formal party, the social event of the year. You can't find your cuff links. In an unusual twist, your wife is ready and waiting, but no matter how hard you search, no cuff links.

- The bus to the big game will leave in fifteen minutes, with or without you. You're dressed out in your Bulldog pants, Bulldog shirt, Bulldog cap, and have an ample supply of Alpo in your tote bag. But you can't find your ticket. You search and disrupt desk drawers, shirt pockets, the glove compartment, over the sun visor, in the trunk, on and inside the refrigerator, and in all the trash cans. No ticket. You harbor a strong desire to blame somebody, but can't. You live alone.

- You have less than fifteen minutes to finish dressing and get to the church for the wedding. The bride is the daughter of your best friend. You tie the shoestring of your left shoe. Next, the shoestring to your right one. The shoestring breaks, the one you've been promising yourself you'd replace every day for weeks.

- You drive 176 miles, from Lake Sinclair to Waycross, to see your daughter play basketball. But upon arrival you learn that the game isn't being played in Waycross, but Stillmore. It starts in fifteen minutes, and you're two hours away.

- You are five minutes away from speaking to 250 members of a ladies' club in Valdosta, and your zipper gets stuck—in the down position.

- You are driving along after midnight on I-16 between Metter and Soperton, heading home from Savannah. It's cold. You are tired and sleepy. Your left rear tire expires, and every breath of air exits through a nail hole. You raise the trunk lid, remove the spare tire. Then, you reach for the jack. No jack! And five hundred cars pass you by.

  No choice. You drive to Dublin, at three miles per hour, ruining the left rear tire and waking everybody on Academy Avenue. You arrive at Brinson's Chevron Service Center at 3:15 A.M. Your left rear tire looks like a pit bulldog got hold of it. You park your three-legged car, leave a hastily written note for Big Dave underneath the windshield wiper, and walk home in the cold.

- You're almost finished writing your Monday column on a rainy and stormy Sunday night. You finger the computer for that finishing touch only to hear a loud clap of thunder (is there any such thing as a quiet clap of thunder?), lightning cracks, and everything on your computer screen disappears to wherever computer characters disappear to following a crack of lightning. What you're thinking can't be put in a newspaper column, and there's nothing to do but start over and hope and pray the lightning holds off for a few minutes.

FOR THOSE BORN

BEFORE 1945

IF YOU WERE BORN BEFORE 1945, CHANCES ARE you can relate to this chapter. I was and I can.

For All Those Born before 1945

We are survivors! Consider the changes we have witnessed:

- We were born before television, before penicillin, before polio shots, frozen foods, Xerox, contact lenses, 7-11 stores and "the pill."

- We were born before pantyhose, automatic dishwashers, clothes dryers, electric blankets, air conditioning, drip-dry clothing, and before man walked on the moon.

- We got married first and lived together afterward.

- Closets were for clothes, not "coming out of." Bunnies were small rabbits, and rabbits were not Volkswagens.

- Designer jeans were scheming girls named Jean or Jeannie, and having a "meaningful relationship" meant getting along well with our cousins on both sides of the family.

- Fast food was what you ate during Lent, and outer space was the back of the local theater.

- We were before house-husbands, gay rights, computer dating, dual careers, and palimony suits.

- We were before day care centers, group therapy, and nursing homes.

- We never heard of FM radio, tape decks, electric typewriters, artificial hearts and by-passes, word processors, yogurt, guys wearing earrings, and cholesterol.

- Time-sharing meant togetherness and visiting neighbors, not condominiums.

- We were before computers, and "chip" meant a piece of wood. Software meant clean diapers.

- "Made in Japan" meant a piece of junk, and the term "making out" referred to how we did on an exam.

GOOD JOKES DON'T HAVE TO BE DIRTY

HOW MANY JOKE BOOKS ARE THERE IN AMER-
ica's bookstores? Probably thousands, and many of the
jokes are repeats.

I collect joke books so it was a pleasant surprise for me
to return home one night and find two books behind my
door that had been left there by a nice lady. One was a collection of jokes by Homer Rodeheaver titled *F'r Instance*. It
was published in 1947.

It is both refreshing and enjoyable. Refreshing because
of its clean, family-type jokes and enjoyable because of the
simple manner in which they are presented.

Some may think many of the jokes and stories old-
fashioned or strait-laced. Not me. I have long held that the
best jokes and stories are clean jokes and stories. And the
jokes have obviously weathered the storm for the past

forty-five years because many of the ones in *F'r Instance* appear in several of my joke books, some less than two years old. If you're looking for something sexy or dominated by four-letter words, you should read no further. I keep the book on my coffee table and won't hide it when my son, daughter, and grandsons come to visit.

Now for a look at a few jokes from the midforties:

• *Boy came to fish:* The small boy had fallen into the stream but had been rescued. "How did you come to fall in?" asked a bystander. "I didn't come to fall in," the boy explained. "I came to fish and fell off that log."

• *Dividing the apples:* "If your mother gave you a large apple and a small apple and told you to divide with your brother, which one would you give him?" asked the teacher.

"Do you mean my big brother or my little one?" asked the boy.

• *Long-winded master of ceremonies:* After the emcee had rambled on and on, far into the night, he finally said, "And now Mark Twain will favor us with his address."

The humorist arose, smiled at the wearied audience, noted the lateness of the hour, bowed politely, and said: "128 Tremont Street, Boston, Massachusetts." Then he sat down.

• *Druggist's mistake:* "You made a mistake in that prescription for my mother-in-law," said the customer. "Instead of quinine, you used strychnine."

"You don't say!" said the druggist. "In that case you owe me twenty cents more!"

• *Long-staying guest:* The guest was getting ready to depart. The hour was well past midnight. "Goodnight," he said. "I hope I haven't kept you up too late."

Host (yawning): "Not at all. We would have been getting up soon anyway."

• *The honest co-ed:* Every year college deans pop the routine question to their undergraduates: "Why did you come to college?"

Usually the answers are as trite as the question; but one young co-ed from a small rural community answered thusly when the question was put to her. "Well, I came to be went with, but I ain't yet."

• *Not well:* The doctor confided to the patient's wife, "Your husband won't ever be able to work again."

"I'll go tell him," she said. "That will cheer him up."

I was having lunch one Sunday with a preacher friend and his wife. The subject of jokes came up, as it usually does when I'm with a preacher. He's a great joke teller. But this time it was his wife, Carol, who occupied center stage.

We were talking about eating out and about how the dining habits of Americans have changed over the past thirty years when Carol said:

"Right. I know a mother of three small children who works and every time she yells 'OK, kids! It's supper time!' the kids run and jump in the car."

And then the preacher husband, Bill, countered with this one: "Well, let me tell you this. Every time Carol cooks, the smoke alarm goes off!"

He'll probably live to regret having said that.

Here are a few more you might enjoy:

• A barber with a bad case of "morning after the night before" shakes nicked the customer he was shaving. The customer flinched and growled, "There! You see what too much liquor will do to you?"

"Yeah," replied the barber. "It sure makes your skin tender."

• An aged woman, born and nurtured in the South, was endeavoring to impress upon her nephews and nieces the beauties of the South and its people, when one of the nephews spoke up.

"Auntie," he asked, "do you think that all the virtues originated in the South and have been preserved by the southern people?"

"No, not all, but most of them," she replied.

"Do you think that Jesus Christ was a Southerner?" asked a young niece.

The old lady hesitated a moment then said, "Well, He was good enough to be a Southerner!"

• Colleges and insane asylums both are mental institutions in a way. But one has to show some improvement to graduate from an asylum.

• Friend: "Has your son's college education proved helpful since you took him into your firm?"

Father: "Oh, yes, whenever we have a board meeting, we let him mix the cocktails."

• Young boy on telephone to dentist's receptionist: "My mother told me to call and make an appointment with the dentist."

Receptionist: "Sorry, the dentist is out this week."

Young boy: "When will he be out again?"

• A state trooper stopped a speeding truck in South Georgia and asked the driver: "Say fella, don't you have a governor on that truck?"

"No, sir!" replied the truck driver. "That's fertilizer you smell!"

• Teacher: "How old would a person be who was born in 1920?"

Smart pupil: "Man or woman?"

• The judge, with many years' experience, pounded his gavel for the court to come to order, then turned to the woman in the witness box:

"The witness will please state her age," he ordered, "after which she will be sworn in."

• "Your name, please?" asked the census taker.

"Matilda Brown," answered the woman.

"And your age?" he pursued.

"Have the Hill sisters next door given you their ages?" she asked.

"No," said the census taker.

"Well, I'm the same age as they."

"That will do," said the census taker.

Then, as he proceeded to fill out the form, the woman saw him write, "Matilda Brown, as old as the Hills."

• An expert army marksman passed through a small town and saw evidence of amazing shooting. On trees, walls, fences, and barns were numerous bull's-eyes with bullet holes in the exact center. He stopped and asked if he might meet the remarkable marksman.

The man turned out to be the village idiot. "This is the most wonderful marksmanship I've ever seen," said the army man. "How in the world do you do it?"

"Easy as pie," the fella said. "I shoot first and draw the bull's-eye afterward."

• A professor who had taught for many years was counseling a young teacher.

"You will discover," he said, "that in nearly every class there will be a youngster eager to argue. Your first impulse will be to silence him, but I advise you to think carefully before doing so. He is probably the only one listening."

• The policeman stopped a man walking down a back street clad only in his undershorts.

"Where are you going?" asked the policeman.

"Home."

"Where have you been?"

"Playing poker at the club."

"Oh? So you're a poker player, are you?"

"No, *I'm not*," replied the man, "but I just left six fellows who are."

TIME TO PUT
OLD GRAY MATTER
TO WORK

TRY THESE MIND-BOGGLERS. THERE ARE NO tricks or deceit involved. All have logical solutions. Trust me. Solutions are at the end:

(1) As I was going to St. Ives, I met a man with seven wives. Every wife had seven sacks, in the sacks were seven cats. Every cat had seven kittens. Every kitten had a mouse in tow.

How many were going to St. Ives?

(2) A man appeared at a prison on visiting day to visit a male prisoner, only to be told by the guard that only immediate relatives were permitted to visit. The visitor then said, "Brothers and sisters have I none, but that man's father is my father's son."

The guard then let him in.

What was the relationship of the prisoner to the visitor?

(3) Is there biological justification for a man not marrying his widow's sister?

(4) Two men are playing Trivial Pursuit. They play three games and each wins the same number of times yet none of the games is a draw or a default.

How did that happen?

(5) What five-letter word is pronounced the same even after you delete four of its letters?

(6) What common household and office item often displays the fraction 24/31?

(7) The person who made it had no use for it; the person who bought it didn't want it; and the one who finally ended up with it never knew about it.

What was it?

(8) What is the only letter in the alphabet you wouldn't need to spell the names of all fifty states?

(9) In top to bottom traffic lights, which color is on the bottom?

(10) Are there more red or white stripes in the American flag?

(11) What letters of the alphabet have been omitted from the telephone dial?

(12) Think of your closest friend. He or she can sit somewhere that you'll never be able to sit.

Where is it?

(13) Every autumn day John raked the back yard leaves into fifteen piles and the front yard leaves into eleven piles. Then, he'd rake them all together in the side yard.

How many piles would there be in John's side yard?

(14) Pitney High defeated Bowles High in a basketball game, 110-34.

Pete, Harry, John, Phil, and Stan scored the most points in Pitney's history.

The five starters went 8, 10, 22, 28, and 30. From the following clues, can you figure out who scored how many points?

The 30 points weren't made by Pete. Everyone scored more than Pete.

The 28 points weren't made by Harry, who scored two points more than Phil.

Stan scored fewer points than John.

(15) How many successful jumps must a paratrooper make before he graduates from jump school?

Answers: (1) One; (2) The prisoner is the visitor's son; (3) Yes. As his widow's husband, he's dead; (4) They weren't playing each other; (5) Queue; (6) A calendar; (7) A coffin; (8) Q; (9) Green; (10) Red—There are seven reds and six whites; (11) Q and Z; (12) In your lap; (13) One; (14) Harry scored the most points—30; Phil scored two fewer than Harry—28 points, John scored 22; Stan scored 10; Pete scored 8; (15) All of them.

WHAT IS A FARMER?

FARMERS ARE FOUND IN FIELDS PLOWING UP, seeding down, returning from, planting to, fertilizing with, spraying for, and harvesting it. Wives help them, little children follow them, city relatives visit them, salesmen detain them, meals wait for them, weather can delay them, but it takes heaven to stop them.

A farmer is a paradox. He's an overall executive with his home as his office; a scientist using fertilizer attachments; a purchasing agent in an old straw hat; a personnel director with grease under his fingernails; a production expert faced with a surplus; and a manager battling a price-cost squeeze.

A farmer likes sunshine, good food, state fairs, dinner at noon, Saturdays in town, family reunions, unbuttoned collars, and a good soaking rain in August. A farmer is not much for droughts, ditches, throughways, experts, weeds, the eight-hour day, helping with the housework, or insects.

Nobody else is so far removed from the telephone or so close to Mother Nature as is a farmer. Nobody else can remove everything from his pockets on washday and still overlook five staples, one cotter key, a rusty nail, three grains of corn, the stub end of a lead pencil, and chaff in each trouser cuff.

A farmer can fix things.

A farmer is a believer and a fatalist. He must have faith to meet the challenges of his capacities amid the possibility that an act of God like a late spring, an early frost, a tornado, a flood, or a drought can bring his business to a standstill. You can reduce his acreage, but you can't restrain his ambition.

And when he comes in from the field at noon for dinner, having spent the energy of his hopes and dreams, he can be recharged anew with three magic words: "The market's up."

- A farmer wears out two pairs of overalls growing enough cotton for one.

- Farmers are made of bent nails, rusty horseshoes, barbed wire, and held together with calluses.

- During planting time and harvest season, the farmer finishes his forty-hour week by Tuesday noon; then, paining from a tractor-back, he somehow manages to put in another seventy-two.

- He buries last year's disappointments with springtime planting because he has faith not in himself alone. He'll finish a hard week's work, then drive five miles to church on Sunday.

- Some years it'll get too wet or too dry, or there'll be hail, wind, early frost, early snow, bugs, and bureaucrats. He may not even meet expenses. Yet the only lines in a farmer's face are from grinning through it all.

- The farmer remains the world's most stubborn optimist.

- The farmer plants in hope, cultivates in faith, and often ends in debt; then, he starts over with greater hope and stronger faith.

- Heaven help the family that depends on the farmer for support.

- Heaven help the nation that doesn't have him to support it.

I can't help but wonder at times why they keep at it with all the uncertainty that goes with farming, like government regulations and an unstable market for their goods.

- A farmer and his wife made one of their infrequent visits to the city and wandered into a very expensive and spiffy restaurant. The farmer inquired of the waiter as to the price of a hamburger.
"$5.75," said the waiter.
The farmer took out his pencil and began figuring on a napkin. Finished, he leaned over and whispered to his wife, "Martha, do you realize we've got a cow at home worth $85,000?"
- A farmer was plowing in a dry and dusty field in South Alabama one hot afternoon when a New Yorker pulled up in a big, shiny, chrome-plated car and said, "I can't see for the life of me how you make a living on this run-down farm."

The old farmer wiped his brow, spit out his chewing tobacco, and said, "Well, mister, let me tell you. I ain't as poor as you think. I don't even own this farm."

• "In my day," recalled the old farmer sitting in front of the general store, "we used to talk 'bout how much you could raise on one hundred acres—an' we meant corn, not guv'mint loans."

NEVER TAKE WHAT YOU SEE FOR GRANTED

MAGICIANS ARE GREAT ILLUSIONISTS. THEY HAVE the unique ability to do one thing and make it look completely different. Flim-flam artists can do the same thing and leave you with a handkerchief full of newspaper cuttings you'd swear was the money—your money—you saw him put in the handkerchief before handing it to you for safekeeping until he got back from wherever.

Con artists do it with slick talk and quick hands. Card sharks do it with playing cards. Circus acrobats? Their stunts can be deceiving as well, as this little story points out.

Two vagrants, R. J. and Roy Lee, both pretty much into the sauce, stopped at a farmhouse near Sarasota, Florida, the winter home of Ringling Brothers Circus, and knocked on the back door. It was a cold and dreary February day.

Shortly, the lady of the house appeared and asked of them why they were there.

"We was just wonderin', ma'am, if you got any work we could do for you to make a little money to buy somethin' to eat?" R. J. asked.

"We been outta work for a spell and we're hungry," Roy Lee added.

The woman looked them over closely before saying anything. She considered their dirty clothes, rumpled hair, and the smell of alcohol—very noticeable. Finally, she spoke: "Well, do you see that pile of stove wood over there by the chicken house?"

Both men looked, and R. J. confirmed that he saw it. "Yessum, I see it."

"All right, if you're really hungry and want to split the wood, I'll cook you a good dinner. Pork chops, vegetables, homemade biscuits, and chocolate cake for dessert," she offered. "Also, I have a brand new ax that has never been used. I just bought it last week."

It was agreed that the two of them would split the stove wood. The lady handed Roy Lee the ax and both he and R. J. shuffled off slowly toward the woodpile.

The lady began to cook and through the kitchen window watched R. J. and Roy Lee reluctantly taking turns splitting the stove wood. They also took turns with the small bottle of liquid heat that R. J. kept in his back pocket. She smiled. Then the telephone rang.

The caller was a lady missionary scheduled to speak at a meeting of the farm wife's church study group to be held that very afternoon at 3:00 P.M. in her home. The missionary's voice was barely audible. She explained that she was calling to report that she had a bad case of laryngitis, and it would be impossible for her to speak to the study group that afternoon.

"Oh, my goodness!" exclaimed the farm wife. "What in the world will I do about a program?"

After appropriate apologies, the missionary hung up, leaving the farm wife in a dilemma. But then, as luck would have it, or so she thought, fate stepped in.

She looked out the kitchen window to check on the two wood splitters. At that moment she saw Roy Lee drop the ax, do two back flips, grab his left foot with both hands, hop on one foot, jump an eight-foot fence, climb up on a tractor, shimmy up on top of the chicken house, let out a blood-curdling Tarzan yell, and plunge headlong into a haystack—never releasing his grip on his left foot with his hands.

"Amazing! Absolutely amazing!" the farm wife said out loud, subconsciously thinking "circus acrobat" and her women's study club meeting.

She ran to the back door, opened it, and yelled to R. J., who was standing nonchalantly on top of the woodpile leaning on the ax while watching Roy Lee go through his routine.

"Do you think your friend would agree to do what he just did again this afternoon at three o'clock for a hundred dollars?" she asked in desperation.

"Don't know, ma'am," R. J. replied. "Ya want me to ask him?"

"Oh, yes! Please do!"

"All right, I'll ask him," R. J. said. "Hey! Roy Lee!"

"Yeah, what is it, man?" Roy Lee moaned from the haystack.

"You wanna cut off another toe for a hundred dollars?"

I Know What
I Hear
While Traveling

PICKED UP OR CONJURED UP WHILE TRAVELING around the country:

- It is certainly not necessary to drink to be a good columnist. It is a great help on the days when you are a bad one, however.
- Marriage teaches you loyalty, forbearance, self-restraint, meekness, thrift, and a great many other things you wouldn't need had you stayed single.
- The surest way to make a red light turn green is to try to find something in the glove compartment.
- Change is inevitable, except from a vending machine.
- Intelligence is when you spot a flaw in your boss's reasoning. Wisdom is when you refrain from pointing it out to him.

• Two shiftless drunks were sitting at the base of the Washington Monument on a bitter cold day in February. One started a fire at the base of it. The other said nonchalantly, "You'll never get it off the ground."

• The new cars are ridiculous. There's one luxury car on the market that is so modern and computerized that when you press a button, *it* presses a button.

• A stunning young blonde walked into a dress shop and asked the manger: "Do you mind if I try on that blue dress in the window?"

"Go right ahead," he said. "It might help business."

• Americans are getting stronger. Twenty-five years ago it took two people to carry fifty dollars' worth of groceries to the car. Today a five-year-old boy can do it.

• I heard a great new song, but it will never make it. I could understand every word.

• One day a fellow came home only to find his new bride standing in the kitchen crying.

"What's the matter?" he asked.

"The dog ate the apple pie I'd baked just for you," she sobbed.

"Now, now. Don't cry, honey," he said, patting her on the shoulder softly. "I'll buy you another dog."

• A poor guy married one of those liberated females only to have her tell him on their honeymoon that she didn't believe in sex after marriage.

• There's a new medical/legal television series in the works. It's about a lawyer who owns his own ambulance.

• The elevator stopped on the fifteenth floor, and a nude woman stepped in and joined the lone office worker on board. She pushed the button for the fourth floor and smiled sweetly.

Dumbfounded and not knowing just what to say, if anything, as they passed the eighth floor he finally said to her, "My wife has an outfit just like yours."

- I was having lunch with a friend in Atlanta when the waiter said to him, "Just help yourself to the salad bar."

He countered with, "I'll be glad to fix my own salad if you'll let me go behind the bar and fix my own martini."

- Three cross-eyed prisoners appeared before a cross-eyed judge. The judge looked at the first prisoner and asked, "What are you charged with?"

"Stealing chickens," the second prisoner answered.

The judge eyed him sternly and said, "Keep quiet! I wasn't talking to you."

The third prisoner said, "I didn't say nothing."

OBSERVATIONS OF A CONFIRMED PEOPLE WATCHER

MY HOBBY IS PEOPLE WATCHING. IT'S INEXPEN-sive, and there is never a shortage of subjects. I've been at it for years.

Yogi Berra is credited with having said, "You can observe a lot by just watching," although I doubt seriously that the famed baseballer ever actually made the statement.

As an avid people watcher, I have observed many things down through the years that stuck in my mind. Just for the heck of it, let me share some of them with you:

- The higher a man rises in his company the harder he is to locate by telephone.

- The prettiest woman at the party will have the mean-est and ugliest husband.

- At any party attended by fifty people, at least thirty-seven of them will stand in the doorway between the kitchen, where the booze is, and the den, where the hors d'oeuvres are.

- No matter how big the room containing the television, a five-year-old will manage to stand directly between you and the television set.

- Give one kid a blue balloon and the other a red one and the one with the blue one will want the red one and the one with the red one will want the blue one.

- Put three kids in the back seat and they all want to sit by the window.

- A wife will never ask her husband where he's been if he gets home before she does.

- Ask two people the best way to drive to St. Simons and you will leave them arguing.

- The more money a man has the harder it is to get any of it.

- As soon as a politician is elected to office for the first time, he begins whispering and everything he says to anybody is very private.

- Flowers for the one you love, on no special occasion, are the flowers most appreciated.

- Political television ads never show the candidate talking to a rich man, but always to some guy wearing a hard hat in a steel mill, standing knee-deep in a cow lot, or entering or leaving a factory early in the morning. After the election? Another story. He rubs elbows with those who financed him and hobnobs with the affluent.

- No matter what time you go to the mall, all the parking spaces near the mall entrance are taken.

- The best dressed people are conservatively dressed people.

- People who regularly employ the use of profanity are, for the most part, insecure.

- Recently engaged girls will find a way to do everything from wiping their noses to covering their mouths when they yawn with their left hand.

- I have never witnessed an ugly wedding or a pretty divorce.

- Nobody really knows exactly what to do with the toothpick after spearing and eating the little sausage at a cocktail party or wedding reception.

- It has never been determined exactly what one should do with his hands during a physical examination.

- The hospital expression "Hold for observation" had to come into being as the result of some poor soul walking down a hospital hallway wearing one of those despicable tie-in-the-back hospital gowns.

- The man who is the worst shot at a dove shoot will invariably wind up on the best stand.

- No grandparent ever had an ugly grandchild.

How to Know If It's Going to Be a Rotten Day

There are good days and bad days, right? It usually doesn't take long after rising in the morning to get some indication as to what kind of a day you're in for. Not long ago a friend gave me a list of ways you can know if it's going to be a rotten day. I've given it some thought and have come up with some of my own.

- You wake up face down on the pavement.
- You call suicide prevention and they put you on hold.
- You are sitting in church as the collection plate approaches your pew and the smallest bill you have is a twenty.
- You arrive at your office and a "60 Minutes" team is waiting for you in the reception room.

- Your birthday cake collapses from the weight of the candles.

- You want to put on the clothes you wore home from the party and there aren't any.

- Your twin sister forgot your birthday.

- You flip the TV on and they're showing emergency routes out of the city.

- You wake up to discover your waterbed broke—but then you realize you don't have a waterbed.

- Your horn gets stuck and remains stuck as you follow a group of Hell's Angels on the expressway.

- Your wife wakes up feeling amorous and you have a headache.

- Your boss tells you not to bother to take your coat off and your personnel file is on his desk.

- The bird singing outside your window is a buzzard.

- You wake up and your braces are locked together.

- You walk to work and find that your dress is stuck in the back of your pantyhose.

- You call your answering service and they tell you it's none of your business.

- You dial Butterfield 8, and Richard Burton answers.

- Your dentist tells you that your teeth are perfect—but your gums have to come out.

- Your blind date turns out to be your ex-wife.

- Your income tax check bounces.

- You put both contact lenses in the same eye.

- You take your date to the drive-in movie and she wants to watch the movie.

- You peep through a keyhole and see another eyeball.

- Your pet rock snaps at you.

- Your wife says, "Good morning, Bill," and your name is George.

- After seeing a triple x-rated movie, staring Linda Lovelace and John Holmes, you run smack dab into your mother-in-law as you walk out on the sidewalk.

- You order two eggs, one scrambled and one fried, and the cook scrambles the wrong one.

- You get a hole-in-one on Number Six, and you're playing alone.

How to Know If You're Getting Old

Just like there are sure-fire signs that one is beginning a bad day, there are signs that age is rapidly approaching. Here are twenty-five ways you can know if you are getting old.

- Almost everything hurts, and what doesn't hurt, doesn't work.
- The gleam in your eye is from the sun hitting your bifocals.
- You feel like the morning after the night before, but you didn't go anywhere.
- The only names in your little black book are MD's.
- You get winded playing chess.

- Your children begin to look middle-aged.

- You join a health club and don't go.

- You decide to procrastinate, but never get around to it.

- You know all the answers but nobody asks the questions.

- Your favorite part of the newspaper is, Twenty-Five Years Ago Today.

- You turn out the lights for economic rather than romantic reasons.

- You sit in a rocking chair and can't get it going.

- Your knees buckle but your belt won't.

- You are 17 around the neck, 42 around the waist, and 106 around the golf course.

- After painting the town red, you have to take a long rest before applying the second coat.

- You remember today that yesterday was your anniversary.

- You just can't stand people who are intolerant.

- The best part of your day ends when the alarm clock sounds.

- Your back goes out more often than you do.

- Your pacemaker makes the garage door go up when you watch a pretty girl walk by.

- The little gray-haired lady you help across the street is your wife.

- You have too much room in the house and not enough in the medicine cabinet.

- You sink your teeth into a steak and they stay there.

- You pay more attention to your food than you do the waitress.

- You realize that you're as old as your mouth but a little older than your teeth.

ARE YOU AS ORGANIZED AS YOU SHOULD BE?

ALL RIGHT, BE HONEST WITH ME NOW. HOW organized are you? Answer these questions for me and see how you stack up.

- Can you locate your U.S. Army discharge within a twenty-four-hour period?

- Can you put your hands on your automobile insurance card without undue delay?

- Have you paid last month's cable TV payment?

- Do you always have to pay the penalty on your water bill because you failed to remit by the tenth of the month?

- Is your checking account in balance, or within fifty dollars?

- Do you have coffee, cream, *and* sugar on hand?

- Do you always have to run like the devil for the last 100 yards on Sunday morning to get to Sunday school before the tardy bell rings?

- Do you enter your place of employment at 8:37 A.M. via the back entrance while devouring a Williamson's doughnut and a cup of Huddle House coffee in a vain attempt to avoid detection by an uncompromising and unsympathetic boss who was previously a CIA supervisor?

- Do *all* the socks in the drawer reserved for them match?

- Do you always appear at the laundromat without an ample supply of quarters?

- Do you always arrive at the airport only thirteen minutes before your Delta flight's scheduled departure? (Delta? Sure. Doesn't *everybody* fly Delta?)

- Do your sausage, eggs, grits, toast, and coffee always get done at the same time?

- Do you board MARTA buses with nothing smaller than a twenty?

- Do you always begin your Christmas shopping somewhere around 6:30 P.M. on Christmas Eve?

- Have you made that will that you promised yourself faithfully in 1958 you'd contact your lawyer about "tomorrow"?

- Can you locate the canceled check for $128.57, dated December 14, 1978, needed for proof of payment of your county taxes?

- Have you *ever* filed for your homestead exemption?

- Is the key to your safe deposit box readily available?

- Are all your receipts neatly preserved and filed in one of those cute little file boxes? Or do you spend most Saturday mornings digging in trash cans and dumpsters?

- Do you throw away your ticket stub immediately after entering Gate G at Atlanta Stadium to see a Braves-Dodgers doubleheader, only to sit there in the top of the second inning with your negligence hanging out while some black-belt karate chopper hovers over you proclaiming for everybody in Section 131 to hear that you are occupying *his* seat?

- Do you habitually show up at the shop to buy that darling little red sweater the morning *after* the sale ended at 9:00 P.M. the night before?

- Do you drop your quarter in the slot early on Wednesday morning, withdraw a newspaper, sit down to your morning coffee and *then* realize that you bought a Tuesday newspaper?

- Do you take a seat at the head table only to have the front of your shirt open up like the Grand Canyon because you neglected, again, to have that missing button in the navel area replaced?

- Do you always arrange to get in the buffet line at just the right spot to ensure that the guy in front of you stabs around in the fried chicken pan and manages to get the last piece of white meat?

- Do you come to the realization that you really are dumb when you reach for the toilet tissue only to grab hold of a cardboard roller?

- Does your magazine subscription expire the very month the final episode of your favorite story that's been running for five months appears—and the magazine is not sold at newsstands locally?

- Does your preacher pay his annual visit to your home the morning after your brother-in-law has returned to Brooklyn, and ring the doorbell while you are cleaning up the guest room he occupied for seven weeks, only to have you greet the preacher at the door while you're holding a *Hustler, Penthouse, Playboy, National Enquirer, Forum* and two empty vodka bottles?

- Do you arrive home at 3:45 A.M. after a night out with the boys and reach for your front door key only to realize that it is resting comfortably on the chest of drawers in the bedroom where you left it?

- Do you stand before a women's club (of which your wife is president) to speak and realize that the notes you have withdrawn from your inside coat pocket and spread on the podium are in reality the point spreads on the Georgia Tech-Georgetown NCAA tournament game in Providence, Rhode Island, or a series of names and numbers: Sally, 286-4492; Rita, 322-8087 (after 10 P.M.); Monica, 404-922-3445 (if a man answers, hang up, or try to sound like a Cuban asking directions to Six Flags)?

If a majority of these apply to you, you're just not organized.

If none of these apply in your case, I envy you.

Helpful Travel Tips Brochures Don't Print

I TRAVEL BY AUTOMOBILE A LOT AND HAVE decided to share some thoughts that might make your travel easier, safer, and more enjoyable. Listed are some of the hazards of road travel that I try to avoid:

- I never pick up two kinds of hitchkikers: male or female.

- I make every effort to avoid eating in any establishment that has a jukebox.

- I'm always leery of stopping for lunch at any restaurant that has its specialties misspelled on the sign. Like, "World's Best Cattfish and Hushpupies."

- I watch out for front door signs that say, "No Shoes. No Shirt. No Service." That tells me something.

- I don't buy gasoline at any place that has a sign on the pump saying, "Pay Before Pumping Gas."

- I pass up any motel that has its night desk clerk imprisoned in a heavy wire cage so that I have to stand outside in the cold and/or rain to register, and then slip my credit card and registration underneath a bullet-proof glass partition like it was visiting day at the state prison, a definite clue as to the kind of neighborhood you're about to go night-night in.

- I shun motels with gift shops that display more playing cards and dice than T-shirts.

- I drive right on by any motel south of West Palm Beach whose sign says, "Welcome, Señor! Interpreter on Duty 24 Hours a Day."

- I don't consider stopping at any motel whose lounge is twice as large as its coffee shop and dining room combined.

- I never make any attempt to race on the interstates with any car featuring raised white-letter tires bigger than a ferris wheel, obscene bumper stickers, one-way smoked glass, mag wheels, and with fuzzy dice, a graduation tassel, or baby shoes hanging on the rear-view mirror.

- I make it a practice never to shoot a bird at any driver of a high-rise pickup with KC lights on top of the cab, a 30.06 rifle and a .12-gauge shotgun hanging in the rear window gun rack, who's wearing a beard, a CAT diesel cap, and tossing beer cans out the window.

- I never argue with the driver of an eighteen-wheeler, or Mike Tyson, Arnold Schwarzenegger, or Rambo.

- I never check into any motel where the beer cans outnumber the automobiles in its parking area.

- I avoid all motels that require a key deposit.

- I scratch any motel that has a sign in the lobby saying "No Loitering" and/or "Not Responsible for Stolen Property or Broken Car Windows."

- I blackball any motel whose honeymoon suite is the back seat of a 1965 Plymouth parked in the rear, way back by the dumpster.

- I routinely do an about face when I walk in the lobby of any motel where the manager is overhauling a transmission on the floor or cleaning fish on the desk.

- I refuse to register in any motel where the desk clerk is twelve years old or under, unless I'm traveling in Mississippi and she's wearing a wedding ring.

- I mark off any motel that only makes reservations by the hour.

- I make a U-turn at any motel upon determining that to get inside the office and register I'd have to walk around or step over hound dogs, younguns, or tricycles.

- I never check in any motel where the cover charge to get in the lounge is more than the cost of the room.

- I avoid with regularity motels at which more police cars are parked than paying guests'.

SEMIPRIVATE HOSPITAL GOWNS AND OTHER ONE-LINERS

I GUESS THE MOST FAMOUS OF THE ONE-LINER comedians on the scene today is Henny Youngman. I had the pleasure of a chance meeting and having coffee with Mr. Youngman in the lobby of the Hyatt Regency Hotel in Atlanta a few years back, a most entertaining experience.

You remember Youngman's most famous one-liner, don't you? "Now, take my wife—please!"

And this one: "I was driving my new compact car on Forty-second Street at Broadway and really got into trouble when I put my hand out to signal for a left turn and ruptured a policeman."

Here are some one-liners that just go to show that it really isn't necessary for one to be wordy to get a message across.

- Card playing can be expensive, like any other game in which you hold hands.

- Most of us would be satisfied with enough if the neighbors didn't have more.

- The semiprivate room at the hospital didn't get me down; the thing that really got me down was the semiprivate gown.

- Probably a man's most profitable words are those spent praising his wife.

- Worse than a quitter is the fellow who finishes things he never should have started.

- God took only six days to create the world—but that was before labor unions.

- It's a sure sign the front yard needs picking up when passersby ask if you're having a yard sale.

- The reason many of us can't always recognize opportunity is that it often looks too much like plain hard work.

- When a man brings his wife flowers for no reason— there's a reason.

- Social Security is the guarantee that you'll be able to eat steak when you no longer have teeth.

- If you insist that you can read me like a book, please skip some pages.

- Anybody who doesn't slow down at the sight of a police car is probably parked.

- I finally found a house I can afford, but the only drawback is the dog won't move out.

- Always keep an emergency candle on hand so when the lights go out you can find the toys that have the batteries that were borrowed from the flashlight last Christmas.

- The age of puberty is when your son quits asking where he came from and refuses to tell you where he's going.

- I think this one was written especially for me: A key-chain is a device that permits you to lose several keys at the same time.

- For most kids, an unbreakable toy is something used to smash those that aren't.

- There has never been a winter on which you couldn't lay a bet and prove by anybody older that those we used to have were colder.

- Conclusions are an important part of any speech, especially when they come as close as possible to the beginning.

- If there were any justice in the world we would be permitted to fly over pigeons occasionally.

- Nostalgia is thinking about the hamburger that only cost a nickel, but a good memory is what reminds you that it took four to fill you up—and you could afford but one.

- It is good to remember that the tea kettle, although up to its neck in hot water, continues to sing.

- A bachelor is a cagey fellow who has a lot of fun, sizes all the cuties up and never Mrs. one.

- An optimist is a person who thinks a fly buzzing around the house is trying to find a way out without bothering anyone.

- A honeymoon is the vacation a man takes just before he begins working for a new boss.

- What with the rate changes that are occurring, anyone nostalgic for the "good old days" is yearning for last week.

- Never insult an alligator until you have safely crossed the river.

- Good government is like one's stomach; when operating properly, one never knows he has it.

- Inflation has reached the point where we all have to run just to stay in place.

- The beauty of the old-fashioned blacksmith was that when you brought your horse to him to be shod he didn't come up with forty other things that had to be done.

- All of us are smart at ages five and eighteen—at five we know all the questions and at eighteen we know all the answers.

- Children do not seem so taxing when we recall they are deductible.

- Economists are finding out that getting the economy straightened out is about as easy as putting socks on an octopus.

- Paying alimony is like feeding quarters into an empty slot machine.

- Grandparents and grandchildren understand each other because they know how to outwit the middle generation.

INVENTORS WHO OUGHT TO BE HANGED

I'M CONVINCED THAT CERTAIN PRODUCTS ARE designed, manufactured, and marketed not for convenience, but strictly to aggravate. Take a look at these, for example:

- *Wire Coathangers.* The darn things breed, right? Hang half a dozen straight as a West Point parade line in your closet tonight then check 'em first thing in the morning. They'll be there, all twenty-three of 'em, as twisted and tangled as Bo Derek's hair. (But they'll look a heck of a lot better.)
- *Toll Booths.* This is what usually happens at toll booths:

You're beat after driving seven solid hours with Willie Kate up front and the kids, eight and six, back in the tourist section.

You haven't passed up a rest room or a McDonald's this side of New Jersey. A monotonous white line has been the scenery from the New Jersey Turnpike to the Sunshine Parkway while you routinely, almost subconsciously, threw away more quarters than a female slot machine addict in Las Vegas.

Suddenly, there it is! Toll Booth Ahead—Cars With Exact Change Use Right Lane says the big sign with white letters. So, you make your move; so do 387 other Florida-bound chauffeurs.

One-handed, you steer toward the wide-mouthed monster that eats quarters, only quarters, while fumbling in your right pants pocket. All the while the back-seat tourists are chorusing a too-familiar refrain. "Let me, Daddy! Let me throw it in! It's my turn!"

Do you have a quarter? No sale. The Coke machine at the I-75 rest area eighty-five miles back cleaned you out. Willie Kate? Don't be ridiculous! She hasn't had one since Six Flags.

So you're trapped in the exact change lane while the monster waits with open mouth. The line of cars behind resembles a presidential motorcade and sounds like New Year's Eve at Times Square. There you sit with six pennies, two nickels, a dime, two subway tokens, a book of McDonald's matches, and a nail clipper, none of which will get you past the monster without lights, bells, buzzers and sirens signaling to all that you cheated!

• *Automobile Hood Release Thingamajigs.* Right here is where we need some legislation. Never mind constitutional revision and supplemental budgets. Let's get on with important stuff, like mandating that hood release thinga-majigs be located in the same place on all cars. Where are they now? Inside, outside, in the grille, over the grille, under the grille, over the bumper, under the bumper, you name it, Mr. Goodwrench. Why? Because the automobile manufacturers are in cahoots with the nail clipper people, that's why.

Ever had car trouble late at night seventeen miles from nowhere, with steam spewing from the radiator like a vigorously shaken Coke, and you try to find the hood release thingamajig? Forget it! You'll have more luck finding a crew cut and a pair of saddle oxfords on U.S. 441 on a Sunday afternoon.

• *A Few More Mind-Bogglers.* I've previously vented my frustrations regarding a few other aggravating gadgets. Like those cute little triangular coffee creamers that spurt artificial cream in every direction except your coffee cup. And those individual mustard and catsup takeouts that are as unpredictable as a woman. Just try putting the yellow and red on your hot dog and see what happens. You end up with both on your bifocals and all over your Timex.

Then there's the one that literally drives me up the restaurant wall: deformed table legs. Ever sit at a table with deformed legs? You must have.

You sit on one side, she sits on the other. You pick up your glass and the table tilts toward her. She picks hers up and it tilts toward you. Only two ways to correct it.

First, practice until you both lift your glasses at the same time. That's a lot of fun and it does give you a feeling of togetherness.

Second, you try everything on the table: folded paper napkins, match covers, saucer, ash tray, a couple of butter patties, and the cap off the catsup bottle. You try, usually unsuccessfully, to make an adjustment by easing the item that most nearly fits under the deformed leg. (Of course, you should expect to tip over a water glass or cup of coffee in the process; that's precisely what the manufacturer had in mind when the legs were sawed.) You can always move to another table and insult the couple at the next one by so doing.

The ultimate pest? Safety medicine bottles. No doubt in my mind, they were invented by a sadist. Just try to open one at 2:00 A.M., in the dark, without your glasses. The thing is definitely an offshoot of one of the most frustrating items ever to come on the market: the combination lock! Grant me three minutes to share a recent experience I had with one:

I had played golf with a friend and rode in his golf cart. Following my usual routine, I removed my watch and placed it in the cart tray along with old tees and dead birdies.

We finished the round, I paid off, and went home. It was 9:00 P.M. before I missed my watch. I heard the time on the radio. I only knew it was Thursday, A.D., and that's close enough for the schedule I follow. I called my friend, explained what I'd done, and asked if I could get the key to his cart stall.

"I'd rather go without my jockey shorts than my watch," I told him.

"No problem. You don't need a key. My cart shed has a combination lock. I'll just give you the combination," he said.

"Fine, go ahead," I told him.

"O.K. Here's what you do. You can't miss. Turn the dial two times to the right and stop on 14. Got that?"

"Gotcha'," I replied.

"Next, turn one time to the left past 14 and on to 4. Stop on 4. Got it?"

"No problem. Stop on 4," I echoed.

"O.K. Then, turn back right to 30 and pull. That's all there is to it," he assured me.

All there is to it? Read on.

This was the one night it's rained in Dublin since World War II. No problem, though, I thought. I'd just zip on out to the country club, twist that little ol' dial a few times, get my watch, and return home.

In the first place, I couldn't see. I barely found the lock, much less the dadgummed dial. Finally, I began twisting and turning while squinting through foggy bifocals.

I tried it on two legs, then standing on one. Tongue in, tongue out. With and without profanity. Twist and pull; twist and pull. I out-twisted Chubby Checker and out-pulled a Wisconsin dairy farmer. Did the lock open? Heck no, it didn't open! I'd have had more success uncoupling a freight car.

I sounded like a quarterback, standing there in the dark, twisting and mumbling, "Right 14! Left 4! Right 30! Pull!" Nothing!

No doubt about it, friend. It takes more than the combination to open one of those monsters, and whatever it takes, I didn't have it. I took the easy way out; I gave up and went home. Oh, my watch? I went with my friend and got it the next day. He opened the lock in less than fifteen seconds.

"See? No problem," he said, gloating.

Oh, yeah? Well, I'd like to see him open the hood of my car without breaking a fingernail on the hood release thingamajig. No way. Absolutely no way.

Things That "Tee Me Off"

In the past I haven't made New Year's resolutions, but in recent years I've taken a different approach. I'm still not making any, but I do plan to try and be a little more tolerant of those little things in life that "tee me off." You know, pet peeves. We all have them and here are a few of mine that I'm going to try and suppress my complete dislike for, or at least make an effort to hide my antagonism:

- People who "save seats" at free public events.

- People who break in line.

- Extremely loud car radios or tape players.

- Loud jukeboxes in restaurants.

- Perfectly healthy individuals who park in spaces reserved for the physically handicapped.

- People who get an armload of mail and then sit in their car for an hour in the post office parking lot and open it while cars are backed up to City Hall waiting for a parking place.

- People who repeatedly interrupt.

- People who pop chewing gum in public.

- People who stare . . . and stare . . . and stare.

- Pay toilets. They should all be outlawed.

- People who insist on getting in the supermarket "Six Items or Less" checkout line with enough items to overload a grocery cart.

- Establishments that sell gasoline but provide no rest room facilities for their customers. I avoid them like the plague.

- Cars that sport "On-Board" signs.

- People who take small children into restaurants and then allow them to run wild.

- People who sit behind you in the theatre and talk during the entire movie.

- People who block the intersection but won't look at you while doing so.

- People who insist on driving 42 miles per hour and won't budge from the left lane on the expressway.

- People who discard their chewing gum in restaurant ashtrays, underneath theatre seats, and on sidewalks.

- People who straddle the line and take up two parking spaces in crowded parking lots.

- Telephone solicitations of any kind.

- People who appear at my front door on Sunday morning just when I'm shaving and getting ready to go to my church who tell me I'm going straight to hell if I don't believe the way they do.

- People who sit in an adjoining booth and jabber back and forth in a foreign language. (I always get the feeling they're talking about me.)

- Any mail that tells me on the outside of the envelope that I have for sure won a prize, probably worth thousands of dollars.

- Has-been jocks in the broadcast booth who can tell you exactly why a certain play didn't work—people like John Madden, the Andy Devine clone; Dick Vitale, ESPN's college basketball color man who sports a .50 caliber automatic mouth loaded from a .22 caliber brain; and Beano Cook, whoever the heck he is. And I never thought I would see the day that I'd admit I miss Howard Cosell.

- Women sportscasters who take great pride in their ability to explain a groin injury in minute detail, and the men who do the commercials revealing all the advantages of using a particular feminine hygiene product. You tell me, how do these people know about these things?

- British commentators announcing American golf tournaments.

- Talk show hosts, all of whom believe they're much more important than they really are.

- Dr. Ruth. Take a good look at her and answer me this: How would *she* know about sex?

- John McEnroe. I automatically pull for his opponent, no matter his nationality. McEnroe is a foot-fault in my book.

- Jim and Tammy Faye Bakker. 'Nuff said.

- Bobby Knight, Indiana University basketball embarrassment. I refuse to watch his team play. I'd rather watch Championship Wrestling (and *all* wrestling is Championship Wrestling; the only thing more boring, and predictable, is watching the Braves and the Falcons).

- Joan Rivers. The ol' gal is right where she belongs—going, going, gone!

These are just a few of my pet peeves, and I honestly intend to tolerate or avoid them. I lean toward avoiding them.

Roots—Will the Real Bo Whaley Please Stand Up?

A FEW YEARS AGO I RECEIVED A TELEPHONE CALL from the program chairman of a North Carolina civic club to which I had been invited to speak. True to form, he was calling to inquire if I had a résumé and, if so, would I please mail him one as he would be introducing me.

Do I have a résumé? Do insurance agents use rate books? Is New York big? Of course I have a résumé. I wouldn't leave home without it.

After hanging up the telephone, I pulled a copy of my résumé from my file cabinet. I scanned it before mailing it to North Carolina. This is what it looks like and is precisely what the program chairman read when introducing me:

"Résumé of Walker W. 'Bo' Whaley"

Born December 11, 1927, Scott, Georgia. Subsequently moved to several South Georgia communities with his parents, his father being a Methodist preacher.

Graduated from Stewart County High School, Lumpkin, Georgia, in May, 1943, and immediately enrolled at Georgia Military College, graduating in December, 1944. Bo was named Most Outstanding Athlete at GMC in both 1943 and 1944.

Inducted into U.S. Army in 1945 and served two years as a combat engineer in the South Pacific before being honorably discharged in November, 1946, and immediately enrolled at Georgia Southern College where he played both varsity baseball and basketball. Graduated in June, 1949, with a BS in History and Physical Education.

Coached baseball and taught history at Georgia Military College from 1949 to 1951. Enrolled in graduate school at George Peabody College, Nashville, Tennessee, receiving the Master of Education degree in 1952.

Coached basketball and baseball and taught history at Dublin, Georgia, High School from 1952 to 1954. Named principal of Wrightsville, Georgia, High School in June, 1954, but prior to the beginning of the school year was appointed a Special Agent of the Federal Bureau of Investigation. He served in this capacity for 21 years in Washington, D.C., Houston, Texas, Detroit, Michigan, Newark, New Jersey, and New York City until his retirement in 1975.

Additionally, from 1949 until 1954, Bo played professional baseball with several minor league teams as a pitcher.

In December, 1977, Bo returned to Dublin, Georgia, to live and began writing a thrice-weekly column for the Dublin *Courier Herald* . . . and still does.

And that, friends and neighbors, is exactly what my résumé says and is what the program chairman read to the North Carolina civic club.

Before driving to North Carolina for my scheduled appearance, I studied my résumé in detail. Remember the television show, "To Tell the Truth"? Well, I thought about it as I read. I concluded that I must do something, so I eased a sheet of paper in my typewriter and typed yet another résumé, one that I could live with and maintain a clear conscience.

This, then, is the résumé that I read to the North Carolina civic club immediately after the program chairman had read the other one:

"True Résumé of Walker W. 'Bo' Whaley"

Born in Scott, Georgia, December 11, 1927. His parents took one look and cried out, "No more!" resulting in Bo being raised an only child. His father exclaimed, "My God! He looks like a boll weevil!" Thus, the nickname.

Bo moved with his parents to the small South Georgia towns of Dudley, Vidette, Alma, Oglethorpe, Lumpkin, and Metter inasmuch as the Foster Parents program had not yet been instituted and they had no choice but to take him along.

In May, 1943, Bo was awarded (and I emphasize the word "awarded") his high school diploma from Stewart County High School, Lumpkin, Georgia, but only after having taken a make-up algebra test in the principal's office three hours before graduation. His grade on the test has never been revealed and went to the grave with the compassionate principal in 1958. A clue surfaced, however, when it was learned that the principal signed Bo's diploma with an "X," possibly to serve as a lifelong reminder that Bo never learned the true value of "X," or "Y" either, for that matter.

By some miracle, and a borrowed $500, Bo's father enrolled him in Georgia Military College, Milledgeville, Georgia (the city in which the Georgia State Mental Hospital is located). It has been long rumored that at the end of the first week the school sent a letter to Bo's father to inquire if, indeed, he had enrolled his son in the intended institution in Milledgeville.

During the World War II years, anybody with a pulse and $500 could get in college. And as long as the payments kept coming, the only way to get kicked out of a military school was to hold hands on campus with the Cadet Colonel (bear in mind this was a long time ago and times have changed) or make a pass at the Commandant's wife. Incidentally, these are the only two subjects Bo passed his freshman year.

While at GMC, Bo played varsity football, basketball,

baseball, and track. This is not surprising, however, as all the real athletes were in the armed forces playing throw the grenade, drop the bomb, or shoot the Japs and Germans. Also, Bo was named Most Outstanding Athlete both years he attended GMC, but only after climbing the fire escape in his shorts after midnight bed check, entering the athletic office, and stuffing the ballot box, thereby also qualifying for the gymnastics team.

Bo fought like hell during World War II, but the authorities caught up with him and sent him overseas anyway, to the South Pacific where he had the dual dangerous assignments of operating the movie projector at night and playing on the baseball team in Manila by day.

After being discharged in November, 1946, and with nothing better to do—the GI Bill money and Georgia Southern College girls looking good—Bo decided to enroll, and did, in January, 1947. He was on the baseball and basketball teams there, primarily because he owned an automobile—a rarity in 1947— and that's the way the team traveled back in those days. Had he somehow managed to lose his driver's license, there is little doubt that his name would have been deleted from the traveling squad.

Two years, three girls, and 4,000 laughs later, Bo graduated in June, 1949. Looking for the easy way out as usual, he returned to the scene of the crime and joined the GMC faculty as basketball coach and history teacher. After all, being as stingy as he was, where else but a military school could he work in those old Army uniforms? He resigned after two years when he had exhausted all valid and acceptable excuses for losing.

Possessing no real desire to work, Bo opted to again climb aboard the federal gravy train and enrolled at George Peabody College, in Nashville, Tennessee, on what was left of his GI Bill. As he sat in the registrar's office, the dean eyed him suspiciously and asked, "What course do you wish to pursue?" Bo eyed a framed document on the wall behind the dean's desk and replied, "I want one of them."

Sure enough, a year and 52 Grand Ole Oprys later, the college surrendered and gave him one, a Master of Education degree just like the one hanging on the wall in the registrar's office.

In September, 1951, Bo put on a coat and tie, shaved, borrowed some deodorant and fifty dollars, and rode his motorcycle to Dublin, Georgia, to apply for the position of basketball coach at Dublin High School. The school superintendent, a basketball fan, hired him in a weak moment.

Bo fooled 'em in Dublin for three years until Uncle Sam rescued him and appointed him as a Special Agent of the FBI, after obviously failing to recruit a sufficient number of qualified applicants to fill the October, 1954, new agent's class.

What the heck, he'd try anything once. He did, and for the next 21 years toured the country with a gold badge, a .38 caliber revolver, a Navy blue suit, white shirt, conservative tie, and a snap brim hat—a Hoover man.

In 1972 Bo became an activist in the Women's Liberation Movement, liberating one in Divorce Court, and for the next few years sort of drifted. Well, really, he was a bum, cruising solo in the single lane of life's freeway.

Finally, in January, 1978, Bo moved back to Dublin, Georgia, the best of more than forty moves he's made, when a longtime friend posed the question,

"How about writing a column for the *Courier Herald* three times a week?"

Bo said, "Why not?" And now, 1700 columns later, that's where he hangs his snap brim hat and props his Western boots on a desk.

And that, friends and neighbors, is the way the cotton pickin' résumé should have been written in the first place.

CALLING MR. GOODWRENCH

I REALIZED THAT I NEEDED A TRAILER HITCH ON my car so I proceeded to inquire about having one put on. "No problem," I was told. "I can put that little baby on there for seventy-five dollars." I decided to have it done. However, in discussing the matter with my friend Ben Canady, on leave from the United States Army in Germany, he assured me that he could do the job for twenty-five dollars. I agreed, and he did it in just about an hour.

I was so pleased at my savings on the trailer hitch that I really went into a thrift syndrome. Overnight I became a one-man fix-'em-up gang, much to my regret.

First, I decided that if Ben could do such a good job on the trailer hitch and save me fifty dollars in the process, why not me? So I gave it a try.

I don't think my car even needed an oil change or new spark plugs but, with my new-found enthusiasm and new worlds to conquer in the automobile repair field, I would have done it if I had just rolled a new Seville off the showroom floor. Also, I would have done it with all the confidence in the world that when I finished, I would be as neat and well groomed as Mr. Goodwrench. So I made preparations to perform surgery on my 1975 Oldsmobile.

First, I bought five quarts of oil and a filter. I couldn't wait to get to the parts store and get the plugs, eight of 'em. Then I hurried home to my back yard operating room to begin.

I found out right quick that you don't just reach under and loosen the bolt and expect the oil to wait for you to move before it starts spurting out in the waiting pan. Nope. It jumps out like a Texas gusher, unexpectedly. Also, there just ain't enough room to jerk your head out of the way when it starts. Instead of a surgeon, I was quickly transformed into an eye, ear, nose, and throat man, because that's exactly the area that was covered with black, dirty oil—my eyes, ears, nose, and throat.

Second, I reached for the oil filter. No problem here, I thought, just twist the old one off and twist the new one on. Right? Wrong! You can't do that without a filter tool. I've seen Mr. Goodwrench do it many times, but he has a filter tool. Into the bathroom, wash up, and head back to the parts store to buy a filter tool. Is the picture getting clearer?

With the filter tool firmly in hand I just took that old filter off before you could say "handyman."

"Nothing to this," I said to myself. However, Murphy's Law began to raise its ugly head when I tried, unsuccessfully, to fit a Volkswagen filter into a hole specifically designed for a 1975 Oldsmobile. Was I defeated? Heck, no! I did something that would make Mr. Goodwrench turn over in his grease pit! I simply put the old filter back on, as every good, dedicated do-it-yourself amateur would do.

Now, it was time to put in the new oil. Very simple, right? Wrong? You see, to make it easier, I had bought one of those seventy-nine-cent thingamajigs that allows you to perforate the oil can and thereby have a spout for easy pouring. The only problem was it leaked something awful!

So, after losing one of my five quarts all over the motor and the grass, I decided that four would be sufficient. Without the spout, I succeeded in pouring those four quarts of oil in without spilling a drop. I didn't spill a drop on the motor, that is, but all I really did was run it through. Here is why. Let me give all you would-be self-oil-changers a simple warning: *Always replace the oil drain plug before pouring in the new oil!*

I now have the blackest grass in Laurens County.

Well, there are times when we just have to accept our limitations. I closed the hood, drove real slow to my friend Tommy Daniel's Shell station, and explained to him that I was a real busy man and needed my oil changed as well as my filter and plugs. I didn't say, "spark plugs"; only an amateur would say that. I just said "plugs." He wasn't impressed.

"I could do it myself, in just a few minutes, you know, if I had the time," I told him nonchalantly.

"Right, Bo. I know." I have the feeling that he does. That's what bothers me.

The only thing I really accomplished was to blow the fifty dollars Ben saved me on the trailer hitch. I wonder if Mr. Goodwrench would like to buy an oil filter tool real cheap, and does anybody need a Volkswagen oil filter?

ALL PLUMBERS
ARE UNDERPAID

HOW MUCH DO PLUMBERS CHARGE PER HOUR?
$12? $18? $75?

$375? It makes no difference. I'm convinced they are grossly underpaid!

Last Saturday made a believer out of me. From this day forward you'll not read a derogatory word about plumbers written by me.

It happened this way.

Every year or two I go absolutely crazy and tackle my storage house. Nineteen eighty-six is my year. I don't know why I thought this year would be any different. I do the same thing every time I take a smart (or dumb) pill and turn on to the storage house.

First, the boxes come out, the same boxes I've hauled all over the United States. Then, I take everything out of them and spread the conglomeration on the lawn. I make a solemn vow that *this* year I'm gonna' throw at least half the junk away. After all, who needs a 1957 calendar, a gear shift knob for a 1962 TR-3, a 1949 identification bracelet engraved "Walker W. Whaley," seven corroded keys that fit nothing in Dublin, three locks with no keys, plus a combination lock with the combination long ago lost and forgotten?

This is not to mention such collectibles as a book on the art of hula-hooping; a jacket the Salvation Army has rejected twice; a pair of trousers I couldn't get into with the help of a sardine packer; a faded and blurred certificate of appreciation from the Pontiac, Michigan, Police Department; twelve pencils; an out-of-date wedding ring; a National Bank of Detroit key chain; a broken seven-iron; baseball glove, vintage 1952; an ash tray from Canada; a broken air rifle that I bought from Hansley Horne at Laurens Hardware in the early '50s; several baseballs; assorted broken sunglasses and cigarette lighters.

I took a look and eyed the boxes yet to be emptied. To heck with it! It was time for a break.

On my way to town, astride my trusty Harley Davidson, for a cup of coffee, I detoured and rode by a friend's house. You never know, maybe she had the coffee pot on.

"Anybody home? How's it going?"

"I'm back here," the voice rang out from the remote regions of her daughter's room, "and I'm beat and disgusted."

"What's the matter?"

"Oh, I've been working for hours trying to fix the drain under the lavatory in this bathroom. Impossible," she said wearily.

It was at this point that I made my mistake.

"Here, let me have that pipe wrench. I'll fix that booger in no time flat."

416

She handed me the wrench but flashed a knowing grin based on her knowledge of my past performances in changing oil, repairing (?) lawn mowers, hunting lost hubcaps, and hanging wallpaper.

Not wanting to see a grown man cry, she moved on to the kitchen. I moved under the lavatory just far enough so that there were two Head and Shoulders under there, as well as more shampoo, hair rollers, rinse, make-up, eye stuff—more creams and junk than in all the drug stores in Atlantic City during Miss America week. No wonder Mary Kay and Merle Norman are billionaires!

I twisted and turned for forty-five minutes trying to connect the cotton pickin' drain pipe. No luck. Then I made a brilliant observation, one that a plumber would have made before turning over the Lilt and getting his sweater tangled up in the hair rollers. (Ever fight eighteen rabid, raging porcupines while imitating a pretzel under a bathroom lavatory?)

There were no threads on the end of the pipe I was trying to connect. Stupid! Just plain stupid! I should have noticed that before I turned the waste basket over with my foot.

I marched past the kitchen and out the front door. She was sitting at the bar drinking MY coffee with a friend.

"Got it fixed?" she called out as I bolted out the door.

"I don't wanna' talk about it!" I called back to her and straddled my motorcycle, stuffing the piece of amputated pipe under my windbreaker.

Once downtown, I marched into the hardware store and cornered Don Jones. He listened patiently as I explained the bathroom lavatory situation in minute detail, holding the pipe in front of me like a wounded snake.

"Simple. You need a new section. This one's got no threads," Don told me.

I pretended not to hear. I merely took the new section, climbed back on my motorcycle, and headed back to the john.

Did I fix the leaky drain by connecting the pieces? Come on now, you know the answer to that.

Back on the motorcycle and back to the hardware store. Another session with Don Jones. His answer?

"You need the whole section," he said.

"Let me have it," I said, without hesitation. At that point I would have signed for a new bathroom.

"Does the main drain pipe you're connecting to go through the floor or the wall?" he asked with a straight face.

Man, I don't know about the pipe but I was ready to go through the ceiling.

"Through the floor," I said with all the nonchalance of a master plumber.

(For the information of all you nonhandymen, it *does* make a difference. Through the wall, and that son-of-a-gun makes more turns than the street in front of the Carnegie Library. I was to learn this little-known fact soon.)

Same song, second verse. Back on the motorcycle and back to the john with a drain pipe sticking out of my windbreaker and above my head. I could have sworn I heard a guy comment as I turned on Gaines Street, "Man, I ain't never seen no diesel Harley Davidson before!"

They were on their second cup when I walked in. I marched right by them. The porcupines were crouched and wiating.

Does that main drain pipe go through the floor? Of course not! It goes straight down into the clump of porcupines, then makes a ninety-degree turn through the shampoo and rinse bottles before disappearing through the *wall* and continues on out Claxton Dairy Road to Dudley as far as I know. I may never know. Only her plumber knows for sure because I stormed to the kitchen and told her to do just that. Call her plumber.

No matter what he charges he'll be underpaid as far as I'm concerned. He'd just better watch out for those darned porcupines. They'll attack at the drop of a pipe wrench.

I would have finished the job myself but I just didn't have the nerve to face Don Jones a third time in one afternoon.

What happened to the stuff I took out of the storage house? The same thing that happens every two years. I put it all back inside where it'll stay until another year. One difference. Now there is a pipe wrench added to the collection and I obviously have no more use for that than I do for the TR-3 gear shift knob, corroded keys, and broken sunglasses.

All together, now, let's hear it for the plumbers. Ready?

"Two, four, six, eight! Who do we appreciate? The plumbers!"

WOULD-BE
HANDYMAN IS
ALL THUMBS

SOME DAYS THINGS JUST DON'T GO RIGHT. TAKE last Saturday, and I wish you had, because it was a bummer for me.

First off, it was a beautiful day and that turned me on. I decided to do something constructive; you know, fix something, just get hammer and nails and start pounding. Ever had the feeling? If not, and you get it, just walk around the block, buy a newspaper or go shoot a couple of games of eight-ball and it'll go away. I well remember the last time it hit me. I broke a hammer, busted a water pipe, got a blister on my finger, and lost my cigarette lighter.

Now that I'm back out in the country where I belong, it isn't quite as convenient to run to the store for materials as when I was living out a fanstasy on Bellevue. Round trip from where I hang my hat now is eight miles and in my car that's a good gallon of gas and a quart of oil.

Last Saturday I decided to start with something simple. You wouldn't think a repair job on a kitchen table leg would pose problems; and it doesn't unless you are Bo Whaley and have two deformed hands, five thumbs on each.

The table needed a leg repaired. I broke one off dragging it from upstairs to downstairs when I moved a couple of weeks ago. Ever watch a table do somersaults down a long flight of stairs? Very entertaining. A New Year's Eve drunk couldn't have done it as well.

It took me about thirty minutes to drive to town, buy nails, and have a cup of coffee with the boys. I really didn't want the coffee but stopped in for a visit hoping maybe somebody would ask me to play golf. Why? Because I was chomping at the bit to answer with, "Can't, I'm repairing my kitchen table."

Nobody mentioned golf so I just announced loud and clear to all present as I rose to leave, "If anybody comes looking for me to play golf, just tell 'em I'm home repairing my kitchen table!"

The telephone was ringing as I entered my house. I caught it on the third ring after knocking over an end table and busting a lamp shade.

"Hello!"

"Mr. Whaley, this is Mary at the restaurant. Did you leave a sack of nails on the table here a little while ago?"

"Uh, yeah, right. I'm gonna' repair my kitchen table, Mary. You see, I was moving and the table . . ."

Mary wasn't impressed and indicated as much with, "Right. Good luck. Whatcha' want me to do with these nails?"

I should have said, "Come on out here and repair this table with 'em." I didn't. I played it straight for a change. "I'll be right down to get 'em. Thanks, Mary."

An hour, another gallon of gas and quart of oil later, I took my nails and headed home. "See y'all later. I've got to get on home and repair my kitchen table."

"How many kitchen tables you got, man?" a smart guy asked. "You just left a little while ago to go repair one."

"Never you mind, Buster! Whatever I got that's busted, I can fix," I countered.

"Why don't you try your hand on that ol' Mercury of yours, then?" another dummy called out.

I didn't bother to reply because I only talk to mechanics about my car. I do pray about it a lot though. Anyway, it's nearly impossible to relate to unappreciative audiences. They're a drag. Pearls before swine, you know.

With hammer and nail in hand, along with a handsaw, foot rule, and marking pencil, I tackled that fractured table leg. Since it was in three pieces, I used masking tape to hold it together for the nailing. So far, so good.

I found out pronto, however, that I was missing a badly needed tool, a vise. Ever try to nail pieces of a table leg together with the thing jumping all over your back yard? Heck, I started behind the welcome center and ended up in Jerry Gay's driveway across 441.

Then there was the kid on the bicycle who stopped to watch. I saw him staring at me. "Whatcha' want, kid?"

"Nothin', just watchin' you kill that snake," he replied.

"Ain't killin' no snake. I'm repairing my kitchen table. You see, I was movin' and . . ."

"Oh, I thought you wuz killin' a snake," he said as he pedaled off, disappointed.

I picked up the pieces and returned to my yard. Up she went on the picnic table. Put your foot on one end and the other tips up, thereby spilling nails, a foot ruler, handsaw, marking pencil, and half a can of Coke. And tell me this— why won't the saw ever start where you mark? I tried placing one of my ten thumbs alongside the thing to guide it like my Daddy used to do, but only succeeded in splitting a thumbnail. Also, try and find a Band-Aid when you need one, especially after having just moved. I can tell you, though, that masking tape will work in an emergency.

Want another tidbit? Putting half a concrete block on one end and sitting on the other won't cut it, either. Finally I had a brainstorm. No, strike that. I had a mental lapse, sticking one end of the leg in the outdoor grill, closing the top, and placing a brick and a half on it for good measure. Then I anchored the other end, which was on the grass, with my foot. You know what happened when I was half through that booger, don't you? The saw became pinched and I would up dancing a polka with a broken table leg. Paul Anderson couldn't have pulled that saw out.

I finally dumped the whole shebang on the porch and opened a can of tuna for lunch before riding back to town to make a purchase.

"How come you ain't playin' golf?" asked a caffeine regular as I walked in.

"Not today, George. Too busy. Have things to take care of around the house. Fixin' tables and things like that," I said, poker-faced.

"Wish I could do things like that. I just ain't very handy around the house when it comes to fixin' things," he sighed.

"Nothin' to it, fella. Just have to put your mind to it. You know, shoulder to the wheel, nose to the grindstone and all that," I bragged.

I finished my coffee and made my purchase, a card table. Now then, if I can just figure out how to open it up without raising a blood blister on one of my remaining thumbs, I'll have it made. I can tell you this, it's a little spooky sitting on the kitchen floor with a card table before you, trying to shuffle a red five to play on a black six at 7:00 A.M., while waiting for the toast to pop up. But I'm gonna' enjoy my new card table if I can just figure out how to open up the legs.

WHEN CHRISTMAS COMES IN JANUARY

A GLANCE AROUND THE DEN REVEALS CHRIST-mas cards stacked neatly under the end table next to the picture you took with your "open me first" camera. The sight of the cards decides your evening: time to pull up a chair, relax, and review them, taking time to carefully read the verse again that was selected with such care, just for you. So you begin.

Some fifteen minutes have passed and all is well—reflections, good friends, loved ones, memories. And then you open the card signed only "Bob and Alice." You have read it nine times since it arrived and the same question arises: Who the heck are Bob and Alice?

I had my Christmas in January last night as I sprawled in front of the fireplace, with Johnny Mathis, Barbra Streisand, and Roy Clark to keep me company.

As I browsed and mentally visited friends from Texas to Michigan, from Las Vegas to New York, I picked up *the* card, which is a little different from Bob and Alice's, for I know the identity of the sender well.

It bears a postmark from Hallsboro, North Carolina, comes every Christmas, always with a little note and a small snapshot, and is signed "Winnie." This one is the fifth since Christmas, 1973.

This card has become real special to me and I would like to share with you how I came to be included on her Christmas card list. I love the story, because it is true and has such a happy ending, the best kind.

It was late, approaching midnight, as I drove toward Savannah from Jacksonville in June 1973. The rain beat hard against the windshield as the wipers struggled in vain to keep up. I pulled off Highway 17 into a service station, joining eight or ten others who had surrendered to Mother Nature.

Once inside the station, I joined them in a cup of machine-dispensed coffee and a cold and stale ham sandwich, the greater portion of which was eventually devoured by a wet dog, the station attendant's companion. I bought it to satisfy my conscience and not just stand and drip on the floor and make use of the restroom for free.

While partaking of the coffee and chatting idly with a fellow refugee from Michigan, I saw her pull in and get out of an old, battered Chevrolet. Instinctively, I noticed the license plate: North Carolina.

When she entered the station she was holding a small piggy bank and appeared very tired and road-weary. Her long, blond hair was in tangles, her white pedal-pushers somewhat soiled, and she was barefooted. She was young, very pretty, with big brown eyes and fair complexion. Somehow, she just didn't fit the old car or the locale this dreary night.

The rain stopped shortly and all had continued on their way leaving the girl, myself, the station attendant, and the dog. I listened as she related her story to Jack.

She left home in North Carolina with no notification to her parents and drove to Fort Lauderdale to marry a boy from her home town. It hadn't worked out and she found herself stranded in Florida with an old car and no money, other than the coins in her piggy bank. She was trying to get back home but was either too proud or too ashamed, maybe both, to call home for help.

As she counted out the contents of her bank for gas, she told Jack that she was going to drive as far as she could toward North Carolina until her gas ran out, then try and work at something for a few days to get some money to go on home.

She ate heartily on the two sandwiches that Jack had given her, continuing to talk as she ate. I heard her say that she was nineteen; Jack was at least fifty-five. She counted out less than $3.00 in change and gave it to him for gas. She was receiving his full attention and I heard him make his pitch.

He had a trailer in back of the station and lived alone. Why didn't she stay overnight there until he got off work the next morning at 7:00? (It was somewhat obious that he would have liked it very much if I left.)

He was glowing as he went outside to put the gas in her car, and I'm sure that had he had a villain's moustache he would have twisted the ends in anticipation.

Now there were three—the girl, me, and the dog. She told me her name was Winnie and that she was scared. She was considering Jack's offer; otherwise she would sleep in her car at some roadside park further up the road. She asked my opinion and I gave it: neither.

Jack could hardly take care of the other cars that were stopping as he kept his eyes fixed on the girl. I bought her another sandwich. She ate it quickly. The dog displayed no interest. I watched her as she ate. My mind's eye made a quick trip 150 miles away as I transposed the image of my teen-aged daughter, with long, blonde hair, to the station and saw her standing there, barefooted, in Winnie's place.

I reached in my pocket and took out a twenty-dollar bill. I rolled it into a tight roll and handed it to her. I told her to take a father's advice and head straight home to North Carolina and assured her that she would be welcomed back there with open arms.

Without waiting for any comment, I walked into the restroom and washed my hands. Maybe they needed it; maybe they didn't. At any rate, when I came out she was gone, and a confused and obviously disappointed Jack was standing by the doorway fingering a small and I'm sure, inexpensive ring.

"The girl said for me to give you this and to thank you. She said it was all she had," he said.

I left a baffled Jack and a sleeping dog and drove north on U.S. 17 to Interstate 95. It had started to rain again. I caught up with her old Chevy, waving for her to stop. She did, after about a mile of waving, horn-blowing, and light-blinking. I walked back to her car and handed her the ring, her birthstone, I learned. "I don't want your ring, honey. I just want you to get on home safely," I assured her.

She asked for my name and address. I gave it to her. She cried a little. (So did I.)

In about a week or ten days I received a beautiful note from her father, enclosing twenty dollars. I will cherish it always because a few months later I received a note from Winnie. Her father had died.

What has happened to Winnie? Like I promised, a happy ending. The Christmas cards started arriving in 1973 and she never misses.

She is happily married, has two fine children, a fine husband, and is living in North Carolina.

Christmas in January—it was good.

BEAUTY AND
THE BEACH
GO TOGETHER

SOCRATES DEFINED BEAUTY AS A SHORT-LIVED tyranny; Plato called it a privilege of nature; Theocritus, a delightful prejudice.

Sir Francis Bacon wrote that "the best part of beauty is that which no picture can express."

And then, there was Confucius who said, "Everything has its beauty but not everyone sees it."

I wish these learned scholars could have been with me on a recent visit to Jekyll Island. Some beauty is so infinite that words are inadequate to capture and preserve it. Such was the case at Jekyll Island.

I arose very early. The sun had preceded me but a few minutes and was not yet at full glow as it peeped over the Atlantic. Its rays danced a rumba to the steady beat of roaring waves.

Walking shirtless and barefooted the hundred or so yards to the rim of the ocean, I understood the vastness and infinity of nature. Thousands upon thousands of footprints, large and small, dotted the sandy path, some going to and some coming from the salty basin.

Once seated on the beach, I became aware that I was alone. A huge ship dotted the horizon. It was impossible to determine if it was going or coming. Its gigantic dimensions were reduced to microscopic proportions when compared to the impatient Atlantic on which it sailed. And I listened. Yes, oceans do roar.

Ignoring the vastness of the ocean for the moment, I cast my eyes upward as I sat in the sand, spent waves teasing my toes. A lone cloud hovered and sauntered about the heaven, carefree and lazy. It was billowy, bright, towering, shimmering, and fluffy—like a just bathed poodle or cotton candy. It fascinated me. And then, it was gone, on to where clouds go, on and on . . .

Socrates was right.

Deserted by the cloud, I returned my attention to the ocean. It was my turn to tease the spent waves and whitecaps as they tiptoed softly to shore and expired. But not before I teased them with my toes.

One took me seriously and slipped up on my blind side as my attention was temporarily diverted back to the sky and another cloud. It attacked and wet my bottom almost as if to say, "Gotcha."

I decided to walk along the beach, why I don't know. One mile of beach is like any other mile of beach. But there's just something about walking on a beach, and it's a good way to dry your britches.

An impatient breeze caressed my face and held my hand. Alone? I think not. The beauties of nature surrounded me. It was good to be alive.

Plato was right.

Having dined heartily on such delicacies as cotton candy clouds, salt water whitecaps, and seabreezes, I retraced my steps in the sand to my motel room to change to dry britches, don shoes and shirt, and treat myself to Sunday morning breakfast. With me it isn't a meal, it's a ritual—a bonus for having survived the night.

Little did I know that I would view the most beautiful sight on Jekyll Island as I shuffled along to the motel restaurant, stopping en route to purchase what for me is a breakfast must, a newspaper.

Inside the restaurant, the smell of fresh-brewed coffee ignited my already gigantic appetite. The anticipation of soft scrambled eggs, sausage, grits, biscuits, grapefruit, and an hour or more with my paper provided additional fuel for a fiery appetite.

I was well into my second cup of coffee and partially finished with my sausage and eggs, when he came in. He was a giant of a man, wearing a black T-shirt with a motorcycle emblem emblazoned across the chest, a massive chest. His biceps strained for freedom, testing every stitch. Immediately, I recognized two areas of common interest with the man, motorcycles and newspapers. He had one tucked under his arm as he walked to his table. (What? A motorcycle or a newspaper, you ask? Friend, the man could have had one of each. He was that big!)

With a terrific breakfast under my belt, I gave full attention to my newspaper and the remaining half cup of coffee.

From a nearby table I heard the last words of a conversation, an obvious reference to my friend in the motorcycle T-shirt.

"Oh, he's just one of them motorcycle bums."

I was finishing with breakfast and nearing the end of the final section of my paper when they came in, a beautiful lady and a little girl, maybe five, six at most. Both were wearing beach outfits and gorgeous suntans.

I had something in common with the child. She had a wet bottom. I soon learned that she'd been to my ocean for a prebreakfast swim. I wondered if she might have seen my cloud. Both lady and child were happy and giggling.

They already had a table. The lady's husband, and the little girl's father, was seated at it. Right, the man in the motorcycle T-shirt. You know, "one of them motorcycle bums."

He rose, helped his wife with her chair and patted the child on her fanny, a privilege reserved for daddies, before lifting her to her chair.

"Have a good swim?" he asked.

"Beautiful! Absolutely beautiful," the wife answered.

The child was as fresh as clean linen and as cute as the little girl in the Coppertone ad, complete with pony tail. The only thing missing was the determined Scottie tugging at her shorts, partially revealing her just-patted fanny.

I folded my paper and watched. The three of them glowed in the joy of each other's company as they made small talk and the "motorcycle bum" explained in detail a small shell found and prized by his daughter. She gave it to him and he kissed her on the forehead. She giggled. Her mother smiled.

Sir Francis Bacon? Obviously a wise man, and he was right.

Their breakfast arrived and I viewed a beautiful sight in the motel restaurant.

Obviously the child was well trained. She knew exactly what to do with her napkin, knife, fork, spoon *and* hands. Just as naturally as breathing, she bowed her head and reached right and left with them—right to daddy and left to mommy. Her pony tail lay as still as a weeping willow on a calm day.

The motorcycle bum? He offered a prayer of thanks for his family and the food before them.

The guy who had labeled the little girl's father, "just one of them motorcycle bums," had left. I wished he hadn't. I would have given my breakfast and newspaper for him to have been there.

Confucius? You be the judge.

As for me, I just have the feeling that I witnessed the most beautiful sight on Jekyll Island that Sunday morning in a busy motel restaurant.

I gathered my newspaper, paid my check, and headed back to Room 516. En route, I met a friend.

"Boy, you're up and at 'em early this morning! Going to church?" he inquired.

"Already been," I replied.

I went on upstairs, opened the door, and walked into my room. I tossed the paper in the general direction of my wet britches, opened my brief case, took out a few sheets of copy paper, and faced my typewriter.

What you just finished reading is what I wrote that Sunday morning. Like I said, words are inadequate to capture and preserve what I witnessed in that motel restaurant. But I can assure you it was beautiful.

Did I really go to church? I have to think so.

"Sick" American Speaks Out on America's Ills

There are those who claim ours is a "sick" society, that our country is sick, that we are sick. Well, maybe they're right. I submit that I'm sick, and maybe you are, too.

Yes, I'm sick.

- I'm sick of having policemen ridiculed and called "pigs" while cop killers are hailed by some as a sort of folk hero.

- I'm sick of being told that religion is the opiate of the people, but marijuana should be legalized.

- I'm sick of commentators and columnists canonizing anarchists, revolutionaries, and criminal rapists, but

439

condeming law enforcement when such criminals are brought to justice.

- I'm sick of being told that pornography is the right of the free press, but freedom of the press does not include being able to read the Bible on school grounds.

- I'm sick and tired of paying more and more taxes to build more and more schools when I see some faculty members encouraging students to tear them down or burn them.

- I'm sick of Supreme Court decisions which, because of some infinitesimal technicality, turn criminals loose on society—while other decisions by this august body take away my means of protecting my home and family.

- I'm sick of pot-smoking entertainers deluging me with their condemnation of my moral standards on late-night television, moral standards which I steadfastly refuse to compromise.

- I'm sick of being told that policemen are mad dogs who should not have guns—but that criminals who use guns to maim, rob, and murder should be coddled, understood, and helped back to society, with no consideration for their victims.

- I'm sick of being told it is wrong to use napalm to end a war overseas; but if it's a Molotov cocktail or a homemade bomb at home, I'm asked to understand the provocations.

- I'm sick of not being able to take my family to a movie unless I am willing to have them exposed to nudity, homosexuality, vulgar language, and the glorification of narcotics and adultery.

And also:

- I'm sick of riots, marches, protests, demonstrations, confrontations, and the other mob temper tantrums of people intellectually incapable of working within the system.

- I'm sick of hearing the same slick slogans, the cries of people who repeatedly chant the same thing, like zombies, because they haven't the capacity of verbalizing thought.

- I'm sick of those who repeatedly say I owe them this or that because of the sins of my forefathers—when I have looked down both ends of a gun barrel to defend their rights, their liberties, and their families and would do it again without hesitation.

- I'm sick of cynical attitudes toward patriotism and equally sick of politicians with no backbone.

- I'm sick of permissiveness.

- I'm sick of the dirty, the foul-mouthed, the unwashed.

- I'm sick of the decline of personal honesty, personal integrity, and human sincerity.

Most of all, I'm sick of being told I'm sick by people sicker than I am. And I'm also sick of being told my country is sick—when we have the greatest nation that man has ever brought forth on the face of the earth, when fully 50 percent of the world's population would willingly trade places with the most deprived and underprivileged among us in America.

Yes, I may be sick. But if I am only sick I can get well, help my society get well, and help my country get well.

Take note, all of you. You will not find me throwing a Molotov cocktail or a bomb; you will not find me perched under a placard; you will not see me take to the streets; you will not find me ranting to the cheers of wild-eyed mobs.

No, but you will find me at work, paying taxes, supporting my family, and serving the community in which I live.

You will also find me expressing my anger and indignation to elected officials if my conscience so dictates because, you see, I'm no patsy.

You will find me speaking out in support of those officials, institutions, and personalities who contribute to the elevation of society and not to its destruction.

And you will find me contributing my time, money, and personal influence to helping churches, hospitals, deserving charities, and other establishments which have shown the true spirt of this country's determination to ease pain and suffering, eliminate hunger, and generate brotherhood.

But most of all, you'll find me at the polling place because there, if you'll listen, you can hear the thunder of the common man. There, in privacy, each of us can cast a vote for an America where people can walk the streets, day or night, without fear.

Yes, I'm sick. But I take great consolation in the knowledge that there is a cure: regular doses of prayer, patriotism, and patience.

THINGS I WISH I COULD HAVE DONE

SOMETIMES ONE COLUMN PROMPTS ANOTHER. Like last Monday's about "places I've been; things I've done and people I've met." It prompted this one.

A lady approached me in the Dublin Mall. She'd read the column but had a question.

"What about the things you wish you could have done? I recall many things I'd like to have done but know I never will," she said.

She's right, of course. We all harbor fantasies about things we wish we could have done. Here are some of mine—places I've never been; people I've never met and things I've never done—but always wanted to:

- I wish I could have eaten fried chicken with Col. Sanders—and watched him lick his fingers.

- I wish I could watch "Mr. Goodwrench" give my Mercury a tune-up.

- I wish I could attend just one wedding reception where club sandwiches and king-size Cokes are served.

- I wish I could dance, just once, with Dolly Parton— up close—to the "Tennesse Waltz."

- I wish I could have met "Kilroy" somewhere along the World War II trail. I never did. Everywhere I went "Kilroy" had already been and left.

- I wish I could walk in a laundrymat, bid $51 on a dirty T-shirt and take it away from some Madison Avenue guy that had just bid $50 on it.

- I wish I could find out once and for all what's behind "The Green Door."

- I wish I could engage in a lengthy conversation with Howard Cosell—on a day when he had acute laryngitis.

- I wish I could board a Greyhound bus, sit behind the wheel and say to the driver, "Relax, fella'—leave the driving to me."

- I wish I had the nerve to walk up to a ticket agent at Delta's Gate 66 and say, "Sorry, but I ain't ready yet."

- I wish I could take a head count just to see if Jerry Falwell really does have a majority.

- I wish I could watch Jane Fonda and Madelyn Murray O'Hair mudwrestle.

- I wish I could watch Perry Como sleep just to see if I could tell the difference.

- I wish I could get reservations for 12 at Nikolai's Roof for 8 P.M.—and cancel at 7:45.

- I wish I could have interviewed Lee Harvey Oswald in the Dallas jail and he'd told me the truth. I'd have asked "Will you tell me all you know about a guy named Jack Ruby?"

- I wish I could book "Miss Clairol" on my radio show and ask her this question: "Tell me, honey—do you or don't you?"

- I wish I knew which twin has the Toni.

- I wish I could hear just one politician say, "Well, to tell you the truth, I'm runnin' for the office because I need the cotton pickin' salary."

- I wish I could ask Gaylord Perry of the Seattle Mariners, "Gaylord, do you or don't you?"

- I wish I could hear some character blurt out from the back of the church, "Hold it! You're dang right I got reasons why they shouldn't be lawfully joined together!"

- I wish I could watch a beer drinking contest between Lewis Grizzard and a fella' I know named Edward. No contest. I'd spot Grizzard a case of longneck Buds and he'd still lose.

- I wish, just once, I would dial a wrong number in California and get Bo Derek on the phone instead of Buddy Hackett.

- I wish I could have ridden "up front" with Casey Jones.

- I wish I could see Rock City—but not on the roof of some North Georgia barn.

- I wish I could meet Mr. Maxwell House and ask him, "What's wrong with the last drop, Mr. House?"

- I wish I could identify the individual who came up with this bumper sticker, and ask him if he's ever played golf with me: "If You Think I'm A Bad Driver; You Ought To See Me Putt!"

But most of all, I wish I could hear my Daddy preach just one more time. That's what I really wish . . .